Praise for *The New How*

"How are you going to get rid of your Air Sandwich if you don't even know what it is? Provocative and practical at the same time."

—Seth Godin
Author, *Linchpin*

"Collaboration is a powerful, competitive weapon: this book shows you how to use it to win markets."

—Mark Interrante
VP Content Products, Yahoo!, Inc.

"*The New How* is a timely, thoughtful, and practical blueprint for corporate executives and group leaders to create highly effective and sustainably successful organizations. Innovatively and refreshingly, Nilofer Merchant points the way for achieving truly productive relationships among all levels in a company. We can all learn from this book; it's also a great read."

—Rafael Pastor
Chairman of the Board and CEO, Vistage International, Inc.

"Want to transform your organization into a collaborative enterprise? Nilofer Merchant provides insightful and practical strategies in *The New How*."

—Padmasree Warrior
CTO, Cisco Systems, Inc.

"Whether you're in middle management trying to connect your team to the strategy coming out of the C-suite, or you're the exec tasked with coming up with a new vision, read Nilofer's book first!"

—Michael Plante
Senior Director, Category Management and Marketing Strategy,
Worldwide Consumer Marketing, Symantec Corporation

"In a world in which the pace of change is ever quickening, collaboration, not control, is the route to a successful organization. This book tells you how to make your organization collaborative. And Nilofer Merchant's writing is a model of clarity."

—Barry Schwartz
Author, *The Paradox of Choice: Why More Is Less*

"*The New How* is filled with insight, good sense, and wisdom that will be very helpful for a professional manager undertaking strategic planning. Nilofer has always made a difference with her presence. Now that presence has a new life in the written word that will transcend different boundaries."

—Andre L. Delbecq, D.B.A.
J. Thomas and Katheen L. McCarthy University Professor,
Department of Management, Leavey School of Business

"Leadership fails not so much from flawed strategy as it does from failed processes of engagement from those responsible for implementing the strategy. In high-performing organizations, everyone acts like a leader, and they own the strategy and take actions to ensure its success. If you care about making a difference, read this book."

—Barry Posner
Author, *The Leadership Challenge*

"Merchant's book is a practical guide for the journey from strategy to implementation. The collaborative tools described here can help companies reach strategic success—and avoid pitfalls along the way."

—Tom Kelley
General Manager, IDEO, and author, *Ten Faces of Innovation*

"Rubicon has always stood apart from other consulting firms because they engender true engagement across an organization. Adobe's first of many engagements with Rubicon was to develop the Education segment go-to-market plan. Adobe's Education market growth over the past decade is testimony to the value of a collaborative implementation of strategy, Merchant's signature, and the foundation of *The New How*."

—Katie Keating
VP, WW eCommerce and NA Channel Sales, Adobe Systems

"*The New How* puts into prose, and backs up with insight, the key thoughts to successful leadership—it's all about people."

—Andy Novobilski, Ph.D.
Dean, College of Sciences and Mathematics,
Arkansas State University

"Nilofer Merchant reveals how to develop and deliver winning strategies by leveraging the creative power of your entire organization. You will learn how to transform strategy from a word to a way of being."

—Kathy Chill
Senior Director, Business Development and Product Marketing,
Citrix Online

"Most business books describe what leaders should do. Many explain why. *The New How* is unique in setting out a clear end-to-end process and framework for co-creating innovation and change in 21st-century organisations. It's also well written, fun to read, and provides practical guidance on how to succeed."

—David Butter
Senior Vice President, Eccpartnership

The New How

Building Business Solutions Through
Collaborative Strategy

The New How

Building Business Solutions Through Collaborative Strategy

Nilofer Merchant

O'REILLY®

Beijing • Cambridge • Farnham • Köln • Sebastopol • Taipei • Tokyo

The New How: Building Business Solutions Through Collaborative Strategy
by Nilofer Merchant

Published by O'Reilly Media, Inc., 1005 Gravenstein Highway North, Sebastopol, CA 95472.

O'Reilly books may be purchased for educational, business, or sales promotional use. Online editions are also available for most titles (*http://my.safaribooksonline.com*). For more information, contact our corporate/institutional sales department: (800) 998-9938 or *corporate@oreilly.com*.

Editor: Mike Hendrickson
Production Editor:
  Rachel Monaghan
Copyeditor:
  Genevieve d'Entremont
Proofreader: Emily Quill
Indexer: Angela Howard

Production Services:
  Octal Publishing, Inc.
Cover Designer:
  Monica Kamsvaag
Interior Designer: Ron Bilodeau
Illustrators: Hugh MacLeod and
  Robert Romano

Printing History:

  December 2009:   First Edition.

All the stories described in this book, except the profile of Hans Grande in Chapter 3, have been camouflaged to maintain confidentiality.

ISBN: 978-0-596-15625-1
[CW]

To all who have taught me to believe that business can be noble

Contents

Part II.   The QuEST Process for Collaborative Strategy

Preface

•

During my nearly 20 years in business, both as an employee and as a trusted advisor to companies, I've seen what you've seen: strategies designed to win are commonly announced with fanfare, but they rarely live up to the ambitions and predictions of their advocates.

Sometimes they're modestly successful, and any gap between reality and expected results is easy enough to explain away as bad luck or poor timing. Other times, particularly for the really bold moves, the outcomes are borderline disasters. Scapegoats are required, blame is apportioned, and one or two executives, often talented, get "reassigned," or leave the company "to pursue other opportunities."

Of course, all around us today, too many businesses are unsuccessful in meeting the challenges placed before them. They fail to defend themselves against the competition, miss new markets, do not innovate effectively, can't reach/retain their customers, and are unable to keep their best people.

Viewed from the outside, these corporate trainwrecks are troubling. Having been on the inside, I can tell you it's worse than troubling; it's excruciating. That's because when you're part of one of these failing efforts, it is personal: it's *your* product that didn't sell, it's that new market opportunity *you* predicted but didn't seize, it's *your* missed results, *your* effort that was wasted. The executive team often complains that their teams "aren't executing well." The rest of the organization grumbles that the execs "just don't get it."

In the end, what we often have is lost opportunity, lost human potential, squandered corporate capabilities, and lost market value. Doesn't that make you mad? It made me mad—mad enough to want to fix it. I was fed up with my own behavior and that of my colleagues. We were wasting our time, rather than focusing on the fundamental problem: what is going to help us to win in the market. We needed to know how to set direction to win, and win repeatedly.

What is the real issue we need to solve? The real issue is the systematic way we go about setting direction and making tough trade-offs. For too long, the business world has insisted that major decisions be owned by only one part of an organization, the executive suite. Execution and tactics are delegated to another part of the organization, those who actually get things done. If you're within one of these companies, you know what this leads to: an enormous gap between the vision at the top and the understanding and alignment of those in the organization that must turn that vision into a ground-level reality.

In Silicon Valley, we call that gap an "Air Sandwich": the empty void in an organization between the high-level strategy conjured up in the stratosphere and the realization of that vision down on the ground. Rather than connective pieces between the vision and the reality, the filling in an Air Sandwich consists mainly of misunderstandings, confusion, and misalignment. This Air Sandwich prevents us from winning. This Air Sandwich is frustrating and, at times, infuriating.

As soon as I could identify the Air Sandwich within the organization, I knew it was the very thing we needed to eliminate. But the Air Sandwich is not the root cause of the problem. It is a symptom of the flawed legacy system of setting direction that may have worked ages ago, but doesn't any more. We need a new system. We need a practical approach that demands that everyone be able to contribute, and lets us gather insights from anywhere in the organization. We need an approach that allows us to make decisions that align with the vision, collectively debate, and gather more reliable and insightful information. We need an approach that helps us to use conflict and tension to motivate the creative process, identify the things that matter, and still drive alignment and resolution. And, given the nature of our times, we need an approach that lets us move faster, not slower, more practically than theoretically—and it sure better help us tap into the power of the people in our organizations.

My team and I have developed—through years of discovery and synthesis, trial and error, some sweat, and a few tears—a different approach that gets everyone to collaborate and create winning strategies. It has been used and tested, in whole or sometimes in part, on numerous real-world initiatives. This approach is the *New How*.

I believe we can make smarter decisions and set direction faster and with better information; that we can more effectively implement a direction; that we can move swiftly as a whole organization with clarity of purpose; and that we can use the best of ourselves and one another to do business in a way that makes us proud.

And if you're reading this book, then you are not part of the "no way, no how" crowd. You're ready for the "new way, new how." The New How has helped bring more joy and more success to my experience of business. I hope it will do the same for you. So, let's get started.

Introduction:
Why Strategies Fail

Failure is the opportunity to begin again,
more intelligently.
—Henry Ford

Before We Fix It, Let's Understand Why It Fails

Watching a failed strategy rip through a company is akin to watching a powerful hurricane hit land and devastate everything in its path. Anyone who has witnessed such destruction hopes desperately to never experience such a thing again. When I witnessed it firsthand, I was working inside the third-largest software company in the world, where I managed revenues for the Americas region. I will tell you a story about my most dramtic experience of failed strategy. (Like all the stories in this book, it is a true story, but some identifying details have been changed to respect confidentiality. The exception is "Profile of a Collaborative Leader" in Chapter 3, in which Hans Grande's real name is used.)

My role had a broad charter to work on product issues, sales compensation plans, marketing, and channel decisions—everything about setting and meeting revenue goals. It gave me a perfect vantage point to watch the events unfold. Unfortunately, I wasn't an innocent bystander; I was complicit in what went down.

It started innocently enough. My boss stopped by my office, excited, with big news: the company had decided to diversify our product line six-fold within the coming 18 months.

The story she told had all the makings of a legend. The CEO had just shared the results of recent market exploration, which had convinced him that this strategic move would propel the company into the future.

After his inspiring talk, the CEO prompted the VPs to join the rallying cry. The way my boss described it, it was part revival and part campaign stump speech. Apparently, she was the first to volunteer. She said she felt compelled to stand up and assert, "I think we need to do this. Sign the Americas up!"

Even though my boss hadn't talked to anyone within her organization about what it would take to make this move a reality, she "just knew" it was the right idea to get us to the next level. Besides, she believed that if anyone in the company could figure out how to make this happen, it would be us. After all, we had a stunning track record—always delivered on our revenue, and the team was competent and smart. I distinctly remember being impressed by the leadership my boss was exhibiting.

The vision for this idea was a classic big, hairy, audacious goal. Not just a few products over two to three years, but six new product lines in 18 months. Sales and marketing would generate demand, with new products developed in parallel. A move of this magnitude would touch every facet of our company: revenue forecasts, individuals' roles, sales efforts, marketing initiatives, product roadmaps, customer expectations, and company reputation. Every part of the company would need to be integrally involved and well coordinated for the whole thing to work. I had concerns, but because I assumed everyone understood the breadth of the impact on the company in the same way I did, I didn't voice them. After all, who wants to be the one to question a direction, which would seem like tossing a bucket of cold water on the company's vision?

So I kept quiet, figuring "the leaders" had it under control. Besides, like my boss, I believed in the team. Failure was not an option. Our CEO had said "we must," and my boss said "we will." With that in mind, the larger team and I charged forward with every intention to do our best and make good on the vision.

A couple of months into the new revenue cycle, I got a call from a lead product manager who was responsible for the launch of our new product suite. We often talked just to sync up or troubleshoot issues as they came up. This call, however, was different. The voice on the other end of the line was anxious and tense. There was no small talk. No sooner had I said "hello," he jumped in and said:

"We have a problem here. You know the lead product? Yeah, the one that's supposed to net us most of this year's revenue? We're not going to be able to ship it with all the features we originally planned."

That spelled big trouble. If the new product was delayed, our revenue stream would collapse. Orders for our existing products were already getting deferred because the new product direction had been announced. This one piece of news changed everything and set us on the brink of a major sales stall.

There was no question the situation was dire. My boss called a quick meeting with a few key people to ensure we could make decisions quickly. Someone began by framing the facts of the situation to date, and then laid out three options, none of them appealing. We could:

- Ship the product without the intended features, then face the analyst and stock market repercussions.
- Ship the product with all the features (even though they likely wouldn't all work) and do a patch release later.
- Delay the product for some undetermined amount of time until we could get it right.

The conversation eroded into mayhem. Instead of a thoughtful debate concerning the trade-offs of each difficult option, the meeting quickly became a blame-fest for the Category-5 hurricane blowing its way toward us. The "discussion" included:

"You are responsible for shipping the thing on time."

"Why did you commit to the deadline if you couldn't make it?"

"You were never supportive of this plan in the first place."

"You're the sales manager. What's stopping you from delivering revenues from our current product line?"

Everyone in the room was smart and hardworking and absolutely certain that it could not be *me* who was responsible for this mess. Accusations bred defensiveness, which in turn led to finger-pointing.

Just as quickly as we decided "we must," it transformed to "we will," then degenerated into "we can't," and we were left wondering "how?"

As you can likely imagine, the team's frustration rose, filling the room with anger and anxiety. Before the meeting disintegrated completely, someone managed to get traction on the idea that we should simply try to meet those commitments that were in our direct control. We ultimately agreed to ship the product on the original release date, knowing full well that it wouldn't meet the customer expectations we had previously set.

It doesn't take a crystal ball to figure out what happened next. There was no *deus ex machina*, no superhero swooping in to save the day.

Nope. Revenues were weak. Several talented staff members resigned. The sales team was demoralized. The company was mired in the aftermath of key customers buying a product that didn't work as promised. The company eventually did manage to recover financially, but the corporate culture took a nosedive. In response to the debacle, people adopted cumbersome and complicated procedures to make sure they didn't get burned again. After taking massive risks with little thought, people sought to avoid risk at all costs. All around, there was a high price to pay for such good intentions.

So what went wrong? How did this well-intentioned new direction turn into such a trainwreck? And who was to blame?

The answer is that none of us, and all of us, were at fault. Despite our best efforts, we were working with a strategy that was doomed from the start because of *how* it was formed. The market direction and vision of product diversification were solid, but the way that strategy was created itself lacked the deeper organizational engagement necessary to enable the company to achieve business success.

Despite best efforts, some strategies are doomed from the start because of how they are formed.

We had no process, framework, approach, or set of organizational mechanisms for embracing the direction as it was set forth. And so we didn't internalize it; we simply took the direction as if that alone were enough. Without a way to consider cross-functional actions, envision different options and their necessary trade-offs, and make some tough choices early on, we missed the things that were essential to ultimate success.

In the absence of both group and individual accountability, it was easy to assume (as I did) that none of us was responsible for overall success or for speaking up whenever something didn't seem quite right. Since there was no review of options by those who would implement, none of us could recognize the risks of the new vision. Nor was there a way to discover all of the essential small tasks and detailed work we had to complete. Not knowing this, we couldn't make trade-offs between functional groups. We didn't know how to form a strategy that would become real. In short, we lacked a way to collaboratively set direction to win.

It was a perfect storm, a tsunami of a strategy failure. And I was left with the lingering questions: why did it happen? And is there another way? I came to learn that yes, there is.

The failure had little, if anything, to do with the rightness of the big idea, and wasn't really about the abilities of the individuals on our team. The genesis of the storm was the original formation of the strategy itself. We went straight to execution. (As in, do not pass go, do not collect $200 million.) It's tempting to view the strategy as correct and blame the execution, but that's off base. A more accurate description of the problem is that the strategy was incomplete.

A fully developed strategy creation process would engage the team, identify the key interdependent tasks that must be done, find the weak spots and make changes, and get buy-in and accountability. All this needs to happen *before* execution. If we wait until execution, the measures and processes merely drive completion of items on a checklist, not overall clarity of purpose. When we recognize this, it becomes obvious that the thinking and alignment are *part of* strategy creation. Some might argue that the execution began immediately in this case because of the urgency, but that's like firing a gun without lining up the sights first. It's OK if you have a million bullets and don't mind a few misses. But if you have just one shot, even in time pressure, getting the strategy right must come first (Figure I-1).

Figure I-1. *Getting the strategy right takes time*

I've shared this tale of woe to give a sense of what a strategy failure looks like. At a glance, the ingredients aren't any different from those of a strategy success: good intent + good direction or idea + talented people + hard work + "magic black box." We know there's magic involved because sometimes it works and sometimes it doesn't, and we understand as much about the inner workings of that box as we did the magician's hat at our fifth birthday parties. We need to replace the "magic black box" with a well-understood process framework, or a "New How" to do strategy creation.

Different Types of Strategy Require Different Approaches

After years of working with name-brand organizations and innovative startups, partnering to build successful strategies day in and day out, I've come to realize that there is no shared definition of the word "strategy." Not among exec teams, or boards of directors, or within a single organization, and certainly not across organizations. Each of us uses it to mean something slightly different, and this lack of a shared definition can lead to misunderstandings. So, before we go any further, let me clear up what I mean when I use the word "strategy," and in particular, what's included in the scope of the definition as it relates to this notion of collaborative strategy.

Strategies are crucial to competitive organizations. Most people would agree on that, at least. And good strategies are essential to winning companies. So, simply put, *a strategy is a way to win*. Although it's seemingly that simple on one level, practitioners know that strategy is also about making choices. It's about deciding not only *what* to do but what *not* to do. And it definitely involves making choices about who to involve, how to listen, which ideas to consider, and how to make tough decisions, as well as knowing what's most important and why.

What's not clear in that definition of strategy is *scope*, and that's where confusion often sets in. My own experience and study suggest that strategy falls into two domains. The first (and more known) is the kind of strategy that deals with *where we compete*, and the second is about *how we compete* (see Figure I-2).

Figure I-2. *Types of strategy and their impacts*

When talking about *where we compete*, many executives use the word "strategy" to describe what a company should do in 3, 5, or 10 years. Most often, the question the company aims to answer within this domain is *which* arena or market space they want to win—either in terms of which markets they want to own, or in terms of what positions they want in the larger market value chain. Strategic discussions like this typically take place more or less annually in boardrooms or executive suites. (Although I believe it can benefit the company to encourage good and diverse input on where we compete, the scope of who needs to be involved in making those decisions can be relatively small without affecting the success of that strategy.) A lot of energy has already shaped this big bucket. Many, many great thinkers, particularly Michael Porter, have shaped excellent frameworks on how best to identify the right strategic domain. My intent isn't to add more to this field of work.

Then there's the lesser-known second domain: the *how we compete* strategy. In this case, strategy can be about day-to-day, quarter-to-quarter operations, as in: "What strategies would drive 50% growth in our consumer division?" or "What strategy is best to grow sales for Product X?"

In these cases, strategy defines the best ways for us to compete *within* an arena. This second domain of strategy, while not as "big picture," has h-u-g-e impact for any organization, because this type of strategy is about determining the best way to win in the chosen space. It can affect which regions, which products, which customer segments, which markets, which product lines, and so on. Once the business domain is set, defining where we want to compete, then nearly every other big decision falls into the domain of "how best to compete." The effectiveness of this bucket of strategic thinking determines whether the other (larger domain) strategy will turn out to be successful—or not.

The kind of strategy in the "how to compete" domain is the answer to the question, "Given what we want, what is the best way to achieve it?" These are the kinds of strategies that can be created at almost every level of an organization. The more complex and diversified an organization is, the more its people need to excel at this kind of strategy creation. And most companies don't know—not yet, anyway—how to do that kind of strategy creation in a way that gets the best results. It is this second domain, the strategy of defining how we compete, that is the focus of *The New How*.

The strategy of "how we compete" is not widely recognized as a form of strategy. Often this domain of strategy is regarded as "tactical" or "execution" or "details," and so it is not addressed in any coherent way. Alternatively, people have treated the "how" as an extension of the "where," and they try to apply the tools they already know from Domain #1. Not good. "How we compete" is a domain of strategy that requires its own set of tools, approaches, and frameworks. But they have a hammer, so it must be a nail, and therefore tools of Domain #1 get brought over and used in Domain #2.

This wrestling match over whether the "how" is strategic or tactical, strategy or execution, is actually an unnecessary and fruitless war. Our individual perspectives on the fight are shaped by our positions on the battlefield. From an executive's viewpoint, the decisions involved in how best to compete look tactical. But to general managers of multibillion-dollar businesses in support of the larger corporation, their decisions don't seem tactical. And, in my operating view of the world, most "how best to compete" decisions are not tactical. These types of strategies shape and influence the success of the larger company vision.

One person's strategy is another's tactics. The unnecessary and fruitless war of what is tactics or strategy or execution must end.

There is no question in my mind that the "how best to compete" includes both real strategic thinking and a number of tactical decisions. Reflecting back to the opening story, the choice of exactly when to announce the new product direction turned out to be a strategic decision—but it was deemed tactical. Unfortunately, the pervasive idea that the high-level "where" of strategy is *all that matters* leaves many strategies incomplete. By establishing and maintaining a culture that stuffs the "how" under "execution," executives unwittingly create a stubborn, persistent structural gap within the organizational entity—one that seriously undermines their ability to succeed.

Perhaps people fixate on execution ("doing what's required") instead of finishing up strategy ("choosing the direction") because it's easier to see progress during execution than during strategy formation and development.

And who would argue that strategy creation (in either domain) is not hard? Typically, new strategies get initiated first under some form of stress or duress: you need to find a new market for revenue growth, your competition is eating your lunch, or you simply need to get higher performance out of your current product line. In any sufficiently complex organization, it seems that there are millions of things competing in our "day jobs" as we also set direction for the future. Nothing slows down to make it easier to define and make changes while running the existing business.

Taken together, all of these tensions reinforce the organizational and cultural gap between strategy created at the top and execution assigned to the doers of the organization.

The "How" Matters

This gap exists for a reason. First, most people think of strategy as a plan, a vision, a direction, a thing. They consider that a strategy is the thing that states something like, "Company X will enter the ABC market and own 30% share within five years." In this way, strategy is a noun, and most of the time, it's a complicated PowerPoint presentation or a dense three-ring binder filled with research findings and analysis. For all the complexity of slides or density of binders, the "where we should compete" strategy usually can be articulated in a single paragraph or slide. All the other dense information we create in strategy formulation of Domain #1 is background, or justification and "proof." That is, all that other info helps the "thud" factor and adds credibility, but it rarely helps us take action and make that vision a reality. Those dense wads often cannot and do not guide the execution.

A strategic direction absolutely needs to be solid for a company to achieve success. But that's not enough. Yet, it is often treated as if it were all things "strategy" and everything else "execution." Then all failure is blamed on execution.

When strategy is conceived of as an answer, a noun, a thing, a tool, it's easy to conclude that all that is needed is the right "thing/idea," and then strong communication to help the organization understand it. That is, a strategy + a strong orator (or even a demagogue) will enable the organization to succeed. This is especially true when the top executive team sees strategy simply as a vision for the overall organization, and doesn't understand that the strategy creation process helps align the substrategies that must line up to support the organizational vision and, ultimately, enable the change. The deeper or more complex an organization, the more substrategies need alignment to create a directional move.

Effective strategies are not solely a plan, nor are they complete before implementation begins. A strategy is not just a plan because, although the word "strategy" is by definition a noun (an artifact such as a document or presentation), in practice most people also use the word to refer to the process by which the strategy is created. In other words, people overload the meaning of the word "strategy" because they don't distinguish *the act of creating the way to win*—strategizing—from one visible byproduct of the process. By missing this distinction, people are unable to see how much the process of developing the strategy is actually part of the strategy itself.

> *Having a great strategic direction or idea without a prepared set of people who "get it" is effectively the same as having a bad idea.*

People and their organizations need both the noun/thing form of the strategy and the verb/process of strategy creation (see Figure I-3). You may have a wonderful strategy document, but if you begin execution without engaging your team in strategy creation, you have a great-looking PDF and an unprepared set of people. If you engage the team, the PDF may have more typos but the content will be richer, plus there is the less-visible byproduct that your team will be wise, committed, and prepared. This nuance is key: if a strategy is, for our purposes, not complete until it has been put into action to create a new market reality, then the *way* you create strategy matters a great deal.

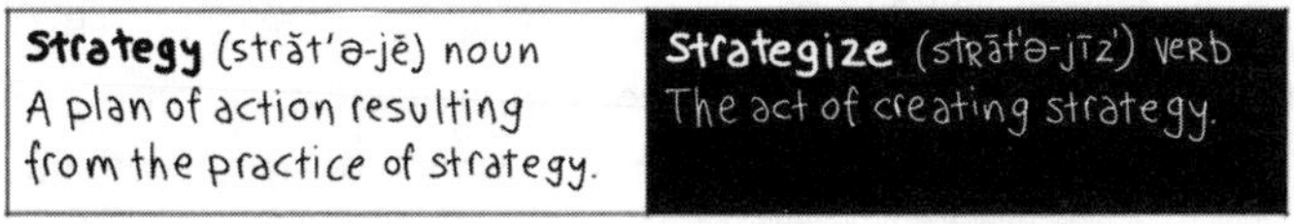

Strategy (străt'ə-jē) noun
A plan of action resulting from the practice of strategy.

Strategize (străt'ə-jīz') verb
The act of creating strategy.

Figure I-3. *Strategy is the noun and needs a verb*

When strategy is viewed as a noun and is not accompanied by a robust process framework to enable solid creation, we are left with something that simply won't work. The thing—the noun—is broken by the very way it was created.

The Air Sandwich

There's a very specific perspective that leads to creating incomplete, ill-formed (aka "bad") strategy.

Strategy gets created incompletely mostly because strategy creation is perceived as an elite exercise, something that only an executive group of people can and should do in a hotel ballroom with walls covered in flip-chart paper. This worldview becomes evident in a number of ways.

One way in which strategy formation fails is when strategies are entirely set or approved by the executive team. The thinking is that execs are empowered to create strategy, so they hole up in long meetings, using models, complex frameworks, and vast amounts of vetted data to decide things. Although the executives' intention is to carry the load, the larger organization of talented, experienced, and competent people see the result of that process as an edict from on high.

Another reason execs do strategy alone is that they want to drive alignment, and they believe that having something written down ("cast in stone") is easier for VPs and managers to communicate consistently. Only a strong organization with a strong high-level vision can tolerate an inclusive definition of the "how." A weaker effort may have a partial, and therefore flawed, vision that will collapse under the scrutiny of the "how."

Another way this worldview shows up is in the form of a mild platitude from an operational leader that sounds something like this: "We don't want to bother you or distract you from your existing work, so we made the strategic decisions for you and want you to validate them in the next 45-minute session of our meeting." Have you heard things like this from the Powers That Be? If so, did it make you roll your eyes (as soon as you were sure you wouldn't be seen)? If you're reading this book, you have an interest in creating successful strategy. You're not looking to be a bystander in the game of strategy creation.

Those Powers That Be aren't trying to do something wrong, but they lack a framework or process to do engaged strategy creation well, so they don't do it at all. Regardless of intent, these examples leave a void in the business. This existing approach to strategy lacks depth and a connection to the realities of the business operations, the needed debate of ideas that result in trade-off discussions, and the need to align capabilities. It lacks a connection to the people who will make that strategy a reality. And it creates an unnecessary separation between the decision of "where to win" and the "how" of winning.

Top-down edicts also typically lack an understanding of organizational capabilities and capacity, as well as an acknowledgment of what the people throughout the organization believe they *can* accomplish. Obviously, this approach lacks collaboration, debates, discussions, and the necessary engagement of the organization.

I've come to characterize this type of strategy creation as one that guarantees an "Air Sandwich." This is where the company's new direction is delivered from an 80,000-foot perspective to the folks holding a 20,000-foot view, who in turn then try to coordinate the people working on the ground—producing a big "Air Sandwich" of strategy (see Figure I-4).

Figure I-4. *Strategy Air Sandwich*

An Air Sandwich is, in effect, a strategy that has clear vision and future direction on the top layer, day-to-day action on the bottom, and virtually nothing in the middle—no meaty key decisions that connect the two layers, no rich chewy center filling to align the new direction with new actions within the company.

What is missing in the middle is the substance of the business— the debate of options, the understanding of capabilities, sharing of the underlying assumptions, the identification of risks, issues that need to be tracked, and all the other things that need to be managed. The middle is missing a set of understandings that would connect the vision of the direction to the reality. By focusing only on the top or bottom, we lose the middle, which is where the value is.

When a company has an Air Sandwich, the most valuable details and decisions that enable a strategy to succeed simply are left out of the strategy creation process. And as a result, they are missing from the implementation plans and the execution itself.

In my earlier story, the strategy formation process was clearly incomplete. If we had done it collaboratively, perhaps we could have changed the direction to ship four products in 24 months—not a huge shift but one that would have let the business achieve better results.

For example, when an organization doesn't test an idea to see whether it's pragmatic or practical, the organization can unwittingly set itself up for failure. This is the byproduct of assuming a given idea will somehow just work. Or, when a critical underlying assumption isn't challenged or a risk isn't highlighted, the people responsible for execution cannot adjust their resource requirements, operating models, or business practices. These disconnects have both direct and indirect costs to the organization (Table I-1). Chances are, you could add a couple of items of your own to this table. And for this reason, we need to find a way to change how strategy is created.

TABLE I-1. *Disconnects and costs of the traditional approach*

DISCONNECT	COST
Data is gathered, but the people with the most insight about the relevance and meaning of that data are not consulted in the interpretation process.	Decision makers do not have the context to understand the situation clearly and correctly, and therefore they fix the wrong problem or create impractical approaches.
Ideas are generated by a few, but not vetted for organizational implications.	Creates impractical approaches. Plus, the missed opportunity of gathering perhaps more useful ideas.
An understanding of which practical steps will support the strategy does not exist throughout the organization.	Different functional groups take different approaches, leading to conflict, frustration, and malaise. Creates an organization of disempowered people.
A misunderstanding between what the top-level executives see in their organization's future and what the people on the ground know about the capabilities or capacity of the organization.	Bad decisions are made in the middle levels, causing a diffusion of resources. Money is wasted; time is lost. Employees are alienated. Customers defect.
A commitment to a common cause may exist at the top, but isn't spread in a tangible way through the organization.	Tension over issues that appear to be about "wrong people" but often is friction caused by lack of clarity or commitment to the strategy.

An Air Sandwich may be filled with nothing, but taking a big bite of one can certainly leave a bad taste in your mouth. Some executives who've sampled an Air Sandwich in the past will attempt to prevent them in the future by managing at a level of detail that undermines the organization's leverage, power, and influence. For example, one approach is to circumvent future implementation issues by delivering top-line visions in an almost who-does-what-by-when format. We've all heard these kinds of directions given as part of the strategy rollout; they look like this:

"Grow X product in the government space by lowering price."

"Please include these three requirements in our product specs that Customer X just requested for our next release."

"Go do a viral video campaign for our PC platform."

Sounds good, right? Sad to say, it rarely works. Directives like this aim to make it easier to implement a strategy, but this technique of spelling out the ways and means to accomplish a strategic goal is generally a setup for failure. In cases like this, here's what often happens: the exec team decides not only the goal or direction, as in "Grow X product in the government space," but they have tacked on the specific way to do it, "by lowering price."

Again, sounds good. But here's the rub: what if price isn't the root cause? Say that the group of people driving government sales at the 20,000-foot level knows for a fact that price is not the issue. Then, essentially, this detailed provisioning of direction becomes a further barrier to success.

The problem here is that the vision itself may be directionally correct, but the details of the directives are incompatible. This mismatch sets up a conflict: which directive is the execution team supposed to follow? Grow product sales in the government space or lower the price? Release the product on schedule as currently designed, or delay the launch until the new features are included? Build a viral video or create something that customers will notice? Should we choose the rock or the hard place?

When the top exec's strategy doesn't jive with what employees know to be true, questions stream continuously through people's minds as internal dialogue:

> *"Is it just me, or is there a fatal flaw in this strategy?"..."Am I supposed to say something?"..."Will I get in trouble if I say something?"..."Will I get in trouble if I don't say something?"..."If I talk about my concerns, will I be perceived as a troublemaker?"..."If I can't see how I can make this happen, will I be told I'm being too tactical?"..."Will I have to pay a price somewhere down the line if I look like I'm not on board with this plan?"*

Questions such as "Should I say something?" or "Do they care about my opinion?" are whispered between coworkers when the organization lacks the tools for involving people and supporting collaboration in the strategy creation process (Figure I-5).

These kinds of unasked questions are a sure sign that a strategy is headed down the path toward failure, because they signal that the

Figure I-5. *The missing questions matter*

strategy wasn't created properly or vetted deeply enough in the organization to be executed well.

Offering detailed directives causes special trouble in high change situations, where dynamics in the marketplace cause things to shift quickly. In cases like these, by the time the strategy trickles down through the organizational structure and multiple levels of decision making, the market opportunity may have long disappeared.

Most people become aware of an Air Sandwich in the organization only after the proverbial shit has hit the fan. Messy.

The New How: Let 'Em Think

The shape and force of outside market pressures will surely impact how a company works to respond. Inside the walls of corporations today, the pressure to continuously improve is relentless. The world of centralized organizations, multi-year product cycles, and one-way communication to our customers and markets is fading fast. All this change brings with it some good news: a more diverse and educated workforce. In 2010, there will be more millennials than baby boomers in the workforce. This new workforce will not only expect to be involved, but they will apply their talents only when they can be fully engaged.

The way strategy creation takes place inside organizations is the key to being able to respond rapidly and fluidly as a whole organization to what's happening in your marketplace.

Winning depends on fully completed strategy now more than ever before. What leaders at all levels are expected to do today compared to even 10 years ago is amazingly demanding. More and better creative strategies are needed to win, and the rapidly shifting market has robbed us of the luxury we once had to ready, aim, fire. Now, it feels more like fire, fire, fire. This situation is highly demanding of people in a number of ways—begging that they consciously improve their strategy for setting strategy.

There are two ways in which I think about strategy: first, as an organization's plan for the future, and second, as the act of creating that plan. In short, how you decide is now as important as what you decide. I've come to see that the model, framework, theory, or PowerPoint you devise (which is typically how strategy is represented) matters as much as the less-observed set of deliberations, discussions, and understandings that happen amongst people who ask "Can we?" and "Should we?" and "When will we?" It is when the team has these discussions and comes together to say, "Yes, we will..." that an entire organization becomes aligned and can actually go and make the strategy manifest. The key area for improvement is to stop focusing entirely on the PowerPoint, and step up efforts to engage the people. A good friend of mine works for John Chambers, CEO of Cisco Systems, who recently shared the changes he is making to lead in this new business climate:

> I was always a command-and-control type. If I said "turn right," all 65,000 employees turned right.
>
> But it's not possible for an organization to scale and take on more when only one person is driving all of the strategy. When you're a command-and-control CEO, individuals impacted by your decision can choose not to buy in, and either slow or even stop the process. This is especially dangerous [in] an industry that moves as fast as this one.
>
> In my view, the days of being vertically integrated and having everything within your control will never return. The entire leadership team, including me, had to invent a different way to operate. It was hard for me at first to be collaborative. When I first got to a meeting, I'd listen for about 10 minutes while the team discussed a problem.

I knew what the answer was, and eventually I'd say, "all right, here's what we're going to do."

But, when I learned to let go and give the team time to come to the right conclusion, I found they made just as good decisions or even better, and just as important, they were more invested in the decision and thus executed it with greater speed and commitment. I had to learn to have the patience to let the group think.[1]

That's a powerful message. His traditional ways of doing strategy that were successful in the past won't work in the future. It's time to take notice. The lesson we can learn from Chambers is that no matter who we are, the way we work and specifically the way we do strategy creation need to be reinvented. *We need to let people think and create strategy everywhere.* This applies to companies large and small. Smaller companies might find this naturally easier because of their focus, but larger firms have more to gain because of the natural complexity of many businesses, people, directions. Companies that learn to harness the value of decentralized power will win against those that simply exploit their people to perform specific tasks.

Chambers's words are a call to action for finding ways to let entire organizations think and create, so that what's created is done better and faster, and is aligned to the larger whole. Chambers tells us that the new approach must share decision-making power, encourage valuable debate, and let the reasoning of "why" something is good be clear and open.

His words suggest that we move from leaders telling and doers doing toward each of us discerning, thinking, and acting. We'll move from vertical strategy creation (top-down telling) to horizontal strategy creation (where we are all share ownership).

Surely, We Can Do This Important Thing Better

Strategies fail for a number of reasons. Some are legitimate reasons, such as the competition created a better offer or a disruptive opportunity changed the landscape. But there are also pointless reasons why strategies fail—ones that we can change by changing how we do strategy creation.

Many strategy failures are avoidable. Treating strategy as a simple noun or set of ideas—rather than including the necessary verb of strategy creation that makes ideas executable—is a recipe for an Air Sandwich, with all its accompanying misunderstandings, inefficiencies, and improper expectations.

Companies using traditional top-down strategy creation models seem to be going slower and slower. At the same time, the volume and complexity of strategic decisions happening today are increasing. These changing conditions demand a model for thinking about strategy creation and a process framework to guide our thoughts and actions.

Without a way to think about and align strategic decisions, the strategies are doomed to fail. We need a new approach to winning that is not dictated from the highest levels of an organization. Inside the most innovative companies, strategic decisions happen at multiple levels within the organizations. For our businesses to thrive and drive the kind of innovation and growth that our economy needs, we need good strategy creation capabilities throughout our organizations.

We can build a community of people who think about strategy creation not as a set of artifacts, but as a powerful process. Then, together, we can redefine ourselves in how we create value. We can embed collaboration into the system as part of both our thinking and our doing. When we add the talents, perspectives, abilities, and desires of the organization into the process, we can make strategy creation an ongoing process of creative collaboration.

Let's move forward and focus on a more predictable and consistent approach to strategy creation: one that combines strategy and execution, engages people in collaboration, and takes into account the essential conditions that are necessary for well-formed strategies to happen.

The first step is to recognize the structural barriers that drive faulty processes. Let go of the idea that when strategy fails, someone—a human being—must be at fault, and not the established system itself. We're smarter than that! Consider the faulty assumptions and rules and the resulting processes. The very way we go about creating strategy determines a big share of its success downstream. To fix the outcome of strategy, we need to look at the total system that produces strategy. That's next.

CHAPTER 1

System Overload

> *If you can smile when things go wrong,*
> *you have someone in mind to blame.*
> —Unknown

> *It's not enough to rage against the lie.*
> *You've got to replace it with the truth.*
> —Bono

Blaming People Only Works for So Long

Watching missed business opportunities is always painful. When products fall flat or sales slow down despite best efforts, it's excruciating to experience the loss of market value. And most of us can guess what comes next: the blame game. Someone must have made the wrong decision, failed to do the right thing, or both. "If only we'd had the right people on the bus, we would have succeeded," is what we say. The mental betting pools begin on who will wind up getting tossed under that very same bus.

Most often, there's some good reason for blaming people. After all, mistakes were made. "Any fool could have seen that our supplier couldn't ramp production that fast." "Engineering missed their committed date. Simple as that." Or "Listen: They've walked before, and they've chewed gum before. All they had to do was walk and chew gum at the same time!" Well, maybe. Who is at fault is not simply an objective question; it is often a political necessity. So we play "he said, she said," pick a scapegoat for the failure, and move on. But is this useful? That is, will blaming people help any of our businesses to be successful the next time?

People *aren't* the core reason why strategies fail. Of course they are part of the dynamic, but we often look to blame people as if that's the whole story. If only it were that simple. When failures happen, I have seen that there are persistent, telltale patterns. As I visit Company A in the morning, Company B in the afternoon, and Company C later that same day, day after day for 10 years, I see that the failures are not simply isolated human missteps that can be avoided in the future by replacing one or two individuals. Instead, the issues are subtle variations of systemic problems. Some problems are dominant in one set of companies, and others are dominant in other firms, but the same few crop up over and over. This is great news, because in the failures we can study the systemic issues, understand them, and create a New How to go forward.

Three situations illustrate the systemic problems. All are byproducts of the Air Sandwich we covered in the introduction, where the top of the organization issues orders at the 80,000-foot level and lobs them down to the folks at the 20,000-foot level, without the benefit of feedback, questions, or even a reality check from below. As long as we're eating Air Sandwiches, we lack the meaty "how" to do an effective job of setting direction and achieving the kind of results we need.

The Three Systemic Patterns

The first situation involves limited participation, the second is about the focus on speed, and the third relates to unresolved questions.

"Tunnel Vision"

Quick, smart, and hard working, Sue was passed over for promotion after promotion, despite good reviews. While personally frustrated at the lack of advancement, she didn't walk away like so many others would have. She wanted to work with *these* people and *this* product set. She didn't just like the company; she loved it. So, she kept aiming to do even better and crack the secret code. One day, she finally got the insight on why she was passed over for the most senior echelon of leadership. Her boss's boss shared, "You get involved and drive the things you are specifically chartered to solve, but you don't jump into stuff outside your domain." Sue was a great leader within her own discipline, but was not viewed as a company leader.

Now, we could say that Sue just wasn't that good. We could say it's an isolated incident involving one person and her individual situation. But of course that's not the whole story. Sue's story highlights a pattern of limited participation and holding back that pervaded the company. The company kept bringing in outsiders as the next echelon of leaders rather than promoting from inside. I knew of other mid-level leaders at this firm who were getting similar feedback from different managers. Each leader shared with me why they behaved as they did, and it came down to this: they hesitated to move beyond their specific assignments, out of fear of treading on others' toes. You see, this firm's culture valued "getting along." The systemic problem was that the culture norm constrained each individual to stay within unspoken, invisible lines of behavior. "Working together to solve the problem" was ranked lower than "getting along." The essential environment for supportive collaborative actions and behaviors was not yet in place.

Remarkably, the executive, Sue, was able to treat her insightful conversation as a springboard to change how the company worked. She used it to set the stage for stepping outside her own domain of expertise and engage with colleagues to drive increased collaboration across boundaries, while the senior execs saw the broader issue and changed the company culture so it was safe for Sue and others to act.

Why does an organization need to drive collaborative actions? Why do people need to step outside their own domains if the business is to thrive? It comes down to this: speed to market happens through cross-silo collaboration. That means companies must work across boundaries and silos to create new things and build greater speed for the company as a whole. The more complex the organization, the more cross-silo collaboration is needed. When members of the organization keep to their isolated sandbox, it leaves holes in the larger tapestry. So firms must seek to avoid the pattern of discouraging productive cross-discipline contribution.

"Ahead of Yourself"

The second costly pattern involves a focus on the *doing* without shared *thinking*. Ian, a general manager chartered to grow "the next big thing" for his division, was entrepreneurial and gung-ho. Working with him and a small group of people in the division, my company had identified a brand-new market where buyers had a "latent need": a deep source of pain they would pay money to solve, but that no offering could solve today. The idea, the competitive landscape, and the size of that market opportunity ($2 billion) were well vetted. The board of the company gave the green light to actively pursue this new market. So far, so good.

That's when things got off track, and perhaps you'll see a bit of your own organization in this next part. With "the big idea" approved, Ian brought together his broader management team and all the extended members of the organization responsible for execution. He shared the results of the board discussion with all the "doers": people from marketing, engineering, delivery, and so on. He finished the update, took a few questions, and then moved on to the next steps. With thinly veiled impatience, he emphasized, "Let's get going!" One person, dialed in via conference call, raised the key question: "Get going how?" Unseen by the questioner, the look on the GM's face left no doubt of his low regard for the person. You probably know the look. Intentional or not, it says, "I get it, so why don't you? What are you, s-l-o-w?" Others present, not wanting to be seen as obstructionist, bit their tongues and got focused on "let's get going."

And so it went. Ian effectively said, "Charge up that hill!" (Figure 1-1) and everyone attempted to do so. The team spent six months trying desperately to make the new market materialize, but got nowhere. People exhausted themselves trying to make it happen, but time and again, something was always amiss, and the execution failed. Ian made the mistake of assuming that what was obvious to him was also obvious to everyone else, even people who hadn't spent close to a year investigating the new opportunity. By going straight to execution without sorting out dependencies and risks, and explaining *why* certain things needed to happen, Ian failed to align his team. So everyone raced off at top speed with no coordination, looking like a tribute to the movie *Keystone Kops*. You already know where this story ends, right? Failure. After six months of zero progress, formerly committed teammates began taking other jobs. Ian was moved to another role. That particular "hill" was never seized, and a lot of business opportunity was lost. Everyone—team members, Ian, execs—was frustrated, though not all in the same way.

Figure 1-1. *Leaders can send the wrong signals*

Of course, wanting to move fast and get a-going toward a plum of an opportunity is not a bad thing! Speed absolutely matters. *But* there are devils in those details that enable people to go fast, in the right direction, together! When people don't understand what is really needed, they can't make key decisions that align with all the other players. Try as they might, they each end up going in slightly different directions. Ian's 80,000-foot take was that what needed to happen next was "clear," and he wanted people to get into gear and *go, go, go.* Ian did not just forget to ask for thinking—he squashed the very notion. Strategic thinking, including things like understanding all that would need to change, deliberating options, making tough choices between those options, and nailing down who owns what responsibilities, does not happen *in spite of* a process. It needs to be *driven by* the process. Ultimately, it is effective collaborative thinking that completes the "how" of strategy and drives the speed of execution. You can align people by the very way that strategy is created. The thinking and "why" of what matters gets encoded into the organizational ethos, the building blocks of every future action. That's when you can outpace the competition. To fix this systemic issue, you have to change the very way strategy gets created.

"It's Not My Job"

The third systemic pattern of failure involves decision making near the source of the problem. A successful firm I was working with, which I'll call Livery, was expanding from a software tools company (making software programs that people use) to a platform company (making software that other developers use to create their own programs). To accomplish this big strategic shift, a lot of things at the company needed to change, from the kinds of products they built to how they built them. Their goals required getting many external software developers involved and committed to this new platform, which meant that they no longer had 100% control of their own destiny. On many levels, it would take a new approach to doing business for them to succeed.

There was no one owner of this shift; it involved everyone at Livery, so everyone had to own a part of the larger strategy. When a significant problem arose, no single party could solve it, because it affected five different leaders and their divisional responsibilities. One leader opted to research the issue, to find its root cause and make recommendations for how to move forward. So far, so good: there was a problem, and someone took responsibility for it. But when this leader came back with recommendations to share with his peers, do you know what he heard?

Rather than a meaty discussion on how to apply the recommendations, what he got instead was pushback. "We've known that for some time," "how will we know for sure" that the recommended solutions would work, and "we've tried that before" were the gist of the conversation. The responses guaranteed that many questions would go unresolved. Zero progress was made. All agreed they needed to solve the problem, but the comfortable focus on things-already-known cut short the rather messy but necessary forward-looking conversation. The five leaders were struggling with learning about the unknown and how to drive change. Each leader had well-defined individual goals, which did not add up to success. The gaps in *between* their roles were not owned and thus compromised the business outcome. Because all of them owned it, no one owned it. They were the right people with the perspective and judgment to make the decision, but they were not comfortable with it. They did not want to bear the risk of the decision, and had other work nagging them for attention. And so, despite clear evidence of a problem and some consensus that the problem was in their neighborhood, the leaders did nothing.

There was a side effect as well. When the leaders show that they're reluctant to tackle change, other people in the organization who start out eager to initiate change and drive new solutions get stuck. "Why bother? It's above my pay grade." They go back to their defined job title–related roles until someone tells them it's time to do something different on behalf of the company. Everyone is exasperated at the lack of progress. The leaders can't see how their subtle insistence on certainty and clear, definitive answers for a new business problem actually stall progress. That risk-averse demand for certainty undermines the collaborative problem solving and tough choices needed to enable business success.

Why does it matter who in an organization handles unresolved questions? Many companies would just let festering issues bubble up to the top echelon of the leadership, but that slows company progress. And besides, does the very top of a complex organization really have the right context to make most calls? Organizations benefit when the people nearest the issue figure out how to solve it. Luckily, when the CEO drove a new way of working, Livery was able to figure out new ways the organization could make decisions closer to the point of action. Some people left because it was so different than their command-and-control way of working, but the overall sense of responsibility within the organization grew, and with it their ability to compete in the marketplace.

The Telltale Signs

Although it would be easy to look at these stories as isolated situational flaws, they are really common systemic issues companies face. They are evidence of how many firms are systemically set up to fail at strategy creation. While many people say they value collaboration, their people, processes, and organizational systems are not set up to support it. Each story highlights a particular element that was missing from the strategy creation process, namely:

- The collaborative actions and attitudes that encourage people to step up and shape the organization's future together.

- A way to work through the energy-consuming and often untidy process of shared strategy creation that reaches beyond the big idea, while still arriving at an end destination in a timely manner.

- The organizational ability to share ownership, do shared problem solving, and make decisions nearest the source of the problem, enabling the whole organization to go fast and stay aligned.

To transform how companies set direction and achieve results, it's important to understand and tune (or in some cases, reinvent) the way we enable people to create, communicate, make decisions, work collaboratively, and take action. To support straightforward examination, it helps to translate these stories into specific warning signs that we can look for in our organizations. There are always telltale signs of the three systemic ways strategy fails, and there are key lessons in those signs.

These telltale signs are clues to your organization's larger view on strategy and the strategy creation process. It's these signs that point to surefire failure (Figure 1-2). When cooperation, co-creation, and a careful exploration of ideas are discouraged, an organization fails to tap the talents, knowledge, and experience of its people.

Figure 1-2. *Telltale signs*

Consider whether you recognize any of the three signs in Tabl
from your own experience.

TABLE 1-1. *The telltale signs*

PARTICIPATION AND OWNERSHIP

Signs	*Lesson for collaborative strategy*
• Pay attention to who is invited and encouraged to be involved in the strategy creation process. Is it just the elite part of the organization, or is a broad range of people involved? Can the people involved bring different and broad points of view to the table? Once there, is there a demand that they step up and participate?	• Inclusive participation with the expectation that "everyone whose job includes judgment and choice must own the solution" is quite different from organizations seeking low involvement, or excluding players, or seeing strategy as owned by the top of the organization.
• Look at how facts are gathered. Are the people who live in that domain involved? Are many voices encouraged to participate and have a point of view? Do leaders say, "I'd like to involve the team, but they'll just slow us down"? If so, the process is biased toward seeking agreement or meeting a preset timeline, rather than discovery, ownership, and getting to the right answer.	• When the strategy process is exclusionary, important viewpoints, perspectives, and data get missed, diminishing the effectiveness of your strategy and hampering alignment and execution.
• If individuals say, "It's not my call," then you have a lack of collaborative rewards.	
• Watch how leaders react when individuals make suggestions or ask probing questions. If they routinely and consistently say, "We've already considered that" or "Let's take that offline," then the larger organization is not valued.	

ORGANIZATIONAL WISDOM AND READINESS

Signs	*Lesson for collaborative strategy*
• See if people are rewarded only for heroically doing their domain role versus working across boundaries to help the company succeed.	• You want to avoid highly controlled ways of doing strategy creation, and instead have the process allow for iterative cycles that support learning by the people involved.

TABLE 1-1. *The telltale signs (continued)*

- Watch for organizations with rigid "turn the crank" planning processes with directives to "fill out this template," as they are focused more on a milestone than on uncovering problems that need solving and building alignment. Controlled approaches that only answer preformed question lead to predictable answers but don't uncover issues or conflicts that need solving.
- See if the leaders approach the strategy creation process as orderly and deliverable-driven. That's desirable, but they often focus too much on rapid closure. Orgs that are excessively action-oriented typically have rigid processes. The focus is on "Did we create the document?" rather than "Did we have the right conversations?"
- Bypassing open-ended ("rambling") discussions means that ideas that merit closer examination often are not uncovered until it's too late.

- Learning and thinking precedes finding and solving key problems. Reluctance to explore options, risks, and issues early on sets you up for strategy failure later.
- Divergence of exploration must be balanced with convergence toward action. Strategy creation requires thought and judgment by co-owners of success. Otherwise, you simply have a team of doers.

DISTRIBUTED DECISION MAKING

Signs

- If you notice that the focus of the strategy creation process is solely on facts, assertions, and what is already known, your process is in trouble.
- Do you hear statements like the following: "This idea is missing x, y, and z," "We can't prove this will work," and "We've tried this before." These statements are used to shut down inquiry and avoid making new but hard decisions.
- Look for where problem solving takes place. And if all decisions are pushed up to the highest levels, then that top level becomes a bottleneck. Meanwhile, the wisdom and judgment of the rest of the organization is lost.

Lesson for collaborative strategy

- The more distributed decision making there is, the more the organization is seeking shared problem ownership.
- Because strategy creation is about creating something new, the process should do discovery and resolution at all levels of the organization. You want distributed decision making based on learning, shared responsibility, and creative problem solving.
- Cultures that value learning support collaborative decision making. A culture of learning values all sorts of intelligence, relishes inquiry, and encourages joint problem solving. "Do we have all of the relevant information we need?", "How have these findings been tested?", and "What else do we need to know?" are all questions of a Culture of Learning.

We all need to avoid focusing on templates or framework outlines and instead focus on getting people to think about what matters and why. Although the people creating those strategy templates are doing good work, they often don't realize that they are not encouraging thinking. Even with well-defined outputs and things moving quickly, the business can go south because the right debates, discussions, and decisions have not yet happened. In other words, without collaboration, strategy can appear to be done well but in reality it lacks the substance to create better business outcomes.

Strategies created in these environments are incomplete and at high risk of failure during implementation and execution. The Air Sandwich gets perpetuated. Let's look at how to set up a successful strategy creation system.

Strategy in the Organizational System

For a strategy creation process to engage people and still work optimally, a host of organizational elements need to come together. We aim to create an environment that supports people working together in the dynamic tension that enables generating excellent ideas, challenging underlying assumptions, vetting those ideas, sharing ownership, gaining a deep understanding, and establishing accountability for success. What follows will paint the full picture of how organizations can come together to form strategy.

First, even bright, talented, and motivated people cannot jointly create effective strategies—ones that people can implement to produce great results—until the fundamental enablers of collaboration are in place. If responsibility-sharing, decision-making, or idea-generation protocols do not enable a co-creative and collaborative approach, individuals can't overcome the obstacles to success. The fundamental organizational enablers for collaborative strategy fall into three areas (Figure 1-3):

Individual behaviors and attitudes
How do people act individually and within groups in the company?

Strategic process
Is there a structure or method that helps people learn the problem, create options, make tough choices, and create accountability while setting direction?

Organizational principles

Where are decisions made within the company, what is rewarded, how are goals set, and how are disputes resolved so learning happens?

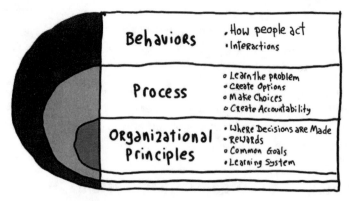

Figure 1-3. Systemic elements of strategy creation

Of course, all three parts of the individual behaviors, strategic process, and organizational principles are tied to the organizational system. By establishing a set of shared attitudes, values, goals, and practices for your organization or team, you'll establish a system of collaborative, productive work. Let's explore each of these elements and how they ultimately come together to help you and your organization establish effective strategy and reach new results.

Individual Behaviors and Attitudes in Collaborative Strategy

As we all know, simply telling people what needs to be done is rarely enough to produce action. Yet that's exactly what many organizations often do in the strategy process. Creating excellent strategy depends on collaboration throughout the organization.

This book will explain in detail a new holistic approach for aligning people to a direction by involving them in fully defining the "what" (the idea) and the "how" (developing options for how to deliver on the idea) and helping them all to understand the "why" (the reasons why something matters). When the what/how/why come together, then people come to own it. They believe in what they are doing.

They know how to make subtle decisions that, in aggregate, ɪ the difference between success and failure. They know how to re few weeks down the road when some change threatens to knouκ things askew. We call this new approach the *New How*.

This has specific implications. For collaborative strategy creation to work, we need to have a way for many people, regardless of title or rank, to participate in setting direction. And we also need their ideas to be valued and their contributions respected. Good strategies require great new ideas that can come from anyone and are often not a product of any single individual. Getting at the valuable ideas that are embedded in your team requires sharing ownership of success within the organization. The act of recognizing ideas based on their merit, not just based on who proposed them, gives some credit and recognition to the individuals or teams behind these ideas. Doing this well moves the focus to the ideas and shared ownership. As will become clear, it is important to be able to build up, tear down, and reconstruct ideas. It's best if individuals don't get too tightly bound to their ideas, or they may perceive criticisms of the ideas as personal attacks. Also, we want the full team to be comfortable adding to the ideas. So we seek shared ownership of ideas, and ranking of ideas based on their merit. We call this dynamic a "meritocracy of ideas."

Quite often, this means that people don't need to have fully formed recommendations before arriving at the table, but instead bring their thinking ability. Thinking happens "in the moment," and so often the individual nuggets and partial ideas are not airtight. Rather than criticizing and discarding incomplete ideas, leaders will build upon the useful pieces and encourage the shaping of options through an iterative process. The sources of individual ideas can see how their contributions were carried forward, which allows them to buy into the resulting strategy.

It sounds good to have a meritocracy of ideas, but it also raises the stakes for all the people involved. It means that people in the organization share a responsibility to play an *active* role, where they take personal responsibility for what gets created. When people are invited to participate, they need to be fully present with their points of view and willing to engage in setting direction. That means putting aside egos and politics and to stop attending meetings as observers, passively awaiting direction. Rather, the expectation on each of us is to show up as full participants in discovery and creation. It is easier said than done.

Later, when the decision is made, each of us knows we've been heard and feels as though the decision is, in a real sense, *our* decision. When that's true, we support the call that ultimately gets made.

Whether people choose to fully engage is deeply influenced by the behaviors and attitudes of the company's leaders. So we'll define what behaviors and attitudes are needed to enable productive collaboration.

But people's behaviors are not enough to enable a collaborative environment. We also need to set up work processes that enable people to come together.

Process for Collaborative Strategy

The strategy gap represented by the organizational Air Sandwich will not be filled with more presentations from above. PowerPoint slides are just another form of air in the sandwich. What's missing from the Air Sandwich isn't repetition of high-level ideas, it's *practical understanding*. Getting more people involved in the process leads to two benefits. First, it increases the diversity of perspectives, which means more potential ideas that win and more potential pitfalls avoided early. And second, it means decisions aren't simply directives from above. By having two-way communication about the strategy as it is formed, follow-on decisions can be made faster and better because the people making those decisions understand the intent behind the strategy, and why X must be done and Y must not be done, and how to choose between W and Z when those decisions arise. This lets management push the decision-making process closer to execution, supporting much faster action and helping to ensure that the cascade of decisions align with one another.

To accomplish this, however, we need to go slow to go fast. We need to involve the right people, do the necessary drill-down, and flesh out the feasibility details so it will work. Unlike what Ian believed was right, people need to create the "how" of strategy. But the process cannot take forever. We need to limit it. We need a process that supports participatory investigation, yet converges in a practical amount of time and generates a concise and specific set of actions. O strategy creation process, and the mindset of the people driving must meet several key criteria to ensure both understanding at quick closure:

- The process and mindset must ensure a shared understanding of the current context. By surfacing both the explicit and the underlying context, all team members can have the same view, and the process will drive alignment and preempt divergence during execution.

- The process must identify right-sized problems. Big problems must be deconstructed so they can be tackled by your organization. Some organizations try to take on the biggest problems all at the same time—what I call *eating an elephant in one sitting* (Figure 1-4). These organizations don't really know their limits, and they don't know what's involved in their tasks. They take on tasks that are too large, and consequently they fail.

Figure 1-4. *Eating the whole elephant at once = recipe for disaster*

- The process must help translate the inherent tensions of a problem into constructive, creative energy. When debate and brainstorming are welcomed, people can both contribute and process new data, insights, and perspectives. Without debate, issues will not be surfaced, and people will find it difficult to aim toward the right target. Organizations that squash debate typically "jump the gun" by getting started on problem solving without first fully understanding the root cause of a problem.

- The process should include mechanisms to identify and resolve conflict. Organizations often struggle with collaboration when the time comes to converge on a unified strategy. Many people are involved, and every idea in the pool seems to be someone's favorite. Teams tend to overinvest in trying to keep every idea alive.[1] For collaboration to work, the process must provide a way to cull the best ideas from all the options. We need to know how to spray weed-killer on some ideas and put fertilizer on others.

With an effective shared process in place, organizations can finally do the necessary discovery, debate, and elimination of ideas so they can lead the march toward progress and, in the end, success. Included in the New How is a specific yet flexible and convergent process framework.

But no process can take hold if the organization doesn't have rules and principles in place to ensure that people cooperate and align with one another. That's a crucial part of a collaborative strategy process.

Organizational Principles for Collaborative Strategy

The notion of harnessing the untapped talent, ideas, and insights of your people and their ideas isn't new.

But collaboration in action is rare because there is trickiness to it. It requires a mindset and a well-tuned process, and they need to mesh. It's very hard to add collaboration to an existing organization. There is a kind of quandary, the business strategy version of a Catch-22. If you're struggling, you're too busy to sort out how to switch to a new approach. If you're ahead of the pack, then why change? But occasionally a large and successful organization will not follow that faulty logic, like Tiger Woods choosing to optimize his swing. John Chambers has told us that Cisco, the dominant firm in networking, is turning the battleship by institutionalizing collaboration.[2]

Organizational rules of engagement can present pernicious problems for doing strategy collaboratively. This is because, in part, these rules are about invisible structures and abstract systems that are embedded in the fabric of the organization. The ownership of these rules feels anonymous. If these rules create motivations at odds with collaboration, then nascent efforts to encourage teamwork can be doomed. And so these rules must be examined closely. The New How identifies four principles for defining rules that enable organizations to collaborate effectively: they involve driving decisions locally, setting up incentives that reward common success, defining common goals, and making learning a key function of the organization.

One thing that helps organizations to collaborate is to view strategy creation less as a rigid turn-the-crank effort and more as a pathway to discovery. This highlights the "how" of strategy, what I refer to simply as "strategizing." Strategizing organizations view strategy as both a noun and a verb. The team members are constantly alert for ways to enhance success, knowing that some ideas will get integrated into execution quickly, and others will be pocketed until the time is right.

Organizations collaborate best when the rewards are based more on organizational success and less on individual accomplishment. Similarly, collaboration works when the results are measured, progress is tracked, and people stay in touch with what is going on. Without tracking, you get poor coordination, weak feedback, and weak accountability. Commitment and momentum will fade. You'll see that the organizational principles provide the glue that connects the people and processes into an organization-wide ability to win.

Naming the Systemic Issues Lets Us Fix Them

In light of all these ideas, can you look back at a strategy creation process you have been involved in—perhaps one where it didn't work out well—and see systemic patterns of weakness? Perhaps you had an experience, like the one I shared in this book's introduction, where you had an inkling that things weren't quite right. There are always early warning signs, but they can be hard to make sense of without a frame of reference. And even if you see them, addressing them is tricky unless the organization is oriented toward taking a systemic view of strategy creation.

We know now that people are not solely to blame. People are just one of the core elements that influence the dynamic of strategy creation, yet they're typically the prime targets when a strategy goes belly up. Blaming strategy breakdowns on individuals gives management the sense that they have fixed something. But when strategy is created in an impaired system, swapping out people doesn't fix much.

Good strategy creation depends on both a good system and good people. If you have a talented team and assemble the right systemic elements—individual behaviors and attitudes, processes, and organizational principles—you have the makings of a powerful organization for creating strategy. The rest of this book is organized into three parts aimed at addressing the systemic components.

Part I describes how people need to "be" in the system, both as individuals and as leaders. How we engage with one another matters a great deal, because people generate the ideas and make the decisions that determine what value we create together. How we behave toward one another is inseparable from how we work together.

Part II focuses on the methodology for doing collaborative strategy. Setting direction is an art and a practice. We need to know when and how to open up the spigot of ideas, and when to close the spigot and accomplish something. Collaborative planning and decision making has a bad rap, somewhat deserved, for never "getting there." By introducing a solid yet flexible process framework, you can be both collaborative and fast. Part II also includes the chapter on the MurderBoarding process, which is the basis of the strategy selection method. Readers interested in narrowing options may read Chapter 6 on its own.

Part III takes us up a level to think about the rules of engagement that organizations can put in place to foster a culture of collaboration and successful strategy outcomes. Changing organizational culture requires more than just bold moves and big announcements. How do you get whole groups of people to alter the way they think, work, and act? To help a new culture stick, you need a small number of big changes, and thousands of supporting small acts. This section covers the principles for incorporating collaboration into your company's dynamic.

Let's get started with Part I.

"Being" Collaborators

So far, we've talked about why strategies fail, the problem of an Air Sandwich, and the systemic reasons why that problem is perpetuated. Closing the gap for the Air Sandwich starts with fixing how we collectively work together. That means we need to explore and name the ways by which people can act to encourage collaboration.

There's a saying: "It's not personal; it's business." Any of you believe that? Of course not! Because what that quote actually implies is that when we are doing work, how we interact with one another is irrelevant. Surely by now you already know I believe the opposite is true: how we engage with one another matters a great deal, because our work is with people and the quality of our work product is entirely based on the ideas we create together. How we behave toward one another, therefore, shapes our creative work as we are co-creating.

In the past, we were complicit in letting strategy get created by an elite few, relinquishing our responsibility to rightly share in its creation. All that changes now. Along with our core beliefs and our rules of engagement, the way we behave as individuals and as leaders must transform. We are not only allowed to shape strategy and debate ideas, but we must do so.

Therefore, how we *act and express ourselves individually* is the first place to start.

Part I is organized into two chapters. Chapter 2 discusses the role *each of us* plays in the system, and Chapter 3 covers the role played by some *as we lead*. After we define how the participants engage the system, we'll move onto Part II: how the specific steps and actions must also change. That'll show us the way in which *how we act* gets rolled into *what we do*.

Let's look at the *ways of being* that will help us end the cold war within our companies and organizations, and enable us to improve our approach to strategy creation. In that manner, the *way of being* is both personal and business.

CHAPTER 2

Each of Us

A bird the size of a leaf
Fills the whole lucid evening
With his note
And flies.

—Wendell Berry

When Individuals Step Up Their Game, the Overall Game Gets Better

At the midpoint in my career, one day I found myself considering a set of difficult questions: What would make me a more valuable contributor? Could I be strategic? What aspects of myself should I cultivate to be the best at what I do? Are there things I could learn to be more influential? How could I make more of a difference?

These questions surfaced shortly after I had won a key argument about how my firm's marketing department should spend a $2 million budget most effectively to achieve the revenue target. I cared a great deal about how they spent the money, because I was directly accountable for a significant $58 million chunk of revenue (out of $400 million overall).

I was, of course, quite sure that my position on how to spend the money was correct. I had studied the issues carefully, formed airtight arguments that supported my position, and worked the halls to build political alliances. To further increase my chances of winning, I told people why my opponent, the marketing lead, didn't really "get" the business. And I had no trouble publicly highlighting the flaws in the logic of her arguments and opinions.

In the end, the decision was rendered in my favor and I received grand accolades from the higher ups. I won. I won because I had armed myself with facts and details. I won because I was argumentative enough and persuasive enough to convince stakeholders and decision makers alike that *I* was right. But at some level I also won by attacking a colleague.

Unfortunately, I did not feel like had I won. I felt hollow. Yes, I had won the battle (as I had many times before), but somehow I didn't feel triumphant; I felt troubled. Something wasn't right.

Up to that point, my work experience had led me to the idea that external trappings of leadership were the goal: actionable insights, responsibilities of budget and people, advanced degrees, drive and determination, status, organizational power, title, etc. And after winning that battle, I had more of that stuff than before. Yet I did not enjoy the outcome. Something—some valuable quality—was missing. If it wasn't missing from the results, then where was it missing? I realized that it was missing from the substance of my *being* inside this corporation. By "substance of being," I'm referring to my identity, and to the quality and nature of my interactions with everyone I worked with. In fact, to some degree, I did not really work *with* many of my colleagues. I worked *near* them or *around* them, but not *with* them. I was not, in a word, collaborative. I worked at being a high-performance individual player, but not a company player.

Before that experience, I had never thought about the choices I was making in terms of who I was and how I would *be* at work. Until I understood that disappointing win, I didn't get that *how* I won mattered a great deal. It turns out that, in this case, it mattered in several ways, and each way became a lesson.

It mattered personally. Remarkably, I already held a core belief in collaboration. But in my striving, I had lost the sense for how that needed to play out within the organization. It sounds trite, but Lesson 1 was that I had been neglecting one of my own values to respect all people, and as a result I had violated that core value. And that's why I was troubled.

Lesson 2 was that stepping on other people to force the "right" decision contributed to an environment where others did not want to speak up. When the multitudes of voices are stifled or silenced, ideas and initiative get lost. My behavior, along with executive support for it, undermined the sense of safety that lets people take risks inside the organization. My actions were creating the opposite of a collaborative culture. So, even if my spending preference was good for the firm, my style of winning did not benefit the organization.

Did it help me personally? Actually, no. Lesson 3 was that I didn't benefit in the long run, since many colleagues lost their ability to trust me, which made my job a lot harder after my "victory."

Each of these lessons is about the *way* I got what I wanted. I certainly did not aim to be "The Villain" of the story, but I did not know a better way at the time to get the "right" outcome. Like others, I was missing a mental model that would help me see how my behavior helped define a culture that lowered the effectiveness of the whole company. In retrospect, I could see that *what* each of us *does* is only part of our contribution. We also need to know *how* to show up, *how* to act toward others...in other words, *how to be*. My internal crisis was about how to excel as an individual while enabling a work environment that would lead the organization as a whole to a bigger success. And this crisis led me to spend the last 10 years reexamining people's individual roles in business overall and, specifically, in the domain of strategy. This chapter is about how each of us can play a more effective role inside companies.

Perspective Change

Without a change in our individual "how," a larger organizational shift to collaborative strategy is not possible.

The question becomes, "How does each of us create the most value for ourselves as individuals *while* enabling value creation for our teams and for the business as a whole?" Each of us, of course, works at creating value at all these levels, and more. Our firms seek to add value to the larger industry, and that industry hopes to add value not just for the shareholders but to society at large. Creating value fuels businesses. It's why we come to work, because I'm fairly sure most of us don't get out of bed each morning just to push paperwork around (or win an argument on how a marketing budget is spent). At our best, each one of us comes to work to create and to contribute to the larger whole.

Curiously, I don't know many people who define success in terms of adding value.[1] Even fewer talk about the personal choices that underlie that definition. Instead, most of us fixate on other indicators as measures of success, starting with GMAT scores, top-10 schools, and graduate degrees. Then it's where we worked, and to whom we reported or had lunch with. Or it's our title, or which VC funded our startup at what valuation.

Although we wave these banners as proof of success, they are more symbolic of positional power than of value created. The symbols certainly don't express the many small, tough choices people make day in and day out that translate into value creation inside a system. Outward symbols don't measure talent, contribution levels, passion, wisdom, or leadership ability. Titles, degrees, and affiliations might hint at the choices someone has made for *how to be* at work, but they are not the choices themselves, nor are they indicators or measures of value created.

To be deeply successful, we must recognize how significantly our individual approach impacts the effectiveness of the teams and larger organizations in which we work. This is a fundamental shift in perspective from the plain "what" we do to the richer "what and how" we do work.

---

*Outward signs (titles, affiliations) don't measure the choices we've made for **how to be** at work, nor do they indicate value created.*

At what time is the *how* of our work especially important? It is most important during times of stress, when we most need others to share their best ideas to define a new map forward. In short, nowhere is our "what and how" approach more important than when we are collaborating to set direction for the company by creating strategies.

So how do we do this? This chapter is about how each of us can shift our perspective away from an exclusive focus on the "what" of what we do, and include the "how" of how each of us works.

Beyond the Title

Think about your work not in terms of *what* you do, but in terms of the *role* you play. Your role is not just your title, but includes sets of behaviors, tools, and approaches to create value for and with your organization. The individual's role in collaborative strategy demands that each of us learn how to make new choices about who we are going to be at work, regardless of our job title or where we happen to be employed at any given moment. Our assignment is to break the systemic issues we discussed in Chapter 1.

Regardless of your formal title, you play various roles at work. Sometimes it involves leading people and sometimes not. Most leadership books tend to emphasize how to use leadership to improve the way people work. Very few books are written about how we as individuals can improve the way we all work together by altering the little choices we make in how we go about creating and adding value. Despite this gap, most of us have little trouble picturing a model collaborator. We may work with someone like that: the kind of person everyone hopes is on their team. Hardworking, high integrity, curious, easy to get along with, but also able to ask the tough questions and challenge everyone to do their best. It's easy to think in terms of playing the role of the great team member, but it's often hard to define the specific actions or behaviors.

I hope this chapter will stimulate a New How for how each of us shows up at work, and about how each of us interacts with our colleagues. My goal here is not to tell you exactly what to do, but to provide a construct; it's up to you to decide what you want to take in and commit to. So, before you dig in, take a moment and reflect on the following questions. How do I contribute today to the organization's larger success, independently of my formal title, positional power, or budget authority? Am I enabling the larger organization, and specifically my colleagues, to be successful through my individual way of being?

Do you have your answers to those questions? OK. Then let's proceed.

In the quest to consider a new way to engage at work and to become who each of us wants to be professionally, we need to let go of traditional definitions of workplace roles, which are sometimes more troublesome than useful in this area of collaborative work. There is a vast crevasse between people in the role of employee and people in the role of executive in business today. Generally speaking, people in each group view their counterparts as "the other." Strategy creation and execution missteps generate reactions like "The execs didn't get the strategy right" or "The employees failed to execute." This classic us-versus-them dynamic contributes to the Air Sandwich described earlier, where the strategy is based on a clear vision and future direction on the top layer, and day-to-day actions are represented on the bottom, but virtually nothing connects the vision to direction to reality.

This us-versus-them pattern promotes a situation in which both the executives and the employees look for "plausible deniability" of responsibility for any poor results. If things don't work out as well as they should have, they can just blame "the other" and avoid considering how they themselves might be implicated. And when we struggle to make progress, the divisive us-versus-them battles impede the larger organization from moving forward together and sharing the ownership for creating new strategies.

To counter this us-versus-them dynamic and establish conditions that improve our chances for winning, each of us must get beyond the artificial boundaries that traditional role designations define and reinforce. Do your best to stick those traditional, formal, or organizational labels in some mental cupboard. In place of those confining roles, I suggest that you consider becoming a co-creator.

Each of Us: Co-Creator

Being a co-creator is a new way of characterizing yourself, one that lets you focus on the value you can create, independent of the formal role you have. It gives you a way of morphing from an individual asset limited by organizational hierarchy to a contributor who recognizes that everything you do creates a ripple effect in the organization (Figure 2-1).

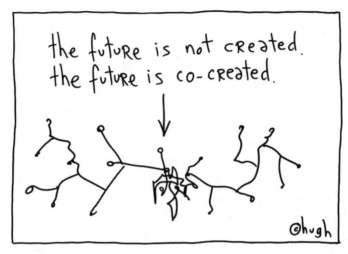

Figure 2-1. *The future is co-created*

As co-creators, each of us takes on a certain amount of additional responsibility for improving the process of creating and executing well-formed strategies. Each of us becomes responsible for co-creating the basis of success. And this is critical, because the business world is moving to a place where creativity drives results and ideas are becoming the core of strategic and competitive advantage.

Once upon a time, some firms had more access to data and information than others. Some firms had more skill at slicing and dicing. In that time, heavy-duty data analysis was enough to form a competitive advantage. Today, everybody has access to vast amounts of high-quality information and the tools to crunch it. What matters now is *the ability to act on* that information: to conceive—now—the nugget of hidden opportunity in a given situation. The key is being able to work with one another and come up with new ideas, build on those ideas, and then add insights based on the data that empower us to act in unique and differentiated ways.

It's not as if we used to be robotic "knowledge workers," copying and collating and answering email, but now any sign of routine activity is going out the door. Given the growing supremacy of ideas, we need a new moniker for individuals at work, one that matches how critical ideas are becoming for the growth and vitality of our companies. This designation is a *co-creator*. A co-creator is an advocate, a champion, and a lobbyist for the creation, development, and adoption of the best ideas to help the company win. Co-creators work as an important part of the organization, engaging people to create powerful new solutions to tough problems, regardless of their formal roles in the organization.

Fixing the way your company creates strategy and adopting a more inclusive process requires shifting how you participate and act. Each of us has contributed to the situation we find ourselves in today. Each of us has made choices in the past. Perhaps you kept quiet instead of questioning something your boss proposed, or chose not to contribute on a project because it wasn't your "assigned" role, or held back while others developed strategy because it "wasn't your responsibility." Or maybe it wasn't *what* you did but *how* you did it. Did you only half-heartedly suggest an idea that, in fact, you believe in strongly? Did you take a cheap shot at someone else's idea rather than making a constructive suggestion? What are the results of choices you made in the past? These behaviors likely debilitated the creation of new business solutions. The point here is not to dwell on the past, but rather to recognize that there is room for change.

A co-creator focuses on advocating, championing, and lobbying for the best idea to help the company to win, regardless of his or her role in an organization.

When we make these poor choices, we are stepping back instead of stepping up. When people lean back, the strategy creation process doesn't get all the fuel it needs to generate a well-formed strategy that would enable the company to succeed. Critical information about the company's situation in the market might be missing. Information about the organization's true capacity is absent. Almost certainly, the resulting strategy would lack some degree of commitment on the part of those who need to implement it.

And that's got to change. The shift involves two things. The first is your willingness to speak up and give voice to your point of view about what you know to be true. The second is to remember that a decision not to act or not to speak is just that: a decision. It's when this voice is let out that it can change the outcome. Held quiet, it never has a chance.

Until now, the executive team has owned strategy the noun, and no one has taken ownership of strategizing as the verb. Executives historically have claimed responsibility for setting the direction that produced "the strategy," and drove a culture that established the Air Sandwich. By not treating strategy as a recurring, progressive process throughout the organization, these executives are encouraging poor business outcomes.

Here is a story about Arthur, the vice president of product management for an $8B consumer products company. Arthur's story highlights how we can add more value as a co-creator:

> Arthur is a very intelligent executive in an interesting situation. Year after year, his company is losing market share and he isn't doing anything about it. Arthur feels constrained by the expectations that he believes his boss, the CEO, has of him. Arthur's formal role is to set product direction. The company is facing a set of complex industry trends and dynamics that are making the firm's products increasingly irrelevant in their current markets. Arthur has a strong gut sense of what the company needs to do to turn the situation around. Arthur is in an ideal position to see what direction the company needs to go and how the company ought to get there. Despite all this, Arthur is sitting on the sidelines.
>
> Interestingly, in private, one-on-one meetings, Arthur will say, "Look, I only have charter for 'x'—I'm only allowed to do 'y.'" As a result, Arthur won't bring up his ideas to the other executives, let alone lobby or champion for them inside the organization to make them actually work, because he doesn't believe he has that authority.
>
> What should Arthur do? If Arthur can't drive product strategy, who can?

While none of us wants to see ourself as like Authur, we all do this to some degree. We limit ourselves to what we believe others expect of us (based on our role or job description). So in this way, this chapter is about *you*: it's about you being able to champion ideas regardless of any specific role you have, and take on a role to help people see ideas in such a way that they want to act on them. It is about you, not as a "direct report" or as somebody who is a leader of *others*, but you as a co-creator—of insights, of creativity, of innovation, of contributions to your organization. Let's go forward recognizing that although coming up with new ideas and being smart is essential, it isn't enough to succeed. Being smart is just the beginning of being a co-creator. Smarts let you be the champion for the right thing, which is incredibly important. The difference is that you don't just want to make a smart argument, you want to turn those smarts into a focus on championing for the right solution.

So what will it take for you to become the strongest contributor to strategy creation that you can be? Let me share a secret: it's not about getting smarter. Sure, strategy frameworks, business models, market knowledge, and domain expertise are essential to strategy creation. But creating great strategy also involves being a good participant in a strategy creation process. And being a good participant is about engaging people in a difficult process, seeing together what matters in a given situation, and together making difficult trade-offs with insight. In other words, becoming the strongest contributor possible involves the set of choices you make in your interactions with others to achieve shared success.

Five Practices for Busting Out

No matter what you do or where you sit in your organization, you are always making choices. You make choices of action and inaction. You make choices about which ideas matter, which ideas you want to champion, when to assert your point of view, and what is worth advocating for the business to consider.

Some choices are about leading people and leading the processes. We'll cover those kinds of choices in detail in Chapter 3. Right now, let's look at how each of us can participate in strategy creation as a peer.

We want to achieve two objectives with respect to choices. First, we want to be more thoughtful and less automatic in all our choices, not just the big ones. And second, we want to establish a clear sense of "targeted intentionality"—that is, we need to be aware of the subtle impact on the big picture that we are looking to achieve through the sum of our small and large choices. The tools that we will use achieve these objectives are embodied in the following five practi These practices will help raise your level of consciousness abo choices that you are already making at work every day. If the practices seem a bit edgy, it is because they are intended to stimulate your thinking as you reimagine ways you can be more influential in how strategy gets created and how you contribute your ideas to the mix. Co-creating is also challenging, and you may find that some of the practices are at the edge of (or even a bit outside) your comfort zone. You may find that you will be expanding your comfort zone as you engage in co-creation. The practices are also designed to help you see the larger impact of your choices.

The five practices are:

- Call out
- Be fully present
- Understand the why
- Live in a state of discovery
- Embrace contradiction

Let's explore each of these practices in depth, to start thinking about how using these steps when you do strategy creation in your company will change the culture of work.

Call Out

Often in folklore we hear about powerful magical dragons or beasts we could control if we just knew their names. Calling stuff out within organizations is just like that. When we call things out, we take away their power. Calling out brings issues to light and helps an organization address them. In our role as co-creators, we must fully engage ideas that matter, *even when they are unpopular.* Co-creators will make choices that demonstrate a bit of boldness as they challenge the status quo by identifying and discussing topics that may have been previously taboo. Such individual choices encourage everyone on the team to participate in a conversation.

Do you see the issues when revenue forecasts are missed? Do you see gaps between divisions where ideas are getting lost? Do you see pertinent information being withheld? This ability to see and—more importantly—to *call out what you see* is the first thing you can do to start leading change.

Calling out starts with understanding the current state of your organization with as much curiosity and clarity as you can. Your ability to call out depends on your ability to see. Get clear on where your organization has strengths, weakness, blind spots, and patterns that don't serve the needs of the company. Identify where there are issues that need to be addressed. Find a way to talk about it that is direct and honest, but holds back on judgment or blame. When you call out, you say things like: "I see us addressing only A here and not B" or "It appears the root cause of this issue is X, Y, and Z" or "This issue can be traced back to last year, when we terminated a product line." Seek to express observations without blame or judgment.

Calling out adds clarity to a discussion. It helps everyone recognize the company's current state, and gets people to deal with the reality of a situation, instead of what they think is happening or want to believe is happening. When issues go undeclared, then teams, divisions, and even whole companies can spend their time and resources on projects that don't create value for the organization. Work at seeing these issues, and when you see them, call them out. Be the kid who called out that the emperor wasn't wearing any clothes. If you have a naked emperor, everybody should know about it.

Here are three recurring scenarios in companies where calling out isn't happening:

- The company fails to acknowledge why customers are defecting, so people work on product features instead of fixing the customer service experience, for example.

- The company wishes to defeat the competition, but rather than giving customers the features they need, the company focuses on new technology.

- The company does not recognize that a viable alternative to its products or services has entered the market, and continues to raise prices, unaware that their offering is becoming obsolete.

These examples show why calling out is valuable in terms of strategy. Calling things out helps prepare your business for what is around the corner. Despite its value, many seem to avoid it, as though the truth is "distracting" or too scary to think about (Figure 2-2).

That's like driving down a narrow and busy road in the dark: should you turn on your headlights or leave them off?

Figure 2-2. *Calling things out is crucial to success*

That said, calling out can be challenging. Have you ever kept your mouth shut in a meeting because you thought you'd be crucified if you dissented from the group norm? Have you held back your opinion because you wanted more time to research the issue? Have you ever agreed to something with the positive belief that somehow your team could figure it out? Calling out takes courage and commitment, because there is always ambiguity. I *might* be crucified. I'm not sure if research *would* support me. It's *possible* my team can deliver to that aggressive date. In these situations, it's easier to:

- Convince ourselves that others know better (without actually checking)
- Focus on only a part (the safe part) of what is there
- Keep quiet (even though you're sure)

All these alternatives to calling out are tactics to avoid pain. Pretending that others know better is an easy way to avoid the responsibility for fixing it. Similarly, when you focus on one part of what exists, you limit your responsibility and risk. After all (you tell yourself), dealing with part of a problem is better than nothing. But only when the full set of issues is known and the choice is explicit.

Working on one piece as a way to avoid issues comes with a risk: you may be solving a symptom instead of the root cause.

Keeping quiet is one of the techniques that all of us use (I'm not immune, either) to avoid extra work or embarrassment. After all, even Abraham Lincoln said: "Better to remain silent and be thought a fool than to speak out and remove all doubt." He was joking, of course; he didn't move the nation forward by keeping silent. Nor can we move our companies forward by doing the same.

We adopt these human tendencies to protect ourselves, but consistently avoiding short-term pain is a trap that results in long-term problems. When we make the choice to begin calling out, we are being subtly courageous, taking appropriate action even though we know there is a risk of short-term pain.

Remember that the aim of calling out is not to be negative or critical. It is not about doomsaying or "talking trash," both of which focus on the negative. Doomsaying dwells unproductively on potentially negative outcomes that have already been raised and considered. Trash-talking is exaggerating the faults of an organization or its products. Neither has any constructive intent, and neither is part of calling out. Calling out is an inherently *positive* activity, because until your company can identify its issues, the team cannot jointly decide how to respond to it.

As you begin to engage in calling out, you will find many opportunities. Should you leap at every opportunity to declare the unspoken truth? You will need some practice to develop a sense for the best situations and best language to use when calling out. But that skill will only come through exercise. The thing that doesn't work is avoiding calling out altogether.

Once you see what needs to be solved and name it, the next action you can take to lead change is to begin a dialogue and engage the issues. Did Wonder Woman walk away from the tough stuff? No, she got out her Golden Lasso of Truth and got down to business...and you should, too.

Be Fully Present

Woody Allen said that 80% of success is showing up. What is the other 20%? *Fully* showing up! Be fully present! Be bold! Show your views. Show your ignorance. Show your worries. Ask "dumb" questions. One of the most important choices you make at work every day—consciously or not—is how you choose to show up!

Many people think they are not supposed to question or weigh in, because they don't have a certain title, or a certain authority, or a certain level of leadership. None of us needs a designated role to have a point of view. That's old-school thinking, and it's totally unhelpful when creating great strategy.

Strategy creation is about understanding, debating, and co-building ideas. Generating great strategies is the creative act of people on a team. Why does that matter? Because if you're not in the room to advocate, deliberate, and contribute what you have to offer—essentially, to fight over the value of ideas for the benefit of the company—then you and your firm are missing a *huge* opportunity. Just by saying that you don't agree, or that you don't know enough yet, or that you've identified conditions that need to be met, your participation is key to making the whole thing work. Without each of us showing up with our best contribution, we cannot change the way strategy gets created. We must show up and engage.

Many people think that they should have an answer before they raise a question. Why? They feel they are expected to "know" something—and sometimes to know everything. Again, why? What is the point of Q & A if everyone is supposed to know the answer? It's worth a moment to consider also why so many of us feel that asking questions makes us look stupid. Some speakers don't like questions for various reasons, and try to discourage them. They may also see Q & A as a time for showing off. These speakers may make fun of people who ask questions, which has the side benefit of entertaining others in the room. But, other speakers do a great job of encouraging questions. "That's an excellent question!", they will say. How do *we* respond when we are asked questions? How does our response influence the culture of our firm?

Culture plays a big factor in how we limit ourselves. In the high-tech Silicon Valley culture, being smart is paramount. The implication: looking stupid should be avoided at all costs. If you show up at a dinner party badly dressed and use poor social manners, people may find you eccentric, but VCs won't be scared off. Even personal hygiene is, ahem, not an absolute requirement. But looking stupid? No, no! God forbid you might look stupid (gasp!). See Figure 2-3.

Figure 2-3. *Looking stupid takes courage*

Now, step back and think about this. Is it really so terrible to look foolish once in a while? It's not. And it's certainly better to look dumb and learn than to keep quiet and stay uninformed. If we're not willing to risk being seen as ignorant by saying "I don't know" every once in a while, we won't leave ourselves open to learning. It's a small act of courage to admit that you have more to learn. And there's a good chance that others need more information as well. Our ability to learn and grow is the single biggest factor that propels our success. Sure, it's not *fun* to look stupid or silly sometimes, but the *fear* of looking bad can be a major obstacle to your own contribution.

It's certainly better to look dumb and learn than to keep quiet and stay uninformed. It's called the **courage to learn.**

What about you, personally? What could be blocking you from bringing your all to your work? What would it take for *you* to say what you actually think? What do you need to do to be fully present in your work? Spend some time on these important questions.

Fear is the main factor that prevents most people from being fully present. Fear is not always a bad thing. It is information, and its value depends on the context and how you react to it. If we always react to fear with a pattern of avoidance, that is very costly. If we treat fear as a signal to pay close attention, then it is very useful. That's how I try to respond to feelings of fear. When I hear the voice of fear in my head, I stop and listen, because it is telling me there is probably some danger I need to account for in my thinking.

Fear can be a paralyzing force that prevents you from saying what is true for you. Or it can be a clear signal that you need to pay attention to something important. Listen not only to what people are saying, but also pay special attention to the needs or *fears* underneath their words.

As described in the sidebar "What They Mean to Say" on page 58, it took time to dig through the fear, but underneath it was a valid issue that the whole group needed to hear and consider.

To be fully present means being willing to share everything—your insights, your perspectives, your questions, your worries, and your fears—because you know that your contributions will benefit the group. When we don't share and reveal with candor what we really need, critically important "stuff" goes underground, which makes it more difficult to consciously manage for optimal business outcomes and often results in unintended consequences. Pushing stuff underground creates the opposite of what we want. To improve our chances of choosing the right strategies and executing them well, we need to share with people why we want or need something. Knowing this lets others help us achieve our intended outcomes in ways that might not be obvious at first. Ultimately, it's the benefits of transparency and a transparent culture that we aim to enable.

Being fully present and sharing your opinion has the added benefit of giving permission to other participants to show up fully and share as well. It is the opposite of hiding. It is the opposite of keeping your cards close to the vest. Author Virender Kapoor says, "It is not your intelligence quotient (IQ), but your passion quotient (PQ) that will take you to the pinnacle of success." He's right, and that's the essence of being fully present.

What They Mean to Say

I once found myself working with an executive team that had just been locked in a conference room with an order from the CEO to "cut costs now." We were given 23 hours to figure out what to cut and what to spare. We spent the better part of the day bickering over who could give up what, and at some point one of the guys announced, "I will not cut any part of my team." As you can imagine, this didn't sit well with anybody. The others quickly ganged up on him.

At some point, someone intervened by asking the guy to share his reasoning (as opposed to his ultimatum). He replied that he had built the team from scratch and hired each person. This was largely true for everyone in the room, so his answer was insufficient. The voice in my head said, "Get real!" But I pushed my frustration aside and asked if there was something else he wasn't saying. And that's when we got to the essence of the situation.

He explained that his team was made up of the best people in the industry. They all lived in the same city and worked well together. He worried that if he fired one of them, they would all leave to form their own company and become his division's competitor. Not only would he lose stellar employees, he would have to face a much tougher fight in the market downstream. The truth for this guy was finally revealed. In speaking this truth, he had finally chosen to be fully present. There was an audible, collective sigh in the room. Everybody now understood what was at stake.

Revealing this executive's fear changed the whole dialogue in the room. The team immediately began to have a much richer discussion about trade-offs and what they ultimately wanted. In the end, they made certain that the cuts they decided to make kept his team intact.

When you are fully present, you bring your passion to the table. Learning to bring your passion is instrumental to being a better strategist. Here are some simple ways to practice being present:

- Share your needs, desires, ideas, thoughts, questions, and fears with others.

- Never discount the power of your voice to influence an outcome, and trust that people will take your concerns seriously.

- If you notice that you have withheld something at a meeting, send a note and follow up later. There is always a second chance.

The next not-so-obvious way you can participate in strategy creation is to make sure you know the "why" of a decision.

Understand the Why

Some people feel like they shouldn't share why decisions are made the way they are. This can include sharing what data was used to inform the decision, which people weighed in, or what risks were considered.

If, say, only a small group of leaders knows why decisions are being made the way they are, it leaves the rest of the organization in the dark. It suggests to people that there's some "all-powerful wizard" behind the mysterious curtain who is the only one with the ability to make things happen, and that each of us is not a co-creator. It can leave the organizational players believing they have no say in what is being decided. By now, you know these two outcomes are taboo.

Everyone is better off when they know why decisions are made with as much accuracy as possible. It gives them an understanding of what matters and provides information on which to base the trade-offs constantly being made at every level. It also boosts buy-in and energy from the organization. When reasons behind decisions are not shared, the decisions can seem arbitrary and possibly self-serving. That is, they may seem like they are made for the good of the decision makers, rather than the good of the organization.

When the "why" is unknown, decisions can seem arbitrary and self-serving. When the "why" is known, it raises everyone's ability to align subdecisions.

We need our people to bring their full brainpower to the game and devise the best ways to get from "here" to "there." That means sharing data and assumptions freely so you get a full organization of great strategic thinking. You get people knowing what matters, so they know what trade-offs to make to accomplish the goal.

One question that comes up is whether to share contradictory data. I'm a firm believer in transparency, even when the data is not quite aligned to the planned direction. Why? Because if it turns out that something changes in the marketplace, we don't go all the way back to the core decision, only to realize we had mixed signals early; we just might want to make a 30-degree turn on a decision to adjust. In any case, choosing to withhold contradictory data is tricky, since the people who already know that data will get the sense that the decision makers were in the dark and that the decision was flawed. Again, more informed now equals more aligned later.

Transparency ultimately gives people the power to adjust the aim when needed, and yet stay in full alignment with the larger whole. Transparency from decision makers also encourages transparency elsewhere, so that useful but inconvenient tidbits of information throughout the organization are not swept under the rug.

The good news here is that even if you did nothing other than calling things out, you still would lead change in your organization. To lead more change, you could be fully present, actively leading by example and bringing a new power to your organization. To lead *even more* change, you can choose to drive organizational transparency. These choices are yours, and that's an awful lot of power one person can have.

These actions, when combined, provide a solid place to start leading change inside your organization. Remember, Margaret Mead once said, "Never doubt that a small group of thoughtful, committed citizens can change the world. Indeed, it is the only thing that ever has." We are the citizens in the world of our organizations. The kind of change that propels our companies forward can start with each of us, if we choose to be thoughtful and committed. Cultures change not because of some edict from on high, but when all people come together and start to act in a way that others follow. It's when our way of thinking, being, and doing fills in the Air Sandwich that we start to create more value together.

Live in a State of Discovery

How many times have you made a decision only to realize later on that you had neglected key evidence that was *right there in front of you?* Why didn't you see it? Were you bound by your own experiences, a prior way of doing things, a preconceived notion of the way things are?

This is totally human. From time to time, we all find that the way we see the world is limited by unconscious notions of what we believe reality is. But there is a contrasting *conscious* choice any of us can make: it's a choice to live in a state of discovery.

Great strategy is at its very core about designing the future, and what it will take to realize that future. If we are not in a state of discovery, we limit the number of possibilities we imagine, invent, and strive for in the future. When we endeavor to live in a state of discovery, we are willing to engage new ideas and revisit assumptions. With practice, we find it easier to let go of earlier ideas to build different ones, and thus tend to be open to the contributions of others. This has an interesting byproduct. When we loosen our grip on our own point of view in order to see others' points of view, we stop appearing "political" to others.

Living in a state of discovery is an active choice. It means consciously continuing to expand our mental frameworks, and staying open to new knowledge, new insights, and new experiences. I call this "being curious": being inquisitive about the world, about other people's points of view, about how things work around you, and even about new notions of yourself. If all that sounds positive and exciting, understand that living in a state of discovery also means being willing to accept facts we don't like, and being able to see old facts in a new way.

Staying curious and open helps each of us stay mentally agile. By contrast, when we treat our experience, knowledge, or insights as "complete" or "done," we limit ourselves to the past rather than embracing the future. As long as we restrict incoming data sets, we screen out the good ideas along with the bad. We lose essential information, constricting our ability to invent, reinvent, and create (and co-create) the future.

ne common challenge in adopting a state of discovery is learning to
;ten. That seems obvious, but again we must resist some of our natural instincts to listen well. Listening is particularly hard when we
have some perspective or concept that we truly value, a key insight or
piece of data that we want to share. In our desire to "express," we
sometimes focus more on outbound flow rather than capturing
inbound insights. And we know that if we impress upon those
around us that we already know all that needs to happen in creating
our future, we leave little room for new options in the collaboration
process. The key? A balanced flow of both. We share and we learn.

In the long run, what truly matters is not what each of us knows
today, but our ability to continue expanding the aperture of what
each of us can see and understand tomorrow. In the short run, any of
us can strengthen our skills by learning how to ask good questions.

Living in a state of discovery is an ongoing practice. It is a muscle you
can constantly flex, exercise, stretch, and strengthen. By choosing to
be curious and accepting of other points of view, you can move from
an unconscious preoccupation with your view of reality to being
open to new ideas, differing points of view, new scenarios, and
unpredicted realities (Figure 2-4). This openness will strengthen relationships and certainly help each of us become a wiser strategist.
This is a necessary ingredient in good collaborative strategy creation. In other words, each of us must be willing to set aside the
preconceived notions we might have about somebody else, just as we
need to stay open to the idea that they might have preconceived
notions about us!

Learning to live in a state of discovery can be a challenge, given the
day-to-day and moment-to-moment pressure we experience on the job.
Here are some straightforward techniques to begin developing this
critical skill:

- Enter meetings with the intention of asking at least three open-
  ended questions. These questions should not be about gathering
  basic facts or about binary issues where a simple "yes" or "no"
  could suffice, but perhaps about what matters and what is possible. For introverts, some preparation can help them know what
  they want to explore. For extroverts, it is more about making
  sure to ask questions that create more learning.

Figure 2-4. *Open to a new reality*

- Set a goal for yourself to be in "discovery mode." There are times in any project where it is clear you need to know more before you even know what questions need to be asked and answered.

- Stop silently criticizing yourself and others for not knowing the answer already. Interestingly, really bright people often make it harder on themselves than necessary by judging themselves for not already knowing. Judgment of yourself and others is best curtailed, because it interferes with your ability to be open to learning. To be open to a new reality is to set aside judgment, if only for a while.

Perhaps the most powerful technique for living in a state of discovery is to temporarily suspend passing judgments on seemingly conflicting data, information, opinions, and stories—in short, embrace contradiction.

Embrace Contradiction

One of the toughest things about being a strategist and a co-creator is that almost all of the easy problems have already been solved by the time you arrive. The easy issues involve decisions that are relatively straightforward and linear, with clear cost-benefit trade-offs. This means that the investments and the barriers to action are largely about money and resources. An example might be a run-of-the-mill marketing program where the decision is clear and resources need to be allocated.

Difficult problems, however, occur when you are breaking new ground. Solving such problems requires that both the means and the ends be found. They are often intuitive or holistic decisions where even the process of discovery itself can be transformative. The complexity of these types of decisions usually means they are mired in resistance that borders on open conflict. To solve the problem, the organizations and humans involved will need to change and adapt in some yet-undefined way. A typical strategic decision is a new market entry or an integration of two companies.

Strategy creation for difficult problems, therefore, is incredibly complex by its very nature. It's rarely clear what the "answer" is, because the problem itself often is not clear. When you roll up your sleeves and dig in, you find a situation of deep complexity where *no* solution appears ideal. The hallmark of thorny strategy problems is that they involve contradiction—that is, they contain a set of conflicting goals or imperatives that create a tension that defies objective resolution. Either something about the future conflicts with some aspect of the present, or two aspects of the future conflict with each other. *If this were not true, the problem would be straightforward.* Your intuitive sense for resolution will often differ from someone else's intuition. And that, of course, is the challenge to arriving at a solution many people can get behind.

> *The hallmark of complex problems is paradox.*

Doris Kearns Goodwin, one of my all-time favorite authors, wrote a definitive book on Abraham Lincoln and his Cabinet called *Team of Rivals* (Simon & Schuster). In her book, she characterizes what so many great leaders do when dealing with contradiction. Goodwin states that when Lincoln assumed his presidency, he rounded up his "enemies" and invited them to join his Cabinet. He assembled a team of his adversaries and put them to work for him. At that time, slavery drove the business of agriculture, and agriculture was the engine of the economic growth for much of the country, particularly the South.

Abolishing slavery would undercut many people's livelihoods, changing the economic structure of the country. Depending on a person's perspective, slavery was either vital or an abomination.

Opponents of the Civil War criticized Lincoln for refusing to compromise on the issue of slavery. Others criticized him for moving too slowly to abolish slavery. Lincoln assembled his political adversaries into his Cabinet knowing he needed their gifts. According to Goodwin, Lincoln, like other great leaders, did not merely tolerate contradictory points of view; he *encouraged* them. In the end, every single Cabinet member helped to shape post–Civil War America. Today, we all recognize slavery as a cruel human tragedy. But in Lincoln's time, the issue of slavery was an economic and moral contradiction.

Contradiction is inherent in all decisions involving significant change. When each of us can live with and explore opposing ideas, we create the space to generate more creative solutions than we first thought were possible. At the time of the Civil War, many felt it would be impossible to reconcile our differences and continue as one nation. Yet we were able to change and progress.

To develop as a strategist and co-creator, each of us will eventually internalize the notion that developing good strategy for complex business problems involves opposing ideas living in tension. There is rarely just one right answer when dealing with complex business problems. Those who constantly insist on black and white perspectives will find progress a constant struggle. Don't just tolerate contradiction; *embrace* it and work with it.

Learning to embrace contradiction is uncomfortable for most people. That said, it's richly rewarding because it allows us to take on tough debates and likely uncover tacit issues, and empowers each of us to arrive at a solution that couldn't be devised without a deep understanding of the situation.

Here are a few techniques to start embracing contradiction:

- Notice how much you value certainty versus uncertainty on any given decision, or peace over conflict. There is no right or wrong answer, but you need to know where your natural set point is so you can manage it during strategy creation.

- Rate how important certainty or peacemaking is to you, and try increasing your tolerance for uncertainty or conflict in small increments. If you find yourself appeasing people to create peace, you are simply camouflaging the problem and it will only continue to get worse.

- Ask yourself, "How could it be possible for both things to be true?"

Without a doubt, learning to embrace contradiction is at the heart of becoming a valuable contributor in the strategy creation process. Refer to Appendix B for more information on dealing with contradiction.

Sitting Forward, Going Forward

We are constantly facing choices in our workplace. On the one hand, we constantly see issues that ought to be addressed today, if not sooner. On the other hand, we are tempted to choose the safety and comfort of checking out and "going with the flow." Why rock the boat? Why risk being wrong? Why risk a potential conflict? Isn't it safer to just avoid the risk of being wrong? Wouldn't keeping quiet be a lot more comfortable than dealing with the issues head-on?

For those of us who seek to do the best thing for our firms, to be strategists and co-creators, the choices are clear, even if they aren't easy. It might seem safer, more comfortable, and easier to sit back, but we know underneath, it's actually not. We know that if we do this, we're depriving the organization of what we know, our insights, and our particular perspective. Our viewpoints can be crucial to helping the company to win. And if the company doesn't win, none of us win.

In order to fill in the Air Sandwich, we can't afford to play only our formal, defined individual roles and neglect what's going on within the team and the business's "field of play."

Adopting the five principles in your individual role is about *sitting forward.* Sitting forward is a way to meet the world so that you are ready for action—ready to listen, to learn, to connect disparate ideas, to help advance options, to create, and ultimately to make something real. You are engaging with the world, not witnessing it passively.

When applied to strategy creation, your involvement is highlighting what's most important, thus shaping the criteria; making sure the right facts are gathered; weighing in on what will work or not; and ultimately making sure that any potential "gap" between the vision and making that vision a reality gets addressed and closed.

When you make a decision to sit forward, the kinds of problems you deal with may not change, but your appreciation of them will. And, hopefully, through your contribution, others will also appreciate the situation more fully.

This basic stance of collaborative engagement is what drives many people to exhibit great leadership, brilliant thinking, and decisive action. Not surprisingly, these people tend to be very successful. But success doesn't come from action alone; success comes from a position or a stance, a deeper way of *being* that consistently creates engaged behavior.

You might find it beneficial to view the apparent problems and challenges in your work life as opportunities to learn something, to make you stronger, to prepare you for something that might happen in the future so you'll be ready. Although the benefits are not always immediately obvious, when you sit forward and embrace problems instead of avoiding them, you learn and grow, and thus get stronger more quickly.

There is a saying in Eastern philosophy that goes: "If you have a fish in a pond and want it to get big and strong, put a stone in the middle of the pond. The fish will swim around and around the stone trying to get to the other side."[2] It is in the fish's nature to explore and move. It is a way of responding to the environment, of being active and present to what can be. Just like the fish, each of us can choose how we respond to our environment. We can choose to be passive in response to the stones in our pond, or we can engage with our environment. One mode definitely changes our relationship to our world and the stance we take when we take on new challenges. One mode makes each of us stronger.

As is evident, we can have a major impact by sitting forward. We can shift how our organizations create strategy today by calling out, being fully present, understanding the why, living in a state of discovery, and embracing the contradiction inherent in complex decisions.

Each of us must do our part to find our voice and participate in the chorus of work going on around us. As we do this, we will start to change how we work together.

You've likely seen these practices at work in real life. Perhaps not as often as is needed, and maybe not in your current organization, but you've seen it. Recall your own experience of when a team is clicking and collaborating, and you'll see that the members are living out the five practices as a norm. These practices are not inherently hard, but they do require personal strength, finding your voice to contribute as an equal member of a whole, and an intent to co-create the best solutions together.

When each of us contributes in our own way as a co-creator, no single person has to carry the load. Not the exec team. Not some smallish cadre of "strategy leaders." We each own our piece of responsibility and the load of carrying our part. Having each of us pick up that load and change how we approach work will enable collaboration within organizations to take place systemically.

Those who lead people or projects (in addition to being co-creators) will expect to carry specific responsibilities for enabling how we work together collaboratively. That's next.

CHAPTER 3

As We Lead

*The road to success is dotted with
many tempting parking places.*

—Will Rogers

Enabling Organizational Velocity

Some of us have the challenge of leading people and initiatives in addition to being champions of ideas. This expanded role offers a lot more *opportunities* in the area of collaborative strategy creation. For most of us, leading is a privilege that comes *in addition to* our regular, everyday workloads, work that each of us must perform flawlessly because resources—talent, budgets, headcount, and schedules—aren't as abundant as we might want or need. Leading collaborative strategy is not as easy as it looks.

Perhaps a story of a newly minted general manager will highlight the point.

Not long ago, a Rubicon colleague asked me to take a meeting with Lucas, who had recently received a prestigious new role at a global media company. The meeting was framed up as an opportunity to explore creative new ways to drive "exponential growth" in what pundits might very well consider a mature business unit.

We talked over lunch at a bustling Greek restaurant. Lucas was sharp, creative, and ambitious. He came across as a confident executive and a strong leader. Nearly two hours disappeared as we spoke about corporate and divisional strategic issues, focused intensely on the questions related to growth. We talked about Lucas's passion for his products and services, and the initiatives he wanted to start and the goals he had. He shared a plethora of detailed facts, keen observations, and expansive ideas.

In particular, his division's current annual revenue was $338M, and he believed that his division was well positioned to outpace the overall company's expected low double-digit growth rate. Based on his fresh perspective and new understanding of the dynamics driving his business, Lucas had concluded that it was possible to drive it toward a much higher goal. Indeed, he was looking at how to achieve triple-digit growth!

Emphatically, Lucas told me that he wanted his team to step up and figure out how to tackle this huge potential opportunity. He recognized, however, that there was at least one obstacle. Lucas was self-aware enough to know that he was enmeshed in too much of his team's individual detail work. He observed himself offering more specific direction than was appropriate given the talent of the people reporting to him. Plus, he had the vague sense his people were somehow holding back.

Between the talking, eating, and drinking, I began a mini-version of my Fact Gathering interview (which we'll cover in Chapter 4) to learn more about Lucas's business and to explore various ways I might be able to help him. We explored dozens of possible approaches to accelerate growth, and looked at creating new product and service offerings to crack open and win new markets.

Whenever I asked Lucas a question that challenged his basic point of view, I saw his eyes light up. "Wow. That's a good idea," he would say. Or, "Oh, I think that would work...."

Lucas responded more passionately to a particular category of questions than others: he had energy around optimizing channels of distribution, creating new offers, performing customer requirement research, and conducting quantitative analysis. Questions that had specific and factual answers prompted Lucas to sit forward in his chair.

In contrast, some questions didn't move Lucas a bit. For example, he wasn't terribly interested when I asked him questions like: "So what do you do to generate ideas from your people?" or "Does your team believe this growth is possible, too?" or "Where, specifically, are your people limited in their decision making and initiative?" His responses were flat. At best, he would mutter something cordial or polite like, "Hmm. That's probably worth looking into."

Over the next couple of days, I found myself mulling over the conversation, trying to put my finger on the source of Lucas's mixed responses to my questions. Only when I had consciously set the topic aside could I see the odd reality of the situation: Lucas was standing directly in his own way.

Lucas was obviously interested in finding creative, innovative ways to win. There was absolutely no question he wanted to be a growth leader, to help his team take real ownership of market opportunities. However, it had become abundantly clear to me that Lucas's natural strength as a gifted problem solver was somehow more compelling to him than his less-developed collaborative skills. This dynamic was holding Lucas back, as it does for many otherwise effective executives, and biasing him toward a definitive, smartest-guy-in-the-room approach to strategizing and winning.

The very thing that helps leaders get to their role of leadership biases them toward a "smartest-guy-in-the-room" approach to strategizing.

Even though Lucas was very much aware he needed his team to step up, he had not recognized his role in getting them to co-own problems and co-create solutions. Meanwhile, the familiar territory of largely solo problem solving had Lucas's sharp intellect literally champing at the bit. I'd seen this before.

If my previous experience was any guide, Lucas's personal challenge was due to conflicting imperatives. On the one hand, he believed himself to be the champion who would be able to find the answers to the tough questions that would ultimately lead to the success he envisioned. On the other hand, he was sensitive to the fact that his team, not he alone, had the knowledge, talent, and capacity to step up and ultimately deliver those breakthrough results. Is it possible to do both? Put another way, can someone in Lucas's position simultaneously find the strategy "answer" *and* get people to step up and engage? This question is the heart of the challenge for most executives.

Talented people are chosen for leadership positions because they possess some keen talent, insights, vision, and/or extraordinary problem-solving skills. And often they find it easier to exercise these skills than to teach them or coach others to use their talents more. To add to the challenge, attempts to promote collaboration are often unrewarded in our current work culture. So it often happens that our Achilles heel as leaders is attempting to come up with the answers and solve the tough problems by ourselves (Figure 3-1).

Figure 3-1. *The Chief of Answers shows up*

Perhaps you see a bit of yourself in Lucas's story? From your personal experience, have you come to believe that you can solve problems faster on your own than you would through any group effort? This is a dangerous type of trap for us leaders, because it lures us into believing that we alone can answer the most vexing questions and solve the toughest problems. And so, rather than collaborating with the people, engaging knowledge, and tapping into the talent within the organization, we go it alone.

If you see yourself in this story, you've got company. This is more than the norm than the exception, and the more complicated the business issue the more likely people are to "go it alone." The upshot is that leaders often figure out "the answer" solo or in small groups, then set direction and tell their teams to "execute." Voilà, the Air Sandwich is manifest, and organizational velocity is not achieved.

Here is what I later said to Lucas—something I wish I could say to all GMs, VPs, directors, and managers in similar situations:

> The answer to today's specific question is only that—part of the solution to today's problem. Next week's problem will require a different solution. And next month's question will need yet another answer. Crowning yourself the Chief of Answers puts you in a difficult position, one with very little advantage. It sets your team up to be the Tribe of Doing Things. And, at the end of the day, you end up feeding the very counterproductive cycle you need to alter.

Our past successes bias us. They reinforce our tacit worldview that, as the smartest person in the room, we can avoid the messy dynamics of group problem solving. All we need are access to credible data, great research, excellent analysis, and clever insights. Our past successes reinforce our misguided belief that we can come up with the best strategic idea faster and far more efficiently on our own rather than slowing down to collaborate with our people.

The Chief of Answers model fails the organization on multiple levels. Here are a few:

- *Scalability.* Having everything go through one leader (or a small set of leaders) limits growth. The number of different kinds of business challenges grows as the market speeds up. The Chief of Answers cannot know the multitude of issues as well as the people who are closer to the problem. The speed of changing issues, the trend of that rate of change, and the speed at which the organization must react is crucial to competitiveness going forward.

- *Ownership.* When people understand the reasons things are broken, why decisions are made the way they are, and so on, they ultimately own the thinking. This means they can own the outcome. Without this understanding, only a few people feel ownership for the success of the strategy; the rest are collecting paychecks.

- *Retention.* Our incoming workforce of millennials expects to play a big role in setting direction. This group of people with new ideas can choose which organization to work with.

- *Motivation.* Sitting outside the room doesn't motivate people. They want a seat at the table. When a Chief of Answers leads, the best people go to organizations where they can make a more meaningful impact.

The Chief of Answers model rests mostly on individual smarts. But we all know that setting direction requires more than an accumulation of facts, processes, formulas, and individual insights. It is about going beyond data, insights, and models. It's about applying many different perspectives and challenging the status quo, making shifts inside the organization and jointly steering it toward a new, compelling future. It's about getting many people to understand, believe, co-create, and co-own the outcome of a strategy, thus turning a direction into reality.

The End of the Era of the Chief of Answers

When a leader crowns himself the Chief of Answers, making him the key person responsible for driving all strategy, he creates a bottleneck in the organization. By not involving other people in the strategy process, things get bogged down (see Figure 3-2), and it's a struggle to do strategy creation effectively. Under these conditions, his people will always be dependent on him, and he will be the limiter of what could otherwise develop into a fast, responsive, adaptive organization. What we want instead is a leader of co-creators.

Recognizing and accepting that the Chief of Answers (CoA) model is obsolete is not always easy. Many of us began our careers during a time when that model was still well regarded, and we've invested a lot in building a set of skills and perhaps a reputation as Chief of Answers (though we don't call it that; we use the terms "whiz kid" or "go-getter"). And some industries move slowly enough that Chiefs of Answers can still manage to keep up. But in the complex and dynamic industries, the CoA model is toast. RIP. And it's critical for this reality to be internalized by everyone who wants to lead a vibrant and powerful team trying to win in those markets. There is a lot of commonality between the failures of the CoA model and why strategies have been failing.

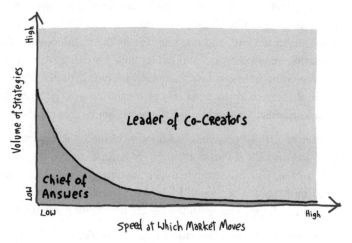

Figure 3-2. *Volume of strategies versus speed of market*

Responsiveness is key to future competitiveness. One person or a very small number of people cannot keep up with a) the number of issues, and b) the rate at which they move. And of course the trend is toward more and faster. Because customers who depend on us are also experiencing these trends, a key differentiator among companies is responsiveness. Responding quickly and well depends on how quickly and accurately information and decisions flow through the organization. Responsiveness also depends on how a company listens, discerns, learns, and organizes itself to respond quickly to what customers will pay for (knowing full well that what they say they want today might change tomorrow).

Many of today's fast-paced industries were just about manageable 10 or 15 years ago, but since then all kinds of complications have been layered on. Outsourcing, localization, increased automation, open licensing, shared APIs, Software as a Service (SaaS) models, and middleware dynamics can all be big factors in decisions, whereas they were only peripheral elements before.

Our shift toward the "information economy" and "knowledge workers" means that we have few turn-the-crank jobs left. We have leveraged machinery, software, and overseas labor farms to handle routine and predictable work wherever possible so that we can compete. Predictably, our teams are now full of highly educated, experienced, specialized *smart* people doing work that requires care and judgment.

'n the one hand, we need these people to care about the work that ley do, and on the other hand, we would love to take advantage of what they see, anticipate, and imagine. We as their leaders want them to get what we're envisioning, and tell us how it's either wonderful or broken. We want to know how they could make it better. We even want each of them to know what others are thinking, to generate concepts and solutions that would not have been conceivable otherwise.

This model of a fully engaged "wisdom workforce" is incompatible with the CoA model. If you don't actively engage people throughout the organization, you will struggle to get them to agree on what's most important and what success will look like. If you've hired well, these people won't be happy sitting on the bench; they want game time!

Yet, according to research, we don't treat them like participants and co-creators of the business outcome.

Only 5% of the workforce understands its company's strategy.[1] Only *1 person in 20* is prepared to answer, clearly and realistically, what her company should be doing and how her individual efforts contribute to supporting it. ("You don't know the strategy? But I sent out the slide deck!") See Figure 3-3.

Figure 3-3. *Everyone needs to know the strategy*

> *Only 5% of the workforce understands its company's strategy.*

Can people really be effective without knowing the strategy? Not likely.

There's a real potential to use the fuller organization to consider and make decisions quickly, based on information that comes from the depths and edges of the company, from customers, partners, and suppliers. This builds a team of professionals.

The Goal Is Repeated Wins

Existing or aspiring leaders who may see a bit of themselves in Lucas's story may be reacting to this collaborative workforce vision in two ways. First, it may seem as though I'm suggesting that you are no longer a key strategist. Second, you may wonder if you need a new skill set to be a leader of champions.

To answer the first question, no, you're not abdicating the role of key strategist. You're simply gaining new leverage. Let's put to rest the notion that the goal is to get to one big win, because the ultimate goal isn't to win once but rather to win over and over again. As leaders, the way to do this is by increasing the quality of ideas and speeding up decision making by helping our teams collaborate and co-create, and by distributing the ability to solve the toughest problems throughout the organization. Together, this creates the conditions for our companies to outshine the competition by out-thinking them, out-creating them, and out-innovating them...repeatedly.

And to answer the second question, yes, you'll need some new approaches. You will want to shift the organizational processes that influence how people input ideas, develop options, and make decisions. And we need to influence the protocols for how people vet ideas and communicate risks and dependencies with one another, so that decisions align to form a unified direction. The protocols must allow for productive deliberations and checkpoints while avoiding red tape, bureaucracy, and politics. By keeping the focus on repeated wins, you are avoiding the parking places on the road to success.

With this in mind, the *way* you lead and set direction makes a big difference. How do you do this, you wonder? How do you help a group of people do more than just find the answers to their current problems? Is it really possible to help other people who are responsible for leading ideas to develop the ability to be more strategic on an ongoing basis and to think for the organization as a whole? In short, how do you get your team to fill the Air Sandwich?

The ultimate goal isn't to win once, but rather to win over and over again.

The short answer is this: you make clear that it matters, invite your people to participate, ask them to help, and provide guidance. As we lead, we have countless opportunities to speed up strategy creation and execution by facilitating conversations across organizational silos, divisions, functions, and departments. So, your job as a leader now includes being a catalyst to connect people and help them combine forces, develop their ideas, and tap their collective knowledge, experience, and strengths. Rather than telling people what to do, you will find opportunities to guide them by sharing your unique point of view, by teasing out insights, concerns, requirements, needs, issues, and experiences, and by asking the question that is on everybody's mind regarding how the needs of the business might be addressed. In some ways, your role is to be a new kind of corporate hero.

Look, it's only natural that each of us aspires to be a bit of a hero. And, as a collaborative strategy leader, you *will* be a hero. But you'll also be a kind of "un-hero." Un-heros are essential. Even Batman needed the un-hero Alfred, because the hero character would be too far-fetched without an amazing helper. You can be *both* Robin and Alfred to your team's Batman. When you contribute toward fostering the new culture of collective strategy creation, you're a hero! When you set the context and allow people to act as co-creators of ideas, you're a hero! When work is challenging, people are valued, and turnover is low, you're a hero! When you lead actively in ways that bolster the successes in your organization and company at large, you're a hero! Your team will be basking in the spotlight, which means you'll spend more time as Bruce Wayne and less time in the cape and tights. (That's OK; they get itchy if you wear them too long anyway.) You'll have plenty to do as an "un-hero" because you will facilitate as much as you decide, catalyze as much as you act, and coach as much as you direct.

Your contribution to the big successes will be clear and critical, but the accolades will be shared because success will be distributed. Others will own, develop, and be responsible for various pieces of the success. In your new capacity, you will lead people through influence and ideas instead of just authority. They will ultimately create, own, and be responsible for executing against the direction that you initiated and they sharpened. You will be the director of a symphony, playing a piece of music co-written by you and the orchestra.

Your real power as a leader now comes less from having the right answer, perfect judgment, and insights about which direction to go, and more from your ability to create the kind of environment where your people can:

- Learn about and understand situations fully (to solve real problems rather than just symptoms)
- Engage with one another meaningfully so any issues or obstacles are identified early on
- Strategize together to build upon one another's ideas and design a new future
- Lead aspects of the strategy you collectively develop
- Hold the big picture in mind when making trade-offs and decisions are needed

Your ability to be effective depends heavily on *how* you go about doing what you do. Stylistic aspects of your leadership, which might be hard to identify at first, will have tremendous impact. This may pose a challenge if, for example, you're the kind of leader who is highly action oriented. You might be tempted to tackle your role in a decisive yes/no and "get it done" manner. (Catalyzed conversations? *Check!* Helped people develop ideas? *Check!*) Resist! Leading idea co-creators, managing and inspiring people in a coordinated fashion, requires a more nuanced and, particularly at first, patient approach.

To be successful, you need to facilitate two things. You must enable and then *encourage* people to step into *their* new roles as co-creators of solutions. And you will need to help your entire organization to think more strategically. Your ability to do these two things forms the centerpiece of *your* new approach to leading.

The way you lead matters a lot, because you are the one nurturing an environment where people bring their creativity to bear. You are the one encouraging people to think about the problem with new options. You are the one encouraging them to own the solution so that execution goes faster in the market. You are creating the forum where people give you and your organization what they most love— their ideas and passion.

But people won't give their ideas and passion if they think their leaders won't treat them with care. So you're going to have to be a trustworthy person who gains people's confidence. You will treat people's ideas with regard; you will be willing to engage creative tension so tough discussions can take place; you will be flexible in your own vision so your ideas can morph into the one that will actually work. Being a leader of co-creators is not for the weak-kneed and spineless. This type of leadership works only if the leader is ready to bring a certain amount of emotional maturity and intelligence. You may not have all the skills you need to do this kind of leadership today, but if you can be aware of and self-manage your learning without fear, none of these skills is out of your grasp (see Figure 3-4).

Engaging your team in a preview of the strategy while it's being developed provides valuable exposure to the thinking around what matters to the organization. When the team knows what's coming, they have an opportunity to think ahead, anticipate obstacles, and imagine possible solutions before the problems even arise. This think-anticipate-imagine process also helps your team to get comfortable with the idea of change. Their participation drives a legitimate sense of co-ownership in the ultimate decision. Understanding, readiness, and co-ownership together speed up conversations and improve the quality of the strategy as it is being implemented.

Remember that at most firms only 5% of the workforce understands the strategy. As *you* lead, strive to help ensure that the team, organization, and/or company achieves a 20/20 score rather than the abysmal 1 in 20.

Figure 3-4. *Self-manage your own issues*

That is how you begin to change the norms. You become more of an organizational leader—in other words, you are putting the success of your entire organization first, creating safety to co-create solutions, and making sure that the how of strategy gets created along with the what. You are creating a New How.

The Seven Responsibilities

Just as for individual champions of ideas, the *way* you do your job has a huge impact on your team's readiness to collaborate. Your approach to leading influences how you establish (or reestablish) connections among your company's people and their ideas. The patterns of thinking and acting that we demonstrate unlock how our people create and execute new strategies for the business. As you lead, you can transform how people work, interact, and talk with one another so that the root causes of the Air Sandwich start to resolve themselves naturally.

In your role as a collaborative leader, you can change the way we work and unlock the power of people and their ideas by taking on seven responsibilities. Together, these responsibilities are about establishing a new mindset for yourself and fostering a similar mindset in each team member. The seven responsibilities are:

1. **M**anage Cadence
2. Generate **I**deas
3. **N**urture Safe Culture
4. **D**evelop Connections
5. **S**atisfice
6. **E**ngage Issues
7. Trace **T**opography

To simplify the job of maintaining your awareness of these responsibilities, I've arranged their labels so that they spell out the word "mindset." Let's explore each of these responsibilities and why they are part of the way we lead collaborative strategy.

1. Manage Cadence

Managing cadence is about setting the pace. From your vantage point, you'll show your team how they are progressing, so they can sense incremental accomplishment and thus maintain a sense of forward motion. You will always keep people informed to let them know where they are and what other mountains lie ahead. You will use whatever means are appropriate and comfortable, regardless of whether you rely on "one-on-ones," email, voicemail updates, or standing meetings.

Pay attention to the frequency, volume, and duration of your communication. Pace matters. Be cautious that you don't drive your people so hard that they fatigue and become less effective. (And this applies to you, the leader, also! Go to the gym, garden, whatever helps you stay balanced, and do it regularly to mentally reboot.) Operating for extended periods at just a few percentage points over their capacity can leave people feeling overwhelmed and apprehensive about participating. Push hard, take a break and assess the pace, and then push hard again.

If you observe that your direction and communication leave people energized and looking forward to meeting each new challenge, then you may have found a good pace. Still, remember that a good pace for the team might be too fast for some individual members of that team, depending on what other responsibilities they have. Stay attuned to pacing at the individual level as well as at the team level.

Also pay special attention to what people are saying about the process, and don't shy away from asking them how they feel.

If and when the collaborative strategy process gets chaotic or confusing, remember to reorient people, manage expectations, and set context whenever the need arises.

You will manage various phases of the methodology covered in detail in Part II. Keep that context in mind when checking on people's response to pace. If you hear your people saying things such as "I don't know which way is up," consider:

- Investing the time to reorient them in whatever way seems appropriate. It might make sense to reassure them that the process is right on track.

- Reminding them which phase of the process they are currently in.

- Informing them of what's likely to happen next.

- Pointing out how much time is left in the current phase.

- Giving them a break from the activity to chill and to reboot their gray matter.

Generally, acting as an "Official Process Guide" is easy if you maintain a clear view of the big picture and where you all are in the thick of it. Remember to communicate it early and often so others know it, too.

You can give your people a sense of security by making it clear that it's your responsibility to guide them forward. This will help individual team members be open to stepping outside of their comfort zones and taking risks that might pay off further down the road.

Keep people in the loop and let them know what else is going on. Feel free to send quick one-liner emails, or use microblogging tools to let the team know that things are on track. It's a great idea to send a quick note when someone on the team has gained a useful insight; for example, "Joelle just did 30 phone calls with customers and learned that the key reason why advertisers are using our competitor is xyz."

Celebrate milestones. It's simple yet powerful to send a message or "tweet" when you accomplish something, even something small. You can even celebrate team learning. Collaborative strategy creation can, at times, be a challenging back-and-forth process, so help your team coalesce and stay aligned by helping them create meaning around what they are doing. If your team has just finished deciding something they deem important to the company, celebrate it. Celebrate the fact that your team has declared, "This really matters to us." Help your team manage perspective by seeing that they belong to something larger than themselves, and that as a group they are contributing to something greater. What you punctuate with your actions and language indicates what is important to you and will be noticed.

When you invest in managing team perspective, you help people stay in motion. This keeps the overall momentum up, and when people sense they are in motion, they are far more likely to continue putting in the effort to make progress.

2. Generate Ideas

Sparking ideas is about illuminating insights, empowering people to see what they already know in a new light. When you perform this assignment, you'll often find yourself generating ideas as you create new connections, as well as reinvigorating existing connections. You will use these interactions to create fresh opportunities that allow ideas to bubble to the surface, expand, and even pop.

New ideas and solutions to present-day problems rarely fall out of a cloudless blue sky. What typically precipitates a new idea is a shift in thinking prompted by the tension between competing ideas, or the pressure of an unexpected challenge in a tight timeframe. Sometimes new technologies can spark that shift in thinking. Another rich source of opportunities comes from talking to others about specific improvements, especially if the improvements are driven by outside market forces. Conducting brainstorming sessions can also be a good source of concept sparks. Such sessions have the added value of helping people to explore the natural tensions that create friction between opposing ideas.

Sometimes ideas come back from groups and they are counterintuitive to a leader's experience or wishes. When that happens, you get to take them on then and there, rather than have that perspective hidden within the hearts and minds of people. Idea generation with the spark of debate leads to shaping each other's ideas, but it also can be about explaining why something really won't work. It doesn't mean that a leader has to succumb to the mass democratic nature of the people generating ideas. Collaboration is not meant to be a democracy, but rather a meritocracy or a benevolent dictatorship in which the larger good of the company is achieved.

Ask your people to find ways to clear their minds and inspire new thinking, such as listening to an insightful industry speaker, hunting down interesting blogs, or watching a TED talk.[2] In each case, the topic may be only peripherally related to work. You might share a radical new concept and push the group to "prove you wrong," just to stir things up and give them practice at convincing you of what they believe. It also lets them see that you don't expect everthing you say to be treated as gospel.

Frequently challenge assumptions. Question the way things are. How did the status quo become the status quo? Probe and challenge in situations where your team can learn that doing so is accepted and valid. Make sure your team is fully supported as they come up with the best ideas possible to solve your particular strategy problem.

People will share their ideas most effectively in the right environment. And so another one of your responsibilities is nurturing a safe environment that invites new ideas.

3. Nurture Safe Culture

Leading collaborative strategy requires nurturing a culture in which people feel safe, so that you lower the sense of risk people feel as they begin to work together to invent new solutions. A simple reality of collaboration is that people can't create together if they don't trust each other.

Some people find that team-building activities let them get acquainted, begin establishing a sense of trust, and have conflict-free conversations before the pressure of schedules, budgets, and conflicting interests enter the picture. Once your people feel safe enough to risk expressing their precious ideas, you must encourage everyone to bring their best selves and creative ideas to the table. Your job is not to control this, but to facilitate it (Figure 3-5).

Figure 3-5. *Control is really not the point*

To create the space for people to express their opinions without fear of ridicule or condemnation, you must temper your own criticism and that of others. Insist that criticism is given constructively so that it pushes the conversation forward and advances learning.

In a larger sense, your job involves welcoming and accepting contradictory voices. Although there is an appropriate time to critique and discard weak ideas (as we will highlight in the process framework), most organizations have a number of team members that are adept at "stone throwing." We need to get all the ideas out in order to discover the good ones, and that is not as easily done if people are afraid of getting stones thrown at their ideas. Ask that people express their opinions and ideas so that they build on the ideas of others rather than chip away at them. A great example of this happens in improv theater where participants learn to say "yes, and" instead of "no, but." This technique keeps the conversation moving forward. Both Google and Whole Foods offer their people classes in improv to teach them how to apply these kinds of techniques in business.[3]

The story of Hans Grande in the sidebar "Profile of a Collaborative Leader" on page 87 provides a memorable example from my own experience of someone who was extraordinarily successful in building a culture where people felt comfortable collaborating.

Profile of a Collaborative Leader

Hans and I met shortly before he stepped up to work on the integration effort between Adobe and Macromedia, two software giants that merged in 2005. Hans's reputation, smarts, and ability to catalyze conversations, coupled with his deep domain knowledge, led to his being handpicked by the then-COO of Adobe to support the integration effort. The COO didn't ask Hans to formally lead the team. He asked Hans to fill another pivotal role: that of bridging the cultural gap.

The formal leaders understood that they required someone with the skills and permission to foster a culture of safety from day one. They also understood that this responsibility did not have to rest directly on the leaders themselves. By all accounts, Hans was an excellent choice. He held an MBA from the Haas School of Business and had been a respected team member on many high-visibility projects within Adobe.

Most mergers do not achieve their predicted goals,[a] and the integration effort between Adobe and Macromedia did not look easy. The companies had radically different cultures. Basic values and beliefs about how to get things done were dissimilar. Adobe people tended to use process-oriented language, whereas folks at Macromedia used a results-oriented style. The more "refined" Adobe people saw Macromedia people as "unruly cowboys" who made up rules as they went along. And Macromedia employees thought of the Adobe people as "stuck-in-the-mud bureaucrats."

Hans was perfect for this culture-setting role because he was likeable, whip-smart, and well respected. Hans would walk up to a relative stranger in the corporate integration room and say something like, "Wanna grab a slice of pizza and talk about X?" (whatever the issue at hand happened to be) or "Any interest in checking out the new bowling alley?"

Hans would act as a catalyst by inviting those who needed to work together to play together. Typically he wouldn't mention that you were not the only person he'd invited. Then, at the pizza joint, the bowling alley, or the coffee shop, Hans brought together people who didn't know each other (and maybe didn't even see a reason to) and used a fun setting to build relationships and get better work done.

—continued—

Fundamentally, Hans helped Adobe and Macromedia create the safe space that people needed in order to make important trade-offs and work together on the toughest of issues. His ability to make connections and foster a context of play outside of the formal integration protocols or pressure of the boardroom was vital to making the integration work. The "whitespace" interactions allowed team members to see the humanity behind cultural stereotypes and to develop a sense of trust and shared understanding before tackling issues that needed to be managed and solved.

Hans did not try to script out in advance how he was going to get people to agree on a given topic. He didn't try to get them to sign up for or commit to something they might be hesitant to do. Hans understood that problem solving would go more smoothly if the participants had some common ground, and that if their only interactions were in an adversarial context, the integration would be doomed. So Hans first focused on creating situations for finding that common ground that would enable people to approach touchy topics as partners instead of competitors.

Remarkably, Hans was not a "softie." People on both sides regarded him as a knowledgeable and respected "quant-jock." Hans could slice-and-dice quantitative data with the best of them. But he didn't approach strategy issues with just his intellect, and the merger was a case in point. Hans's unusual combination of strengths (emotional resonance, intellectual prowess, natural intuition) was key to his success. His analytical ability gave him "street cred" among the hardcore rationalist leaders, which bought him the permission to use his gift for creating a safe space for people from both companies to get acquainted and break down stereotypes before attempting "productive" conversations. By creating this kind of culture and shared framework first, Hans got people thinking strategically and working together collaboratively.[b]

a   Source for merger statistics: *http://blogs.computerworld.com/node/255*. Fifty-eight percent of mergers failed to reach the value goals set by top management. (1999 A.T.Kearney study of 115 transactions cited in the book *After the Merger*, published by Pearson.) Fifty-three percent of mergers failed to deliver their expected results. (2001 Booz Allen & Hamilton study of 78 deals.) Seventy percent of mergers failed to achieve expected revenue synergies. Twenty-five percent of merger execs overestimated the cost savings by at least 25%.

b   Hans Grande was an incredibly humble guy who would have protested my honoring him in public like this. He passed away shortly after the integration effort. I share his story because he believed, like I do, that the way we work together matters and helps us create value. Thanks to Dave Burkett of Adobe for sharing his memorial notes. More of Hans's story can be read here: *http://www.haas.berkeley.edu/groups/pubs/calbusiness/winter2007/alumni06.html*.

As we reflect on how Hans approached his assignment, we can see that he did more than simply create safety. He also established connections. It's a part of our job as leaders to build the bridges that bring people together and create a group or ensemble to address particular challenges or problems. Developing connections across boundaries—across corporate silos, divisions, functions, departments, and teams—is at the heart of building a truly productive and collaborative environment.

4. Develop Connections

Developing connections is about bridging divides, large and small. When working on this assignment to assemble the right group of people to tackle an issue, you will be linking departments, divisions, and individuals across the organization in new and sometimes unexpected ways. You will use your understanding of how different parts of your organization operate, and you'll encourage conversations across the invisible boundaries that might have kept people from working together in the past.

As you compose any team, think about individual personality types and styles. Whether you rely on systems such as Myers-Briggs, colors, or the Enneagram, or you use your own "spidey-sense" intuition, keep in mind that certain styles can be quite compatible or incompatible, and that "compatible" may not mean "similar."

Do what you can to encourage that every connection is a kind of creative partnership. However, if a specific connection doesn't click, try building a connection with a different person, one where there's better chemistry between people.

As you build each connection, carefully think through the choices you are making and how it will impact the team, because it will determine who's at the table and who needs to play what role. By figuring out who specifically needs to engage and by catalyzing the right connections, you will help different parts of the organization come together and work on the problem at hand.

Developing connections is particularly important because addressing the toughest challenges in business requires getting the right people to work together in alignment with a shared vision of success.

And connecting people across organizational boundaries lets you leverage the company's strengths, wherever they happen to be found.

As you initiate connections, provide context of business issues to discuss. Kindle each connection with the spark of a new idea to test the chemistry. New ideas provide the fuel and the energy to develop creative new solutions to ever-changing problems. New ideas provide the power for collaborative strategy.

One thing that everyone will want to know is when you have arrived at a destination. Please note that there are many destinations along the way to the end of a project. As simple as this might sound, you'd be amazed to discover how difficult most people find the process of recognizing the finish line. When there is no checkered flag, how do you know when you're done? As a leader, you can clarify where the finish line is by influencing how and when decisions are made. In particular, you can orient your team to recognize situations where seeking the absolute best option is not justified. Quite often, it is more than acceptable to achieve a milestone or result that is "good enough," meaning it meets or exceeds the needs of the situation. This is the process of *satisficing*.

5. Satisfice

The job of figuring out when done is done (or when you need to keep trying) is a judgment call. When I discovered the concept of *satisficing* many years ago (in *Scientific American*, of all places), I found the word that describes the perfect stopping point.[4] Satisficing is a decision-making strategy that uses criteria for adequacy rather than perfection. It's a concept that helps us know when we're done. Satisficing is about defining when enough is enough and it's time to move on. It is a pragmatic alternative to maximizing, minimizing, or optimizing. When you engage this technique, you choose to stop one thing and move on to another while managing to time and resource constraints. You help your team make the best decisions for the situation at hand, knowing that you might need to make more decisions later.

Satisficing is the opposite of trying to achieve the "perfect" solution. As Voltaire said, "The perfect is the enemy of the good." When you're balancing a dozen competing demands, there is no clear notion of "perfect," so seeking it does not add value. Other times, investing in some element makes no difference to the larger outcome. Does your website need a custom feedback form? Or is an email address enough? Would travelers choose Southwest more often if it served almonds and cashews, or are they really driven by low fares and on-time arrivals? Satisficing is about helping your people recognize they've succeeded given the scope of what you were working on (Figure 3-6). Sometimes peanuts are a perfectly acceptable answer.

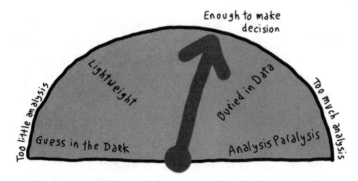

Figure 3-6. *Satisficing is knowing when enough is enough*

6. Engage Issues

When you engage the issues, you lead the simple act of getting people to talk. You pose questions such as: What will it take us to address this problem? Is this something we are willing to look at right now? Do we all agree on what the full problem is? Do we agree this is a priority for *us* given where we are on other things? Which factors are most critical to our success?

Engaging the issues is an act of bravery because you demonstrate the ability to deal with issues head-on. Engaging the issues does not mean having the answers, but it does mean being committed to learning. For example, where someone says X is the most important problem and another says the most critical issue is Y, the question to ask is: how can both be true? It is possible you will learn that X is most important to customers and Y is most important to finance (or operations, or channel partners). By engaging the issues, you create the opportunity to learn what the organization is willing to do in more detail.

Engaging the issues accomplishes two things that can dramatically shape culture. It allows you to:

- Communicate to the people working around you that you value openness and risk taking.
- Lead by example, showing your people they can acknowledge the truth and talk about it.

People at all levels actually *want* to be able to understand the issues, they want to be able to talk about what is really going on, and they want to do it without fear.

By engaging the issues, you lead this effort, giving others permission to speak to what they see, ask questions, and contribute freely. By choosing to engage the issues, you shed light into dark corners and take the discussions in your company to a higher level. You also diffuse pent-up concerns that something important is being ignored.

Most people don't see how conflict can serve business. They think appeasing everyone creates peace, but that just waters down solutions. It is our ability to work through tension that resolves issues and creates new solutions.

In general, people tend to shy away from engaging the issues in an effort to protect themselves. They fear difficult conversations, and they want to avoid feeling uncomfortable, incompetent, unsuccessful, or blamed. They don't want to be perceived as causing conflict. When a culture lacks a pattern of dealing cleanly and fairly with tension and conflicting viewpoints, those natural avoidance behaviors are understandable. Not healthy, but understandable.

However, engaging the issues does not mean blame, judgment, or conflict. It does mean having conversations about present and future risks, such as customers defecting, competition winning, or markets disappearing. We have these conversations because the benefits of engaging the issues will ultimately outweigh the consequences of staying silent.

Engaging the issues requires some consideration about how people might receive information. Avoid getting personal, and keep the discussion focused on the business impact. For example, don't say, "What Kristine did is causing a lot of pain." Instead, you might say, "This situation is impacting us a lot. What would it actually cost us to solve the problem?"

Often problems arise through reasonable actions, and it can sometimes help to acknowledge this: "It seems that in the rush to meet our last milestone, we took some shortcuts. That's understandable, but as often happens, some of the shortcuts have caused a problem, and we need to deal with it. Do we have the capacity to solve this problem now? What would be the impact of waiting six months?" By showing the impact and asking questions with room for choice, you empower your colleagues to decide how best to move forward.

By engaging the issues and opening up a dialogue, you enable your company to begin talking about key decision points. It is not necessary to get commitment about solving a problem, only to get the conversation going, so that it can be solved at some point in time. In some situations, you may find that a group's decision to postpone dealing with a particular problem can be the absolute right decision, if, for example, there is a larger issue that needs addressing first. If you find yourself unable to deal with conflict and you avoid it to the detriment of yourself or your business, figure out the underlying reason and resolve it by participating in the Hoffman Program referenced in Appendix B.

To make it easier to engage the issues, here are some helpful hints:

- Take other people's perspectives into account, and speak as though you are peers. Refer to Appendix B for resources on how to speak the truth with clarity and power.

- How do you tell a powerful leader that you think he is missing something? The answer is to get inside his mind and see through his eyes. This can sound like: "It seems like we're doing A, B, and C because we're assuming X, Y, and Z are going to happen. But there's a real chance that Y will not turn out quite the way we're anticipating. We might be better off doing D, E, and F instead. Can we talk about that?" The more articulate and specific you can be, the more you can have a conversation about facts, and not about who is right or wrong.

- Keep the conversation on topic. The curious thing about dealing with the issues is that people often want to go off into the weeds. Tangential topics can pop up, and people will get uncomfortable and want to change the subject. People often want to defend their actions, even when no one is targeting them. They may feel anxiety and implicit blame. You can defuse much of that anxiety by taking a brief moment to acknowledge that the current situation may very well have arisen from legitimate and reasonable efforts. Make the point that the discussion at hand is focused on moving forward, not looking backward.

- Name your intent (and keep reinforcing it if you need to). It often helps people to accept your involvement when you tell them why you are involved and what your interests are. It's also helpful to tie the topic to what the person, company, division, or team wants. When asked to research an issue, it's useful to share with everyone involved that your purpose is not to find the flaw around what's not working (and to blame), but to help the team find out what to do next and regain its success.

- Be open about your own mistakes and culpability (if they exist). Be up front about your past contributions to the situation, if any, and focus the conversation on the present and the future. Show your humanity and lead by example. Don't leave it to others to tell you that the emperor has no clothes.

- Stay focused on simply engaging with the issues versus finding a specific outcome. When well-intentioned people engage on a topic, they will often uncover misunderstandings, and it may take some time to find a resolution. The less attached you are to a particular outcome, the more you can simply focus on getting people to start talking and making progress.

- Engage a professional facilitator or someone from elsewhere in the firm (like Hans Grande) if you personally expect to be an active participant in the discussion. A facilitator will be able to help you by tracking and managing the rational, emotional, and intuitive parts of the discussion. This will leave you free to participate fully in the conversation.

- Be open to learning. You will likely find out something you don't yet know or don't want to see. Without being open to whatever comes, you can't work through the tension.

You set the tone by what you allow to happen and by what you reinforce or ignore. Whenever you are involved, engage the issues in a healthy way. I've had executives watch an aggressive power play happen right in front of them and say, "I'll let you two work it out." That rarely works; instead, it signals that it's OK to do power plays within the organization. If you let power games go unchecked, you are setting up a catastrophic failure in your business. You may not want to choose sides, but you can strongly urge that the merits of the issue get addressed instead of allowing the issue to become political.

Keep power games and passive-aggressive behavior in check. If you let them go unchecked, you end up letting people work from positional power, which undermines the power of good ideas. It ends only when we say that it's not OK to work from positional power. To get from us-versus-them to a collaborative culture, that stuff is no longer allowed (see Figure 3-7).

Figure 3-7. *Don't tolerate behavior that limits collaboration*

Our cultural norm going forward is about having each of us co-create our future, defining together what we want to build for our teams, divisions, or companies. So we need to start *demanding* that people focus on the problem and get on the same side of the table to do it.

Tell your people that any energy spent showing one another up is wasted energy that could have been spent on winning the market. (A tip: when I see a power play, I find just chuckling and saying, "What's that about? Are you taking that approach because you don't have a good cost-benefit argument for your position?" works wonders to get people to cut it out.) And if you tend to hush up issues as a way to avoid conflict, just know that you are missing out on opportunities to learn. Conflict is a signal that there may be an opportunity to improve on the status quo. Until some shift happens (like learning a new fact or point of view), change and growth never can.

When creating strategy, maintaining forward progress is essential to overall success; satisficing supports this. When you engage this responsibility, you establish what is ahead and make sure that people don't get stuck in one place for too long. The next responsibility is about navigating the terrain.

7. Trace Topography

The collaborative strategy process is most effective when teams use the phases of the process described in Part II. But it's not always easy to do. Nuisances and distractions unavoidably crop up. You must manage these things. When you perform this assignment, you'll be holding the "topo map" of where you are, even when your team is mired in the details of the rugged terrain. You'll remind your team of the larger goals and guide them away from paths that you know lead to a dead end.

In this role, you'll answer questions. You'll give directions. You'll encourage your team to keep going even when they feel lost. When there is a decision to make, you will know what this decision looks like at the ground level and how it fits into the larger landscape of what you are trying to do. This, of course, means that you keep perspective and don't get caught up in the act of doing.

One common nuisance is that some team members will tend to arrive at a new phase of a process unprepared for what they are about to do. This is normal when people have a lot on their plates. Still, it's essential to ensure that participants do not accidentally sabotage the process with their lack of adequate preparation, and part of this responsibility is pushing the members to be prepared.

Conversely, other team members will be all fired up and itching for the next phase before the rest of the team has agreed to close the current one. This is also normal. Normal or not, collaborative strategy requires that people support constant progress. They must work together in a loosely coordinated fashion to ensure that the necessary work gets done at roughly the right time and is of adequate quality to support constant progress. Your job is to help them.

All the nuisances and challenges of keeping creative, motivated human beings focused and working together require sequencing. Sequencing what, you ask? Sequencing is an advanced, high-level skill related to managing the following:

- Logical flow of conversations among people
- Steps of work that follow one another
- Hierarchy decision making

It is about managing the readiness of change.

The best way to manage orientation is to stay on top of events and activities as they unfold over time. You can achieve this simply by staying keenly aware of what's happening as it's happening.

By doing two things consistently, there is a simple way to accomplish this: establish an explicit purpose or intent for everything the team must do, and refrain from holding regular meetings out of habit, regardless of cultural norms or the convenience of setting up an automated, recurring calendar event. Yes, I'm giving you permission to have fewer meetings. That biweekly meeting in which you see eyes glazing over like Krispy Kremes? You're allowed to cancel it.

Instead, convene people in ways to keep the team fresh. Move in small groups or in other flexible ways so you are not designing strategy "by committee." Spend less time knowing the answers in advance; instead, clarify the agenda each time you meet with any department, team, group, or subgroup, and start each session with what you need to accomplish together and why it matters.

Maintaining strong momentum through the process requires that you proactively work to minimize the nuisances. As we lead, our deep understanding of collaborative strategy phasing gives us a leg up and helps emphasize when we need to:

- Foreshadow what's to come
- Begin preparing the next phase
- Celebrate meeting all of the objectives in the phase you're working on

In short, you know and signal when team members can embark on the next phase.

It can go without saying (but I'll say it anyway) that preparing for the next phase includes making sure the current phase of the collaborative strategy process is being done thoroughly enough, and that critical resources—especially time—are available in sufficient quantities to complete the next phase.

Here is a simple example of sequencing that recently took place with one of my long-term strategy clients:

> *The head of sales operations and her extended team were working hard to redefine part of their channel strategy, but they were facing a dilemma. On the one hand, they were under pressure to implement some near-term changes to reduce costs. On the other hand, they wanted time to think through longer-term product assortment issues, i.e., which products are sold by which channel.*
>
> *The key was to figure out what issues needed to get resolved immediately while simultaneously leaving the door open wide enough to change the product assortment in case the product team later arrived at another conclusion.*
>
> *In this case, sequencing the conversation, workflow, and decisions meant that the sales team could begin talking to the channel partners to make short-term decisions they needed to act on. At the same time, the internal product teams could begin working and have enough time to get answers to the larger questions in front of them. As the leader, the head of sales operations recognized how to organize and sequence these activities to improve the collaborative approach to developing the strategy flow.*

Launching some activities, deferring others, and cueing up the next conversation, task, or decision as the active thread completes are all important because they keep the collaborative strategy creation process moving forward.

Nobody waits—not the world, not the competition, not your customers—for you to get it all right. Figuring out what needs to happen at what point will give people a sense of what is on the horizon, so they have enough time to learn and reflect and act with grace.

Be a Collaborative Leader

These seven responsibilities and their corresponding assignments— managing cadence, generating ideas, nurturing a safe culture, developing connections, satisficing, engaging the issues, and tracing the topography of the conversation, workflow, and decisions—are task-independent. Meaning that, when you do them, you are leading cocreators, not just a leader of any particular effort to solve a problem.

By enabling people to interact this way, you are helping them fill in the pervasive Air Sandwich that limits an organization's success. As a leader, you will foster the necessary learning, discovery, debates, and discussions; provide the context; set the cadence; decide when to move on; and know what happens next. It's a tough role, but it's a fun one, because you get to help an entire crew of people bring their passion and ideas to the table to benefit the company.

And without someone managing these responsibilities, the collaboration process won't work. While intentions can be good and people can aim to be collaborative, they need a way to participate, take on the tough topics, and still move forward quickly. The leader's role as described in this chapter is central to the work of collaboration.

Sure, being the Chief of Answers is fun. But being a conductor of cocreators is even more fun. Somewhat like jazz, collaborative strategy is a structured yet improvisational performance. As the leader, you get to be the band arranger. The responsibility for how the performance is structured falls to you. And you get to invite the "players" to jump in at the right points. The quality of the "music" your ensemble creates will then be shaped by the stage you step on, what each musician brings to the piece, and how well you all co-create the future together. By taking on this role, you are enabling the organization to have more velocity in its ability to set and achieve direction.

Up to this point we've covered a lot of ground. Without changing the role each of us plays and how we lead, we can't take on the tasks of collaborating well. For some of you who are already behaving collaboratively, you may already know the importance of the "how" in the business results. We are ready to apply what we've covered in a practical, roll-up-your-sleeves-and-get-dirty kind of way.

So let's now turn our attention toward putting all of this into practice. Let's explore how leaders and individuals can take their new understanding of roles and responsibilities and apply it to the phases of the collaborative strategy process. That's next.

PART II

The QuEST Process for Collaborative Strategy

We started this book with the notion that we need to change how business works. If business is to thrive, institutions must move from an us-versus-them opposition to an us-versus-opportunity stance. By doing strategy creation collaboratively, we are demanding that each of us take responsibility for the shared outcome, to improve business performance. We will move fast, get aligned, and welcome the creative conflict as we work together.

Part I, which we've just finished, covered how we need to show up at work to enable the creative and productive act of collaborative strategy. We focused on the role each of us has, and what we need to do as leaders.

We're about to enter Part II, which covers the actions we need to take to reach the needed outcome. There are four stages of collaboration: Question, Envision, Select, and Take, or QuEST. These stages are shared in the four chapters that follow.

First up is "Question," which focuses on seeing the full picture of what needs to be solved. We'll learn a process for making sure the problem we have identified is the right problem, as well as getting a clear picture of "what is true," so we have a solid basis for how to get from where we are to the future we decide we want. The most crucial aspect of this phase is getting early organizational understanding of the problem.

The second phase is "Envision," where the emphasis is on creating options from a full marketplace of ideas within the organization. To know which options should matter more, we start to capture the criteria that come up, which will later shape the process of sorting ideas. Criteria form the lens through which we can see what matters to us in this time and situation.

Next, and perhaps most important, we enter the "Select" phase. This forces us to make the tough choices that business absolutely needs to make, to avoid the malaise caused by the perpetually repeated assertion that "we'll do everything and do it all well."

Last, we "Take" to create accountability in the system. "Take" means taking ownership, taking responsibility, and taking charge.

These four phases form the QuEST collaborative strategy framework (Figure II-1).

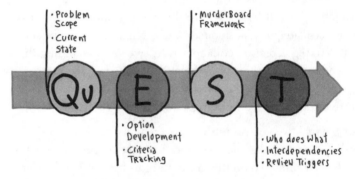

Figure II-1. *QuEST collaborative strategy framework overview*

You can get a quick sense of the framework by understanding the specific goal of each phase within the process, together with the approximate duration of each phase (Table II-1).

TABLE II-1. *Collaborative strategy process framework (QuEST)*

PHASE/PHASE GOAL	PHASE DURATION/COMMENTS
1. *Question: Know what you need to know*	*Medium: 1–10 weeks*
The key here is to avoid shortcuts, and to rigorously collect all relevant information to enable a clear, deep, and rich understanding of the need or opportunity you seek to address.	The duration depends on the size of your scope, people's availability to discuss things, the priority within your organization, and the complexity of the issue. Cap at 10 weeks or less, since energy fades after that point.
2. *Envision: Create options that matter to this organization, at this time and place*	*Short or long, depending on scope (typically 1–6 weeks)*
This creative phase focuses on the generation of strategic ideas from everywhere in the organization to find viable options, and the reasoning behind why those options matter.	The duration depends on the geographies involved and how many disciplines and teams need to discuss options.
3. *Select: Make tough choices*	*Short*
The goal of this phase is to use the original MurderBoarding process (described in Chapter 6) to sort ideas, and then fix, merge, tune, and toss them until one final winning strategy remains.	Typically 1 day, but can be from 1 day to several days.
4. *Take: Create accountability*	*Short*
The goal of this phase is to specify, *with as much fidelity as possible*, the following details of the final strategy: who is responsible, the actions required to execute the strategy, the changes needed to enable the strategy, and the means of detecting how well the strategy is hitting the intended target.	Typically 1 day, but can be from 1 day to several days. Has a tee-up and post-process follow-up. Usually followed by a systemic process (like a quarterly business review).

These four phases form the new building blocks of collaborative strategy creation. Each of the phases is collaborative in nature, but in different ways. The Question phase is about fully shared understanding of the problem, and so it depends upon all participants expressing their perspectives on the challenge. The Envision phase uses collaborative creativity to develop a pool of ideas for later selection. The Select phase pushes for explicit agreement (not tacit acceptance) on the choice of strategy option, and collaboration is essential for that. The Take phase is about working together to build a unified and detailed plan of action.

Before proceeding to the specifics of each phase, take a moment to consider the mindset you'll need when using this process framework. Creating great strategy requires multiconversational, multidimensional discovery that involves three ongoing tasks: learning about what is relevant, defining what matters, and determining what the organization needs to do to make something new happen. As such, new information and new insights will sometimes mean you have to revisit previous phases so that your decisions can be aligned with the new information.

This potentially nonlinear aspect of strategy creation can seem messy, but this messiness is a byproduct of thoroughness, which always pays off in the final execution of a strategy (Figure II-2).

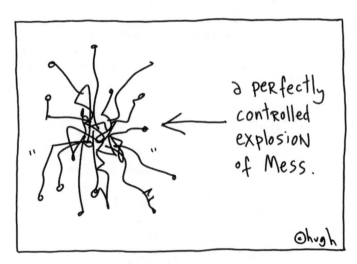

Figure II-2. *Strategy creation is a controlled messy process*

The process framework helps you be explicit and informed about the choices you are making so you can move forward quickly.

When the process feels messy, that's OK. Not only is it OK, it *needs* to be messy. Creating something new is almost never neat. The good news is that when you dig deep early, your team can discover potential obstacles that might otherwise have remained hidden during strategy creation. Digging deep is essential to preventing the Air Sandwich.

Your willingness to let the process be messy from time to time increases the chances of finding a strategy that will work, as well as discovering when a strategy won't work. Both discoveries are valuable when making decisions about where to spend valuable resources.

By following the QuEST process framework, you make sure that:

- You have unearthed the real problem in such a way that everyone sees it clearly.

- Your team can generate many options, but still make tough decisions quickly.

- The people who implement the final strategy understand the fundamental assumptions and the rationale behind the strategy, so they can explain what matters and why.

- As a result, they know which trade-offs to make on the fly as they encounter unexpected things.

Ultimately, everyone involved will have an internalized understanding of why the strategy is important and what it is designed to do to serve the end goal of winning. They will not be just the "doers" but also "thinkers" who serve the organization.

After we finish Part II, we'll step back into the larger view of the organizational rules of engagement to establish the new QuEST standards in an organization. That's what Part III will detail.

For now, we need to dive deep into Part II. This methodology builds on the foundation of the "ways of being" covered in Part I. So let's get into the specific phases.

CHAPTER 4

Phase I: Question

> *It is tempting, if the only tool you have is*
> *a hammer, to treat everything as if it were a nail.*
> —Abraham Maslow

Know What We Need to Ask and Answer

Isn't it tempting to do what we've already done because it's the road we know? It is for me. The next section we're taking on is the "how" of creating better business outcomes.

Above the inside door of my office, there's an Italian clock, and above that, there's a little sign printed on regular laser printer paper. It reads "All Roads Lead to Rome." My team gave it to me after an arduous time helping an e-commerce company hit their $24M product launch goal. The phrase had become the mantra for the last few weeks. "All Roads Lead to Rome" was what we kept repeating to our client (and to ourselves) to focus everyone on the process rather than fixating on getting to a specific answer, so we could create a strategy together that would actually work.

You lovers of history may recognize the phrase. I learned it during a college course in Western Civilization. The Roman Empire, you might remember, drove the greatest economic expansion in history— connecting remote places and people together through commerce. One way it did this was by building a vast network of roads connecting widespread communities so that Roman legions could deploy and harness resources wherever needed. The city of Rome was effectively the center and genesis of their universe, so the Empire built its roads from that place, outward. If you were somewhere wandering lost in the land, you could be guaranteed a way back "home." By following any dirt road, you would eventually connect to a wider road, until it reached a paved road, and all paved roads would eventually lead to the center of Rome.

This analogy comes in handy when a team loses its way and is wandering through the vast confusion of strategy creation, lost between the goal and all the data, various perspectives, and too many options. "All Roads Lead to Rome" is a phrase that can remind you to follow and trust that the resilience of the process will deliver you to your destination—that is, to the winning, workable strategy.

At another level, the phrase reminds you that most of the time people already have the wisdom and the knowledge required to get where they need to go; the trouble is that the key ideas may be scattered far and wide throughout the organization in the minds of various doers and functional leaders or in the larger ecosystem.

Of course, the approach the Romans took worked for the Roman Empire. Other empires have relied on different ways to connect remote places and people. Similarly, creating strategy relies on a process, but not just any process. The notion that "All Roads Lead to Rome" depends on having a process for creating strategy in a collaborative way: a process that's flexible yet robust, and has been tested enough so that you can place your faith in it to give you business results.

The key for building great strategy is to figure out the way to connect seemingly disparate parts together so that something results from it and you "get there." So how do we do this? And how do we do this collaboratively so that what is decided gets made into a reality?

Let's get down to business and explore the meat-and-potatoes steps of creating strategies using the QuEST process framework. What follows are the details behind each phase: *Qu*estion, *E*nvision, *S*elect, and *T*ake. The QuEST process framework will guide you through a structured, directed way of developing better business outcomes.

You will learn the actions, steps, and responsibilities to execute each phase. I'll also highlight some issues, which I call temptations, that you will want to watch out for as you move through the strategy creation process.

How It All Works

First, let's take a minute to clarify the meaning of the phrase "process framework." A *process framework* is a structure that allows for a set of actions (processes) that are related to one another and should be done in a preferred order.

I call it a framework, and not a methodology, because the structure is generic and is flexible enough to be applied to different applications in different contexts, meaning different industries, businesses, kinds of companies, and business units.

The process framework is flexible because, even though the phases take place in a given order, at the end of one phase (and the beginning of another) there is a "gate" you have to pass through. Before you get to a gate, the process framework recognizes that a learning loop happens inside each phase. And it's not so rigid to suggest that you always follow an inflexible series of process steps, because the act of strategy creation involves people learning and formulating ideas. Creative processes are not linear, and nor are they purely analytic. Much like life itself, there's a flow to it. Strategy creation is unfortunately much messier than an "A to B to C" kind of model. Instead, the New How provides a framework of sequenced phases so you know what particular things you want to accomplish, and in what order, to optimize business outcomes. And, as you exit a particular phase, it's important to make sure certain things have been completed. That's the role of each gate.

The QuEST process framework allows you to create strategies in a way that is structured but fluid, messy but controlled, fast but deliberate. It addresses many common concerns you might have along the way. You might shy away from creating strategy with other people because you fear that involving others will slow you down. However, the QuEST process framework allows you to keep things moving by involving people for specific reasons so that you can make decisions that roll forward and continue building on each other.

Remember the idea of satisficing from Chapter 3? It applies right here. Keeping things moving will force you to define when enough is enough, when it's time to move on, and when you can stop one thing and start another. It's the opposite of trying to get things 100% right and achieve the "perfect" solution. The QuEST process framework allows for satisficing, which is essential to the larger success because it lets you keep going and continue making progress.

This process framework also allows you to have a certain cadence of conversations that leads to timely decisions, so people know what they're going to do first, second, third, and so on. It lets them know what is coming next and what they'll need to do to prepare for the next thing. Most importantly, QuEST accommodates the messiness of strategy creation, given that it is a creative act and one that's almost never neat and tidy. It helps you to make the messy choices in a conscious and engaged way.

The QuEST process framework is built on four repeatable core phases that focus your team on the essential decisions you need to make by the end of each phase. The process framework helps you turn business opportunities into visions, visions into strategies, and strategies into specific and measurable plans of action. It leads you through a set of steps that allow you to clarify the problem as a team, figure out what success looks like, ask and answer the right questions, generate ideas, sort ideas until you arrive at one final best strategy, and then create clarity and accountability for what needs to happen.

The Question Phase: How It Fits

The first phase of the QuEST process framework is the Question phase (Figure 4-1). During this phase, you build a rich understanding of the situation you are facing by asking and answering the right questions. It precedes the Envision phase because you need to know what the problem is and have everyone understand what you're trying to accomplish. The Question phase is done before the Select phase because you need to be clear on the problem scope (which I'll discuss in the next section), so the resulting strategy will match the problem.

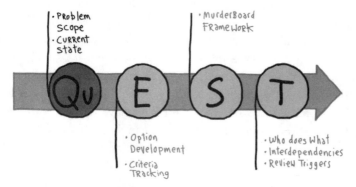

Figure 4-1. Question is the first phase of QuEST

Working Parts of the Question Phase

The Question phase is about making sure you understand the problem with enough fidelity, gather all the facts you need to get a clear picture of where you are today, and organize and share the results of the fact-finding to build understanding of and agreement on the problem being solved.

The Question phase is about going in with an open mind, so everyone is open to new information, insights, and directions. It requires stepping into the initial discussion of the problem in an inquisitive way to look at what the problem actually is, and to gather all the relevant information necessary to understand what needs to be solved.

There are three steps to the Question phase: identifying the problem, gathering relevant information, and sharing the findings to make sure the problem being solved is well understood. Let's talk about the first step of the Question phase, which is necessary to accomplish this: identifying the problem scope.

Step 1: Identifying the Problem Scope

How many times have you jumped straight to the resolution of a problem, only to realize later that if you had been more thoughtful and asked more questions first, you could have come up with a far better solution? This preliminary step in the Question phase, then, is about deciding that a particular problem needs to be solved, a difficult issue needs to be tackled, or a new challenge needs to be confronted.

For the purposes of our discussion, I'll be using the word *problem* as shorthand, even though some people perceive *problem* to be a negative word. Think of it as a way to talk about the gap between where you are today and where you want to be. I could just as easily call it "opportunity," so if it helps you, you can mentally substitute that word. Once you've identified and clarified the difference between what you have and what you want, you have defined a *problem*. And this is the point at which you can begin to develop your thinking and start to engage the organization to work toward a solution collaboratively.

Establishing the problem scope is identifying what you *intend* to work on or *believe* needs to be tackled. Note that I use the words "intend" and "believe." What I'm pointing to is not a definitive "this is *the* problem," but rather the problem scope is a hypothesis to be tested. It's not about "following your gut" and jumping to a conclusion (Figure 4-2), although the problem scope will surely be shaped by your gut or intuition. It's about identifying the right people to involve, or the characteristic of the right people, similar to the way that Adobe chose Hans because of his natural gifts (see "Profile of a Collaborative Leader" on page 87). Perhaps even more importantly, it's about setting the stage to create a solution by clarifying the underlying nature of the problem, which lets you develop an early understanding of what you, your organization, and your company are up against. Because strategy is never a theoretically perfect solution, but rather the solution that would most likely work given your context, competitive situation, capabilities, and so on, the problem scope needs to take into account the lay of the land.

I often refer to this step as the problem architecture. You are defining the shape, size, and perimeters of the problem you want to take on. Just like you might architect a house to be a "3,000-square-foot Craftsman on a hilly property," you would architect a business problem to be "enterprise-customer-focused in the North America region affecting product line X." To know what we are building, we need some architecture of what it generally looks and feels like. This is because encountering new problems—and beginning to think about solving them—is unavoidable. It's the natural result of having solved other problems earlier.

Figure 4-2. *Problem architecture shapes the scope*

The problem architecture is about characterizing the problem, getting a handle on the parameters of it, and then naming it. Getting to the essence requires that you stay open to the size, scope, basic nature, and even the name of the problem itself. It's about clarifying who's involved and what they care about. It also includes identifying what's stopping or preventing the problem from being solved now. But more than anything, defining the problem architecture revolves around trying to connect what *appears* to be the problem with what the problem *actually* is...to the *even more important* thing that people are trying to solve.

The fact is, most complex business problems are not clear-cut, meaning there is no obvious right or wrong answer. It's almost always about data gaps, human issues, understandings or misunderstandings, and gaps between what is and what needs to be. The problem architecture step includes both facts and data, as well as making sure you understand the human side of the business problem so you ultimately solve the full problem in such a way that it'll stick to the organization and accomplish something.

It's essential to determine the problem scope as the first step in the Question process phase because everything that follows depends on it.

Without it, things don't line up. When everything does line up, people can make conscious choices about how they're going to bound the problem well enough to start building the team, confirm the scope, and, ultimately, develop the strategy to attack it.

Defining the scope of the problem necessitates embarking on a small discovery process. To do this, you may want to engage in discussions with your peers, talk to a few key people who are close to the problem, and/or have a discussion with your boss about possible new angles and questions such as: "What do we really need to do here?" or "What do we need to fix?" or "Where can we have the greatest impact?" Do everything you can to challenge your own assumptions about what needs solving. Aim high, but not so high that you lose sight of what you are actually looking to achieve.

When the focus is correct but not clear enough to act on, you're on the right road and headed in the right direction. However, you'll need to do some additional work to make sure the problem is bounded, but with a clear charter. Bounding the problem gives you the scope: it says what's in and what's not.

Table 4-1 lists some examples of statements that are directionally correct, and others that are properly bounded with a clear charter to create scope statements.

TABLE 4-1. *Scope statements*

DIRECTIONALLY CORRECT	PROPERLY BOUNDED WITH A CLEAR CHARTER
We are going to figure out how to drive international expansion.	We are going to build a plan to expand the video line by 20% to affect fiscal year 2010.
How do we find volunteers to support our nonprofit growth?	What are the key areas where we could use volunteers based on our 2010 goals? What skills will they need? How big will the tasks be? How many volunteers will we need?
How do we sell more health care software to small businesses?	We will find and identify the customer group that represents an underserved part of the hospice market. Target companies should range between 10 and 1,000 employees.

When you define the scope of a given problem, it's important to strike a balance between identifying a problem that's big enough for people to get excited about and one that's so big that they feel as though they'll never make a dent. Your job is to define a scope that is bounded by a well-formed outcome or tightly coupled set of outcomes. Once you're clear on the scope of the problem you intend to address, it's time to identify the people (or the characteristics of the people) to talk with to learn more about the problem itself. These are the people who have something to add and aren't narrowly defined by their job titles.

Problem scope: Roles and responsibilities

In the problem scope step, you (as the operational leader) and your team have certain responsibilities, as listed in Table 4-2.

TABLE 4-2. Step 1: Problem scope roles and responsibilities

LEADER'S ROLE

- Define the scope.
  - Do an early discovery process.
- Create a bounded problem statement. Possible boundary dimensions are time, market segment, divisions, product lines, and budget.
- Create the space.
  - State the vision for the project.
  - Select the team. Remember that you can have a core strategy team drive the majority of the process and an extended team that must be engaged in some way.
  - Identify individuals needed on the team and specify why.
  - Set ground rules for interacting and collaborating. You can leverage Chapter 2 for this.
  - Review the QuEST process framework.
  - Talk about what to expect.

COLLABORATOR'S ROLE

- Question/challenge/debate the problem statement and clarify anything that doesn't make sense.
- Commit to co-creating a solution.
- Participate actively (see Chapter 2).

When you're ready to invite people into your process and launch into the next step of the QuEST process framework, you'll want to have a kick-off meeting where you clearly state the purpose of the team and answer what seem like basic, context-setting questions such as:

- Why are we here?
- What do we need to accomplish as a team?
- Why does this matter?
- How will we know when we are done?

As simple as these questions seem, getting the team to articulate their answers is essential. Being clear about the answers at the outset will help team members know why they, specifically, are on the team and what you are trying to accomplish as a group.

Managing Temptation: Being Overly Ambitious

When you first identify the problem, you will find it tempting to assume that you already see the problem clearly, or, alternatively, to be overly ambitious about what you and your team can do. Resist these temptations. All but the simplest business problems are complex in ways that prevent people from easily seeing all angles and implications. You may also want to consider aiming for smaller goals with the assumption that the scope will probably expand once the team fully grasps the details of the situation.

This preliminary kick-off meeting is the place to begin establishing a culture of safety, because it gives you ample opportunity to set the ground rules for how you hope team members will interact, both with each other and with those who are not on the team. Getting both individual team members and the team as a whole to understand your role as leader and what you expect of them is another excellent place to establish group norms.

This meeting is also the right place to review the overall QuEST process framework, as well as the leader's role, the collaborator's role, and how all team members will be expected to engage during each phase of the strategy creation effort.

From here, you can move on to Step 2 in the Question phase: fact gathering.

Step 2: Fact Gathering

The second step of the Question phase, fact gathering, involves interviewing people throughout the organization (and possibly beyond—customers, partners, suppliers, etc.) to generate a deeper level of understanding of your problem or opportunity. It is about exploring what questions you need to ask (and answer) to know your strategy problem well enough to solve it.

The goal of this step is to create a comprehensive picture of the problem, so that you can discuss and share it up front, eliminating the possibility of not being on the same page about the problem your team is solving, or worse, being out of sync with the reality of the actual problem. Fact gathering is not about proving your hypothesis. It is about learning/testing to see whether the hypothesis is accurate. Whatever you find while disproving or proving your hypothesis, you learn something important.

The fact gathering step of the Question phase is critical, as many people launch into solving a problem with incomplete data and therefore an incomplete understanding of the problem they are trying to solve. This step allows you to avoid this pitfall by getting you to define four things:

- What you know (and can prove) about the problem that you want to solve

- What you believe (but can't prove)

- What you doubt

- What you suspect are outliers or "red herrings" (conflicting or misleading "facts" that are not relevant)

Also, fact gathering creates a forum for people to voice their hunches, questions, and concerns about doing something new *early on* in the strategy creation process. This lets you factor in nuances such as politics and other important aspects of the situation and include them in the ultimate solution you create.

During fact gathering, you'll learn what matters most to the organization and, therefore, what solution should you choose when it comes to selecting a strategy. So be sure to make special note and keep track of what people say is important, because it will become part of your criteria for success and you'll want to come back to it. We'll talk more about criteria for success in Chapters 5 and 6.

Fact gathering activities

You will engage in several activities during the fact gathering step:

- Elephant hunting
- Interviewing: mining wisdom
- Researching: gathering data for reference

Let's look at each of these activities in detail.

ELEPHANT HUNTING. For the fact gathering step to achieve its goal, you and your team need to be "inquiry experts." This means you need to stay open to what you don't know, particularly if everyone on your team has significant expertise in the subject matter area of your problem, or if a good portion of the team has been in the organization for quite some time. It's often the case that a group of experts or seasoned employees will be aware of topics and assume that everyone understands them.

To account for this, the fact gathering step must seek to reveal "two kinds of elephants" (Figure 4-3).

Figure 4-3. *Two kinds of elephants*

The first is the elephant in the room. This is the big issue that almost everyone knows about but it's a somewhat taboo topic, so no one brings it up and the issue never gets addressed. Big, unaddressed "elephants" in your project can cause lots of trouble, so you definitely want them revealed. If left unaddressed, big elephants can stampede around and cause trouble in your project, so get them out in the open.

The second elephant is one that looks different from every perspective: an important but multifaceted issue that many people see, but each in only a limited way. We each have our own limited aperture— what we're willing to look at or what we see. Sometimes our area of responsibility in the organization limits our perspectives. Other times, it's a function of our own lack of understanding.

If I were to put an elephant in the room you are in right now (and cut off your olfactory powers and blindfold you for a second) and have you touch it, I could have you describe what you felt and ask someone sitting on the other side of the room to describe what they felt. As you both report it out, the two of you could appear to be in violent opposition. The tail is going to feel different from the tusk; the toes are going to feel different from the back. So one of you is going to say, "It's smooth," while another says, "It's hairy." Both are true. Applying this to business, typically each of us sees only a part of the full picture because we work inside complex organizations. The silos that separate us can be huge. But it's when we can break down those silos that great learning can happen.

This second elephant is about getting to a clarity or consensus about the nature of the problem. It's only possible to understand the full concept of an elephant when you have more complete information than each individual point of view and when you add that information up. When important issues lack a joint understanding, they'll lead to problems down the road. But when everybody can look at the same picture, together you can solve that problem.

In order to successfully "reveal the elephants" in your project, it is important to adopt the right approach to the fact gathering step. People often come at the task asking simply, "What do we need to know?" This seems logical, but putting a focus on answers can undermine the Question step and put pressure on people to "find relevant data" to "get it right." Factual answers alone don't encourage people to talk about the elephants that need revealing.

A more effective approach is to put the focus on the kinds of questions that people need to ask instead of the kinds of answers that need to be found. By way of example, here are sample questions that might start a fact gathering session for a team that is strategizing on how to defend against a competitor:

- What do we know about what has been done before?
- Who has been involved?
- What results did they generate?
- What do we need to know about why this worked or didn't work?

By beginning with process questions, you'll treat the fact gathering step more like a discovery process, and it helps you stay open to what you might find. Adopting a position of inquiry doesn't take much time, but if you miss it, you can't add it back later. Make sure to commit to this step before moving on to the legwork of the fact gathering step: interviewing and researching.

INTERVIEWING: MINING WISDOM. When you're ready to begin fact gathering, you'll want to interview people. This involves talking to people in your organization, and sometimes outside it, who are interacting with some aspect of the problem. You will learn how they experience the problem, so you can understand what they know about it. The process can be a bit like building a mosaic. Up close, things may look random and unordered, but stepping back reveals the entire, clear picture. At the end of the process, when you've put together all your pieces from all your sources, you will have a complete set of valuable information. You will know what has already been tried and has failed in the organization, how people feel about the current problem, what they believe to be true, and what key data they think is central to consider.

Interviewing is an efficient way to find sources of quantitative information, and it's the best way to gather qualitative information; in other words, the kinds of perspective, knowledge, and insights— valuable nuggets of organizational wisdom—that help you make meaning out of the data.

It's remarkable how often I see teams focus on numbers from formal reports and spreadsheets. They do this because they think numbers are more concrete than qualitative (subjective) information. Perhaps it doesn't occur to them that quantitative information has its own kind of "fuzziness" and can be misleading for any number of reasons. Numbers don't provide the empirical set of facts we often think they do.

Remember that, according to Benjamin Disraeli (and popularized by Mark Twain), "There are three kinds of lies: lies, damned lies, and statistics." This quote is well known because it's so easy to manipulate numbers so they say what you want them to say. That's why it's so important to gather the human intelligence as well.

Mining wisdom requires that you recognize the need for a balance of both quantitative and qualitative information. Sure, quantitative data is critical. It's the language of business. But keep in mind that because numbers appear concrete, people tend to discount the "soft stuff" during strategy creation, even though subjective information— such as insights about what's most important in a given situation or what the organization is actually capable of—is just as crucial.

In addition to being an important way of collecting data, knowledge, and insight, interviews offer the added bonus of helping you build support for your strategy early in its creation. So, with that in mind, whom should you talk to?

Pay attention to whom you ask. In the Question phase, *whom* you ask shapes *what* you learn. Many people only ask key questions of people at the very top of the organization, thinking that they must know more. Although the people at the top do hold important knowledge, be aware that as information gets farther from its source, it is distilled, distorted, and stripped of its critical nuances.

Be sure to interview deep within your organization, where things are actually happening. Make sure you talk to the people who are more familiar with how things are working day to day.

To expand your list of interview candidates, ask your initial group of candidates to nominate three other people within the organization to talk to, and pay attention to names that get nominated multiple times. These individuals can be a great resource, and they can often nominate three other people to talk to.

When the problem is a product that isn't achieving revenue goals, talk to the salespeople who are missing their targets. Resist the impulse to go only to the people who are achieving their quotas, because they have most likely found a way around existing obstacles, or might never have encountered them in the first place. The people who are losing deals are much more likely to be aware of what needs to be fixed in the product (or channel, or sales operations) to achieve growth. When finding out about lost deals, be sure to probe for other factors that may be influencing the problem, such as pricing or the sales exception process.

For example, when you want to find the obstacles preventing the business from scaling, talk to the people handling customer service calls. Ask them what their customers complain about, because unsatisfied customers will tell you what's not working and why they won't be buying the next whiz-bang gizmo. The people handling these calls hear these complaints every day, and they hear them first. Chances are, they're keeping a list, and this list often contains the raw data of what is *truly* happening on the front lines.

When the problem is to discover the next big opportunity, look outside the company. Opinions inside the company typically are limited and held down by "what can we do." Instead, try talking to non-customers to find out what you might do. Ask partners, or developers, or people who run industry associations about what they need and what problems they wish the company would solve.

I know how important it is to dig in and keep digging. In my company's early years, we worked with an organization that was trying to reconcile the pricing of a product. The product management team thought the price was too low, and the sales team thought the price was too high. Each team believed the other team's view was self-serving and was therefore putting its revenue growth projections at risk. Both teams had talked to customers and had gathered facts that supported their different points of view.

When we took the time to interview customers, we looked beyond the questions the teams had already asked, and kept digging to find something that would allow both sets of facts to be true. What we found was that two distinct kinds of customers were using the same product in two different ways. One customer group was willing to pay a lot of money, whereas the other believed the product was over-priced. We brought these results back to the company, who shifted their discussions from pricing to figuring out how to differentiate the product into two different product lines. This fact gathering step was critical for uniting the two conflicting points of view and finding a strategy that would allow both teams to focus on the shared goal of revenue growth.

Managing Temptation: Sharing Sensitive Information

When you're doing fact gathering well, your interviewees will tend to open up and share all sorts of information. You may come across sensitive information or learn about situations that could compromise certain departments, divisions, or people. You may be tempted to share this information and its source so that the situation can be brought to light quickly. However, it is vital to handle the information you gather with 100% respect and sensitivity. In some cases, you can report findings, but don't attach these findings to a name unless you have permission. Sometimes even the information itself must be kept under wraps.

For example, you may learn of an impending business deal or significant personnel change that is relevant to your strategy. In such cases, you may or may not be able to include a small part of the team in this awareness. Without sharing the information, you may still be able to use it, but doing so will require you to depend on your personal judgment more than you would otherwise. In order to explain some of your decisions, you may need to disclose that you've received important confidential information that is influencing you. The good news? These situations do not arise very often.

Consciously manage the temptation to disclose sensitive information. In particular, you must never use any information you learn to undermine someone. Maintaining confidentiality is important because it builds trust and supports your ability to do thorough fact gathering in the future.

Interviewing techniques matter. For the fact gathering step to be as fruitful as possible, you'll want to conduct your interviews carefully.

Let's review how interviewing fits into the Question phase. I'd like to highlight some suggestions that you'll want to consider before you begin the interviews. For deeper guidance on how to conduct interviews well within your organization, check out the "Tips for Interviewing" section in Appendix A.

First, conduct your interviews in person whenever possible, especially when dealing with complex problems (but don't skip an interviewee if the phone is the only practical option). Remember that most times the business problem you're investigating affects the people you are talking to, so what you learn from them matters to them. Talking with people face to face will give you insight into the factors influencing their input, as well as who the people are beyond just the role they play. Although some people might think this exercise is only for extroverts, in reality it can be done by every type of person. This is not a social exchange; these interviews are about learning, and the process is about discovery.

Knowing who the players are, what makes them tick, and what their deeper, underlying needs are will allow you to tailor the eventual strategy so that it can take those needs into account if appropriate and ultimately achieve your goals.

For a strategy to work, it has to meet the needs of the people who must support it.

Interviewing opens the door to finding things that you may not even know you're looking for. Questions pop up in the heart of a discussion that don't arise when you're sitting at your desk staring at a blank piece of paper. More often than not, the more unusual the question is, the better the discovery. If you find yourself wanting to ask some unscripted question, do it. Crazy, off-the-wall questions in the heat of the moment are a signal to your interviewee that this is a wide-open conversation. This can take the interview to new place, or prompt the person being interviewed to recall something that she wasn't aware she knew. I frequently ask, "If you were king/queen/ruler of the universe for a day, what one thing would you do/fix/change?" (see Figure 4-4). "Tell me what I need to know" complements this.

Although many people are comfortable with the concept of interviewing to gather data, knowledge, and insight, the idea of asking for *help* seems foreign. But asking for help during the Question phase can produce excellent results. Approach each interview as an opportunity for partnership. Ask people to help you understand what is happening. Ask them to share what they believe you ought to know.

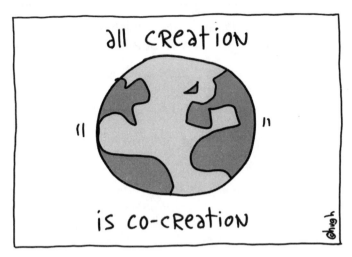

Figure 4-4. *Get people enrolled in the process*

Ask them what matters most in this situation. Asking for help will open more doors than demanding information. When you ask people to help, they will often share the most vital information you need. Remember to tag the topics that matter most as potential success criteria for use in later phases.

As mentioned earlier, one area where you might want to ask for help is in gaining access to quantitative data as good reference content. If you do ask about this, try to do it toward the end of the interview. Asking for this kind of information too early may push the conversation in a quantitative direction, causing you to miss the chance to learn about the more subjective nuances, which are important. When you do talk about data, be sure to ask basic critical questions and especially about any caveats the data brings with it. Is there anything else you should know about the data you'll be gathering? For more on asking good questions, see Appendix A.

RESEARCHING: GATHERING DATA YOU CAN REFERENCE. Quantitative, hard numbers from reports and databases are an important part of the Question phase, but use them with care. The ubiquity of computers and vastness of the Internet mean that quantitative information is everywhere, and much of it is free and of dubious quality. Still, numbers can be a gold mine, as long as you know how to interpret the data.

> ## Managing Temptation:
> ## Believing You Already Know What Problem Needs Solving
>
> As you start capturing facts and criteria, you and your team will be tempted to rush through the process because of the erroneous and all-too-common belief that you already know the essence of the problem and have nearly all the info you need to solve it. This belief is the result of having been around the block often enough to think you know what matters. It's particularly tempting because your gut sense about problems like these may actually be very good indeed.
>
> Resist this temptation. In unexpected situations, it's possible (even likely) that key stakeholders will call upon your team to verify that they have the right information, to ensure that decisions are, in fact, based on real, verified data (or, when necessary, on unverified data that everyone agrees is unverified, and is therefore a calculated risk).
>
> In addition, although it's tempting to shut people down when you've heard something two or three times before, there is value in having people in the organization express what you already know. You'll get independent confirmation of what you know, and they'll know that they've been heard and are valued.

The first step in knowing how to interpret your information is knowing where it came from. If you identify that the 2008 consumer software total available market (TAM) was $X zillion, it matters where that data point was found. Were the numbers from a 2009 study? Or from a 2007 projection? You may need to revisit the source of a "fact" in order to evaluate the assumptions and vocabulary of the source. Keeping track of your information sources also increases the credibility of facts in discussions down the road.

Beyond the source, try to get perspectives on the validity of the data. If you gained access to databases or reports during your interviews, hopefully you also got some sense of the accuracy and reliability of that data. For external or web-sourced content, see whether you can find other people in your company (or externally) who can attest to its usefulness.

Finally, check that your team has some data analysis skills. If they don't, borrow someone with those skills. Two particular skills will be useful.

First, if you have raw data, it will be very important to have someone with the ability to slice-and-dice numbers in search of insights. Second, you need someone who can "see through" and comment on conclusions drawn from statistics, particularly on information from polling data. For example, was there a sampling bias? Did the wording of the question make it impossible to answer accurately? What did the analyst mean by "open systems"? The skills of an insightful number cruncher can be very useful in this phase.

Managing Temptation: Choosing Certainty over Clarity

Even though the fact gathering step may take only a week or two to complete, the tension of wanting to move fast and get to an answer quickly can tempt you to shortcut it. The minute you do, you miss a critical opportunity to create shared organizational understanding, which recreates the Air Sandwich and will likely cause a failure downstream.

This temptation can be especially strong when you're working with internal groups who think they know enough about the situation and/ or the organization to take a stab at defining the solution.

The common mistake is to head straight to a quick-and-dirty sketch of the final picture without first gathering facts. The risk is that you end up with a strategy that doesn't deliver because the picture of the problem was incomplete, and the resulting solution didn't anticipate a major obstacle or was misaligned with the hidden issues. Creating a quick-and-dirty picture isn't unwise, necessarily, as long as you cycle back to the fact gathering step and carefully challenge the picture you've created.

Making a habit of skipping this step entirely puts you in danger of missing vital information when you actually need it. Doing fact gathering up front, each time, ensures that you are working on the real issues and the real problem. You know if you're truly being diligent about the Question phase when you have the facts uncovered in some easily accessible form. Without these facts, you cannot effectively challenge the understanding you are creating.

Fact gathering: Roles and responsibilities

As you'll recall, each phase and step of the QuEST process framework relies on a set of unique activities. Accordingly, your role as leader and participant will by necessity vary somewhat, depending on the point in the process.

Because some of what you're responsible for might seem straight-forward and simple, you might be tempted to skip activities or ignore certain responsibilities without realizing how painful the long-term consequences could be. Moreover, as you lead, you will undoubtedly be tempted to rely on clever, familiar techniques and shortcuts to keep people, activities, and the process moving along. After all, these skills and traits have helped you get this far, right? Why ditch them now?

We avoid taking shortcuts because the goal of capturing facts is to explore the scope of a given problem as fully and completely as possible. The picture we paint of that problem must be as vivid and comprehensive as we can make it, a picture that people across the organization can validate, question, and challenge.

As the leader, you are responsible for this. The artifact of this process (discussed a bit later in this chapter) involves creating a summary document, which you'll want to share with people as it makes sense.

In the fact gathering step, the leader plays the role of facilitator, and each participant is a discoverer. As a facilitator, your job is to make sure that every person involved leaves with the sense that they have really been heard, and that their contributions will be seriously considered and incorporated wherever and whenever possible.

From the leader's perspective, the important part of this step is going the extra mile to set appropriate context. Remind interviewees why you want to talk to them, let them know how it's important, and share with them who is involved and any key events that have happened. The leader can do a lot to create a safe environment for the people being interviewed so they share as openly as possible. It can't be overstated how worthwhile it is to make the extra effort and foster the kind of environment where interview subjects don't hold back. Unspoken concerns and silent objectives will only surface later.

Responsibilities during the capture step for both the leader and the team are listed in Table 4-3.

TABLE 4-3. *Step 2: Fact gathering roles and responsibilities*

LEADER'S ROLE

- Do good discovery.

  —Select one or two people to do the fact gathering interviews and make sure they're good at asking probing questions. Remember that the goal is to ask things devoid of judgment and full of curiosity. Choose interviewers who have personal credibility in the organization and are free of "political baggage" that might hinder people from talking openly.

  —Instruct the people doing interviews that not all facts are the same, so they need to listen for how confident the interviewee is about what they are saying (and highlight those observations in their notes).

  —Make sure to choose a range of interviewees to generate a valuable diversity of opinion.

  —Consider calling interviewees ahead of time to let them know that this project is important and that your team truly wants to hear their opinions, hypotheses, feelings, data, and perspectives. That said, I'm reluctant to send people the questions in advance, but I am happy to send them the topics. Sending questions locks you into a survey-like fixed flow. Just the named topics without specific questions allows greater flexibility to go where the conversation needs to go.

- Foster open sharing.

  —Match the style of who is doing the interviewing with who is being interviewed, so the interviewee feels comfortable enough to give you good information.

- Evaluate data.

  —Study data and underlying assumptions to make sure you're not being lied to with data.

COLLABORATOR'S ROLE

- Conduct interviews.

  —Seek out and organize relevant quantitative facts, with clear sourcing from documents and databases.

- Discuss/debate/synthesize findings.

- Report findings to the organization. This is not an optional step.

Step 3: Sharing the Findings

Through interviewing and researching, you will discover a good collection of "facts," hunches, insights, and perspectives. Some of this information will be objectively true and validated in many ways. Some pieces of information may conflict with others. Some may not make sense at all.

The final step of the Question phase is to create a report back to the team or larger organization of stakeholders and players. I call this "sharing the findings." The goal in this sharing phase is to create a shared understanding of the problem and the current situation.

Before we can share findings, they need to be organized in a form that will make it straightforward to share with everybody, so they can develop a shared understanding. Ultimately, this shared understanding will become the information basis that in effect enables the organization to think about the problem fully, and helps the team develop a strategy that will solve the problem at hand.

You'll have to sort through the information and organize it into logical buckets to create more meaning. The way you organize these facts will change for every situation, but in general, the categories tend to include what is known, what you believe, what you doubt, and what doesn't fit, like this:

What is known and can be confirmed

This is information that is irrefutable, confirmed, and can be presented as fact. This can include hard numbers from validated sources, or it can be a series of facts gleaned from stories people have told in the organization. Create two subcategories for this kind of information: one bucket for information that has already been confirmed, and another bucket for information that needs to be confirmed. Note that if your data comes from a previous project, make sure to put it in the "unconfirmed" bucket. Don't treat last year's market share numbers or customer buying habits as automatically confirmed for this year!

What you believe, but don't have enough facts to confirm

This is typically something you know or sense from your own experience or something many people believe, but that you lack sufficient data to support. It's OK to have unconfirmed facts; just make sure you tag them as such. Later, when you're making decisions based on pivotal information, you'll want to avoid the risk of making a key decision on information that you never backed up.

What you doubt

This is information that somehow you don't quite believe. It could be data from a source with a reputation for fluffy numbers, or some signal from your nonsense detector that something isn't quite right. You can tag something as questionable, even if you don't know exactly why you doubt it. Quite often, it is these points of doubt that show you where there are noticeable gaps between various people's views of the situation.

What doesn't fit

This section is for identifying any "red herrings" or stories that people believe but that aren't relevant to the task at hand. For example, perhaps there was some big sales deal that occurred in the past and it's used as an argument to take a particular course of action. However, on closer inspection, the story is debunked by some hidden assumptions or special circumstances. Another example is when an issue that's broadly recognized as a thorn in the side of the business is inappropriately tied together with the problem you're trying to solve, because people think they can get their problem solved if they can associate it with something that is going to get resolved and/or resourced. This is like an unrelated attachment to a piece of legislation that's obviously going to pass. When something is perpetually a problem in the organization, people often find a way to drag that issue into every project or strategy because they hope it can be solved "alongside" the core mission *you* are carrying. However, this will dilute your efforts. So be clear about this type of issue so it can be set aside and not revisited in every meeting. If it really is an issue, solve it discretely.

At this point, you've filtered and categorized what you've learned and put it into logical buckets so you can look at everything more clearly. The next step is to create a document called a *summary of key findings*, which lets you share what you have learned, what you believe, and what you understand with the people throughout the organization. The buckets we just talked about are a good exercise and will help you develop your own deep understanding of what you have discovered during the fact gathering step. However, they aren't the final output of your report. Your report back is a much more comprehensive view and a story. When you're confident that you have a solid framework of key findings, you need to share it. For recommendations on doing this, see the "Building a Findings Framework" exercise in Appendix A.

There are two compelling reasons for sharing the findings with your whole team. First, you want to be certain that they have the opportunity to weigh in on what you've learned, and to shape and add to it. This ability to add perspectives is particularly valuable for multifaceted issues, so make sure the team knows that their feedback is welcome.

As you share your findings, the team will have the opportunity to see the comprehensive range of things they need to address. They may have some new insight to share that will shape the view, or they may simply see the situation in a whole new light. Be sure to capture any feedback or insights that come up during sharing.

Second, the sharing provides an opportunity for many team members to learn things they didn't know or weren't comfortable admitting, which is essential to forming a common understanding. Part of the "team learning" aspect is coming to terms with the unvarnished truth of the situation. This can be an uncomfortable conversation, but it's one you need to have in order to move forward. If it helps, consider yourself a reporter in this role, describing "what is" so that it can be dealt with. Figure 4-5 illustrates how the output of the Question phase is all about shared understanding.

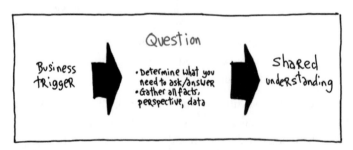

Figure 4-5. *Questioning produces the key artifact of shared understanding*

Another way to look at the sharing activity is to think of it as publicly revealing the elephants that you discovered in the fact gathering step. Getting your team's perspectives about the multifaceted topic gives shape to the different parts of the elephant that the blind men couldn't see. One thing that commonly happens during the sharing step is the naming or spelling out of the elephant(s) in the room. In other words, this is the place to openly identify and discuss taboo topics so that people can understand them more clearly.

For specific help on how to share sensitive information so that people can learn from it, review the "Speaking Truth with Clarity and Power" exercise in Appendix A. There are three high-level things to keep in mind:

- Present everything you say in terms of "early findings," not as truth. Early findings suggest you are doing thorough fact gathering. Truth suggests you are making judgments (see Figure 4-6).

- Don't gloss over anything. Say exactly and specifically what you want other people to know, using as many distinctions and details as necessary. You want people to learn about the situation with as much fidelity as possible, so that everyone has a chance to question, learn, and ultimately come to a shared understanding.

- Tone matters, so approach this session assuming that people want to hear what you've found and want to do something about it. Don't unnecessarily shelter them from the findings or appear to be confronting them in an aggressive way.

Figure 4-6. *Keep things open as "early findings," not as "truth,"because force-fed truth never tastes good*

The key part of this step is to ensure that team members *call out all of the issues* (and not try to duck, discount, or hide them) *without necessarily trying to solve them.* You may want to talk about company history. You may want to list what hasn't worked in the past so you can make sure to avoid those pitfalls. You may want to bring up any unspoken elephants in the room. Good. You may even want to draw out implications for what you think all the findings might mean. Again, good. Do all of that, but do so without making any recommendations.

Sharing the findings: Roles and responsibilities

Table 4-4 outlines the roles and responsibilities for leaders and collaborators during this sharing step.

TABLE 4-4. *Step 3: Sharing the findings roles and responsibilities*

LEADER'S ROLE

- Manage the process of reporting findings back to the organization, so that later recommendations are based on a fuller understanding of the problem:
  - —Invite people to this reporting process who are key to solving the problem or who need to have the full picture in order to support the effort.
  - —Let collaborators know that this is an early check-in process. Your role is to shed light on the problem, and their role is to validate what they hear, not to make decisions or act on the information.
  - —Ask people to confirm your assumptions about which data is relevant and not relevant. If people believe data that you have considered irrelevant isn't, you want to know this now—not later, when your assumptions have become the foundation of a strategy.
  - —If you are going to expose an elephant in the room, let people know it is coming. You can say things like, "I want to let you know that this next information may be a surprise to some of you. We heard XYZ, and we found that about half the group sees this as a problem we need to address."
  - —Call out issues, but make it clear that the point of the session is not to solve them, only to surface them. (Solving them happens later; getting caught up in them now derails efforts.)

COLLABORATOR'S ROLE

- Discuss/debate/synthesize and ultimately organize the findings.
- Report findings to organization. This is not an optional step.

Don't run from any conflict, deal with it; it's a necessary part of the process. One benefit of reporting the findings and getting resistance is that it alerts you to areas and issues that might generate resistance later in the process. Better to know now than later. Better to know what you still need to ask/answer to address those issues. Face into that tension to learn what you need to learn.

Another thing that comes of this shared findings work is making sure those working on the problem don't have confirmation bias—where people more readily notice things that confirm what they believe and discount facts that contradict their beliefs. Confirmation bias skews the facts when data that supports a belief is included preferentially and data that is contradictory gets filtered out. When the report back is public, people are less likely to become victims of confirmation bias, because at some level they think that any distortion of the facts will be exposed. There is a natural self-correction built into the system when findings are shared publicly.

Sequences of the Question Phase

Often people want to know the sequencing of Question and how many meetings it takes. We've talked about the three steps in this chapter; now let's add fidelity on what types of forums are needed and who to involve. Although it varies by situation, the average Question phase for a relatively complex problem takes 1 to 10 weeks. Table 4-5 captures the steps and some key forums, and summarizes the outputs.

TABLE 4-5. *Sequencing Question steps with roles, forums, and output*

STEP 1: IDENTIFYING THE PROBLEM SCOPE

Who			Forum	Output
Initiates	*Consults*	*Decides*		
Operational leader	Experts; multilevel influencers	Operational leader	1–3 group meetings	Statement of scope

STEP 2: FACT GATHERING

Who			Forum	Output
Initiates	*Consults*	*Decides*		
Members of strategy team	People in all parts of the organization who might have insights/ perspectives		One-on-one interviews	Raw data (quantitative and qualitative)

STEP 3: SHARING THE FINDINGS

Who			Forum	Output
Initiates	*Consults*	*Decides*		
Operational leader	All involved parties; open invitation		Group meeting plus follow-up email	Summary of key findings and implications

The entire sequence of Question steps goes quickly, yet it involves a lot of talking and gathering information with people to learn the problem. The operational leader will most often be the best person to serve as the process overseer (though depending on skills, another member of the team can take this role, or you may bring in a skilled outsider). You, as the leader, will oversee the interviews, create the summary findings, and organize how facts get reported back. Take care in choosing the people who are doing the interviewing, that a representative variety of people are being interviewed, and that the information you gather is fully validated and understood by your organization before you move forward. Although you might wish to delegate the task of reporting back what the fact gathering step uncovered, ultimately it's still the leader's responsibility to manage the discussion that surrounds the event.

The Goal: Getting Shared Understanding

The Question phase creates buy-in among the organization because if you have the courage to call out the issues and publicly report back what you think needs to be solved and why, the broader population generally comes around and starts to naturally support the effort. That doesn't mean this part is easy. It just means this part is necessary.

Recall that we talked about how when we know the problem, we can solve the problem. That naturally happens in the Question phase. Even if you didn't get the right problem statement at the start of it, you will have a chance to test it and change it if necessary.

We've described the process as talking to key people and engaging them in conversation without trying to solve anything. There's an openness to doing the questioning so you can keep learning. It's this learning during Question that lets you understand the situation fully and with a broader view than if you jumped straight into problem solving. You also will see the individual problems that often are part of a single big problem. Until you unravel the issues with a degree of clarity, you cannot address all the holistic or core issues.

Of course, we complete the Question phase by naming the problem in public. This may seem unnecessary, but it is a key output of this phase. By naming all of the issues, the people involved won't be ducking, discounting, or hiding them. At this point, you've already achieved some success. But there's still something else that needs to happen.

The purpose of sharing the findings is to build a full, 360-degree view of the problem in people's minds with minimal bias, so that team members have a larger understanding of the problem itself. This creates—or rather, supports—an organization that *thinks* rather than simply does the bidding of others. If you blur the lines between this effort and the next phase, you're less likely to have clarity amongst the people involved. This means you'll have accomplished part of the goal of Question, but will miss an opportunity for people to click on their brains to get it, challenge it, and make it their own.

After sharing the findings, you and your team have a clear and shared picture of the problem. You now enter the second phase of the QuEST process framework, Envision. Envision is where people get to work on the creation and development of your strategy options. This is often the most enjoyable part of a project, because you get to start working on the solutions to all these problems. So, let's have some fun.

CHAPTER 5

Phase II: Envision

*Every man takes the limits of his own field of vision
for the limits of the world.*

—Arthur Schopenhauer

Create Options That Matter and Know Why They Matter

Knowing that insights reside everywhere and new solutions can come from anywhere, we need a systematic way to gather, analyze, and develop new, creative options to solve the problem—without being bogged down. That's what the second phase of the QuEST process framework, Envision, is all about. It's where we generate a wide range of options for solving the problem, and begin to track the criteria that will ultimately let us choose the best options based on our shared vision of success.

If you are like most people, you start this chapter with some context for how to approach problem solving through idea generation and brainstorming techniques.[1] The weakness with these tools and techniques is that people use them assuming that the best idea will become apparent. However, people often generate a range of ideas without a clear idea of whether those choices will actually work, given the organization's internal capabilities and market situation. The Envision phase lets you use whatever approach you want for idea generation, but adds a nuance to the process by recognizing that not all solutions are right for a particular company.

Envision aims to answer the question, "What is the right set of options for *you*, given your problem and particular set of circumstances?" It's not about blue-sky thinking and generating the broadest set of options. It's about focusing and generating options that are most likely to work, knowing that best *theoretically* and best *practically* are two entirely different things.

The Envision phase (Figure 5-1) is important because, until we've had a chance to gather all the viable options, we won't be able to select among the best of them. Envision lets an organization use collaboration to generate solutions. Because you have named the problem already in the Question phase, you can now open up the floor to the best ideas from unexpected sources. This is done in a flat structure that allows for open input. Because so much is known about idea generation, this chapter is going to focus on how best to do options development, and then how these options and the selection criteria feed into the next phase (Select).

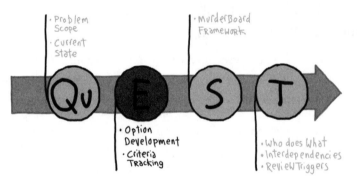

Figure 5-1. *Envision is the second phase of QuEST*

Let's look at how the Envision phase will help you come up with viable options to solve your strategy problem and generate the necessary outcomes for your business.

How to Do It

There are two short-and-sweet steps to the Envision phase:

- Developing a rich set of options
- Tracking criteria that will be used to shape decisions in the Select phase (Phase III)

As you leave the last step in the Question phase, you have a group of people with a shared understanding of the real problem. At this point, they are champing at the bit to actually solve the problem, and this is the time to let those people loose to identify viable solutions.

In the Envision phase, the goal is to tap into the latent power in your organization by asking people to contribute toward fixing the problem. In this phase, we include people at all levels in the organization so we can generate a diversity of ideas on the table. Ideally, this ensures that the aperture for potential solutions is as wide as possible. This is a good place to use those collaborative tools (listed in Appendix A) that let you do mass idea generation and brainstorming so that gathering options goes quickly. Some of these tools also let you camouflage the source of input so you can protect people from the risk of looking stupid or naming a political issue that stands in the way of the organization's success.

> *There is no such thing as "the right answer."*
> *There is something that is best for you, given your problem and particular set of circumstances.*
> *Envision that.*

The other part of this phase is to keep the focus on "why" something matters. In order to make any of these options viable or practical, you need to figure out *which ones* matter for your company or organization, and know *why* they matter. This is the reason that we call out criteria tracking in the Envision phase. It lets you gather many, many ideas, while starting to draw distinctions as to why one option might be better than another. So let's talk about both of these pieces—option development and criteria tracking—in this chapter.

Step 1: Option Development

In option development, you slow down enough to involve many people in thinking things through and understanding all of your possible choices, so that when you're ready to make a choice, you have a rich pool of options to evaluate.

Be sure to involve the people who do the hands-on work in the business; they're better able to see the day-to-day challenges and act as a source of new options and key insights. Include people outside the business (partners, suppliers, channels, etc.) if you want to be open about solving the problem and could use their outside-in perspective. You'll have many good options, and later we can understand the distinct impact each would have on the business.

Face-to-face meetings traditionally have been the source of brainstorming work, but there are several compelling ways to do this kind of problem solving with collaborative tools. Whether you hold several brainstorming and discussion meetings in person or host a brainstorming session online, the focus of each session will be driven by the dynamics of your specific situation. For example, you may want to have an entire meeting devoted to developing a particular idea, looking at product options, exploring regional alternatives, or whatever type of results you are considering.

In option development meetings, the focus is on exploring possibilities: "What if we...?", "Is there a reason why...?", and "What would happen if we tried...?" You may need to integrate different techniques for different aspects of the project. In addition to including various domain experts, you may want to bring in people with inquisitive, provocative, or energetic styles, though be sure to balance that energy with the sense of safety that the team needs to feel in making contributions.[2]

It's important to explore many different angles on the options you could pursue, and to make sure that you engage everyone on those options that are relevant to them. This doesn't have to mean bringing everyone together at the same time (although that is an option if you're confident they won't get bored and check out).

Ask people if there's anything new, from their perspective, in the current project. If so, how can it be handled? How do proposals from other functional groups influence them? How does our competition do it? How will our competition respond? What if energy prices rise? What if? What if? However you approach this, make sure you probe for a broad set of perspectives. Often we are limited by our specific near-term experience. To ensure a holistic viewpoint, task a knowledgeable and open-minded person with representing each aspect of your project during ideation.[3]

As you begin to produce some ideas and options, you or someone else on the team may realize that there are embedded criteria being used to either create or filter the options list. That is fine, and indeed is part of the reason these two steps are part of the same phase. But you must ensure that you make criteria explicit and keep them in different buckets while developing options.

Some of the more creative ideas may require some investigating before you can answer questions such as: "Can we actually do that?", "What would it take?", "How does this currently work today?", "What are the current barriers?" In this case, you may need to revisit the Question phase to dig up more information. Don't let this deter you. If the idea is compelling, further digging may take you to an exciting and powerful new solution—or not. You won't know in advance. What's important is to be sure that you keep the team aligned around what you are doing, and how that affects the eventual picture of what success could look like.

Leading the option development step

Option development generates a full range of ideas that offer potential ways to solve the problem, as well as a solid understanding of how these ideas compare to each other in terms of their impact on the organization.

Option development is directed creative problem solving. There are myriad ways to structure and manage such processes. Again, check out the resources section in Appendix B. Choose whatever method works for you and your team.

For the option development step to be effective, you need to foster an environment in which people feel safe enough to rigorously debate ideas, share their wide-ranging opinions, and keep their defense shields down long enough to build on one another's ideas. Safety is an interesting notion: it's when judgment is suspended and risks are encouraged. As the leader, your key role is to make sure there's a safe environment. If you are interested in passionately advocating and building your set of proposed solutions, make sure someone else is facilitating and driving the process for everyone.

Managing Temptation: Saving the Ideas You Personally Like

The value of facilitation is often overlooked. You will be tempted to lead the meeting and not acknowledge that your own passionate point of view can limit discussion. But here is the truth: you cannot be both the content player and the group owner without sacrificing the quality of one or the other. I know most leaders think they can do both at the same time, but when they've been freed to focus just on content, they see how they were straddling too many things to do content *and* lead the process well. If something is incredibly important to the business (like a strategy), you need to make sure all points of view are heard. For option development to succeed, the process must be led without a bias toward choosing one option or one leader's voice having too much dominance. When the leader is opinionated (and what leader isn't?), someone else has to manage the flow of conversation to make sure all points of view are raised/heard/managed. Therefore, the process must be managed by a specific someone with that distinct responsibility. Don't let that get sacrificed, or you will have done the business a disservice.

Leaders as facilitators serve more like the host of the party than the guest of honor. You are hosting a party where people are expected to come ready to play and to have a good, productive time. In your role as facilitator, you will oversee the details of the event, as a skilled party planner would. As your guests arrive and while the party is in full swing, you'll manage their interactions, keeping things running smoothly so people want to come again.

Leaders who are not strong in the role of "host" or "facilitator" may choose to delegate or outsource this role. For more information on the role of host, refer to "Facilitation" on page 254 in Appendix B. Use a trained, high-quality facilitator from outside the firm, or choose someone within your company who has demonstrated this natural skill. This approach has the advantage of freeing the leader to participate on an equal footing with others.

No one party can overpower another in these situations; equal footing matters. Remember, everyone's ideas have merit.

As the facilitator or as the content leader, you should get the ball rolling by proposing some semi-outrageous notions, such as, "Should it be solar powered?", "Should it have speech recognition?", or whatever outside-the-box suggestion you might have. As the leader, you will have a certain amount of permission to take such an approach.

Table 5-1 lists the responsibilities that leaders, facilitators, and collaborators have during option development.

Managing Temptation:
Wanting Harmony Instead of Productive Conflict

In the option development step, you may be tempted to promote group harmony instead of facilitating productive disagreement. This is totally natural. People on the team will say or imply that harmony is what they want. This is because they value keeping their working relationships as smooth as possible, and they may not look forward to disagreeing with each other, especially in a public or semi-public forum. Your job, then, will be to lead option development so that opinions and disagreement are welcomed, invited, and expected, and even investigated as potential sources of creative energy. Here's the thing: our business challenges come with inherent tensions. By acknowledging and addressing those tensions as we develop ideas rather than smoothing things over, we'll end up with an even stronger, more viable set of options. It's one of those pay-me-now or pay-me-later choices. The tension is going to be there. The question is whether you harness it during options and solutions creation or wait until a strategy failure occurs, like the one I described in Chapter 1.

TABLE 5-1. *Step 1: Option development roles and responsibilities*

LEADER'S ROLE

- Pay attention to who you invite to the meetings, and be sure you aren't inviting the same set of people repeatedly. The purpose of these sessions is to generate fresh perspectives.
- Invite those with on-the-ground experience about what is going on, what works, and what needs fixing.
- Invite people who can give you a lateral perspective on how other departments or divisions will be affected.
- Invite constructive critics who almost always start their sentences with "But you haven't thought about...." These critics can remind you of what you need to consider.
- Set context. Let people know at the outset that you're looking for fresh perspectives. Tell them you expect them to step outside their domain areas and create new solutions. Let them know that you want to hear not just why Bob's idea has a flaw, but also how they could take it one step further to either remedy the flaw or build upon the idea itself.
- Make note of options that spur a need to cycle back to get more data.
- Advocate/champion/lobby for ideas that pop up that you believe need to be fully heard.

FACILITATOR'S ROLE

- Establish the norms of the group at the outset of the meeting. For example: "If you're here, you need to *be here*." (In other words, no email, no phone calls, no text messages.) Reinforce these norms as needed.
- Manage the flow of the conversation and the tensions inherent in decision making.
- Seek a balance between support and confrontation, and a fair balance between whom you support and confront.
- Ensure that people are able to express a diversity of opinions. The session should not be treated as "open mic night," but rather as a guided experience of creativity where everyone gets to weigh in and contribute.
- Monitor the quality of conversations so that they are as productive as possible. This may mean switching from a structured format to a more improvisational one (drawing versus talking, small groups versus large groups, creating Post-its as individuals). You make the call as to what is needed.
- Be alert to the environment in terms of physical comfort. Does the room have enough natural light? Is the room warm enough? Cold enough? Do you need cookies in the afternoon? (I have found the lack of cookies to be one of the biggest impediments to quality idea generation.)
- Manage the environment in terms of people's emotional comfort. People generate good ideas when they feel free and safe to do so. If your team is facing heavy layoffs or is preoccupied with some other serious concern, you may want to consider postponing the session.

CO-CREATOR'S ROLE

- Bring your ideas and creativity to bear on the problem.
- Advocate/champion/lobby for ideas you believe need to be fully heard.
- "Sit forward" into the process. Engage.
- Build on other people's ideas. This does not mean tear down everyone else's ideas.
- Figure out how to step outside your specific domain and contribute to the shared business problem.
- Support the norms of behavior.
- Speak up if you're not comfortable with the environment.

In the option development step, everyone is undertaking a deeper creative act than any one person could do alone. You get to bring together experts in different domains—engineers, marketing, and sales channel specialists. Inspire them to work together to generate ideas outside their individual expertise. Co-creating like this simply doesn't happen when people are hesitant to speak their minds for fear of stepping on toes, damaging new working relationships, or driving into a "career cul-de-sac." As described in Chapters 2 and 3, the tone for this dialogue is set by everyone.

Step 2: Criteria Tracking

As a part of the option development step, you and your team will invest a bunch of creative energy in finding a good range of potential approaches to solving your problem. In the process, you'll probably touch on various notions of success. Capture those ideas while they are fresh. This is called criteria tracking because you are identifying the footprints and patterns that seem to dictate whether one option is better than another. Criteria tracking does not need to be treated as completely distinct from option development. That is, the two steps can overlap somewhat. In practice, this means you'll initially focus on option development with occasional moments of criteria tracking. Later, in the Envision phase, you'll be doing some criteria tracking that will spark more option development.

Criteria tracking is parallel to option development in another way: it is about creating a rich set of potential criteria for evaluating visions of success. This criteria list will be sorted and prioritized during the upcoming Select phase. Criteria tracking also serves another useful function: it provides some effective separation between the idea generation space of the Envision phase and the idea rejection space of the Select phase.

As you build your list, include criteria from each area: product development, sales, operations, and so on. The intent behind criteria tracking is to gather what matters to the team and your organization so that during the next phase, Select, you can make the most well-informed choice among all your strategy ideas. You are seeking to answer several questions: How will we know when we're winning? What does success look like? Where do we want to be? How does this influence what other moves our company can make? Some people have described this as tightly linked to a corporate mission. Often that will be true. But sometimes the criteria for a particular strategy will be unique for its own reasons.

The point to remember is that the criteria you develop now will determine how you choose amongst all these options. It's important that these criteria align with the larger mission of the organization, to make sure that you're not abandoning your core principles just to make an extra buck. Dollars matter in business, but not at the expense of core values. Doing things in alignment with the core mission and vision of a firm can accelerate success (Figure 5-2).

Figure 5-2. *Knowing what matters to us*

There are two key points to remember about criteria tracking. First, you want to expose tacit assumptions about the project goal and help your team come to a shared and explicit understanding about what matters. People in different roles often disagree about what success will look like. Finance may want the new project to address an anticipated revenue shortfall. Business development may want the new project to win a potential new partner. Engineering may see the project as a chance to learn a new technology. Resolving these tensions in an agreed-upon way is vital to the project. This can make a big difference in the ultimate success of the business solution. For example, the product development team might be motivated and even incentivized to keep capital equipment costs down, but when they understand that doing so is less important than schedule or quality (or whatever), they can take this to finance and explain why they need more in their budget. That's an example of a decision that teams make after selecting criteria because they understand the inherent criteria and trade-offs. The full debate on criteria can wait until the Select phase, because at this point you want to focus on bringing things to the surface.

Debating why something matters instead of which idea is best lets people think collaboratively.

Second, explicit shared criteria give the entire team a shared vocabulary for "where we want to be" and will help each team member know how to make decisions at any point in the process where they need to make a trade-off. They will be aware of the underlying logic of the strategy and be able to articulate it. This is a benefit of collaborative strategy. The leader won't hold the criteria alone; everyone will get it.

People sometimes don't understand what forms criteria, so Table 5-2 lists some examples that can be useful for spurring the creation of a rich list of potential criteria.

TABLE 5-2. *Sample criteria*

WHAT MATTERS	EXPLANATION
Size/revenue	It will be big enough to be a significant focus for the division.
Timeframe	It will match our needs in number of quarters/years to yield.
Portfolio	It will match our portfolio of products/services/offers.
Region	It will be available in regions where we are strong.
Certainty	We will have the right data available to make a good decision.
Affinity	We will need to follow what our e-team wants, and they really want to do this.
Defensive move	We will do it because we don't want others to.
Sales model	We will already be set up to sell it.
Customer	The account type will match buyers that we know how to reach.
Leverage	It will use our core strengths (product, channel, know-how) best.
Service	We will be able to perform to meet customer satisfaction expectations.
Profitability	It will support add-on of items, such as professional services.

Criteria are ultimately another way to foster the culture of thinkers and strategists who can arrive at their own answers and drive forward the business without needing explicit direction. Criteria include all aspects of what is important to the business. Sharing these makes everyone aware of what matters. When everyone knows this, they are all *thinkers* rather than "just" doers. When we have shared criteria, we enable a healthy and thriving culture of problem solvers rather than simply doers. This is a key notion of the New How.

Start with an open question

One simple question to start the criteria tracking step is: "How will we know when we are done?" This question gets people thinking about what the solution should look like, without specifically considering any options. Another question is: "Imagine you are looking at a series of options of what we could do and pointing and saying, 'That's the ONE!' What about that solution makes you sure?" This question helps people start to consciously identify their decision-making criteria and helps them communicate explicitly what will drive the decision for them.

Lead the criteria tracking step

The goal of criteria tracking is to create a shared understanding of what success will look like. The understanding must be *shared* so each person on the team has a chance to talk about, internalize, and agree on the criteria or *evidence of success*. Consensus is important, but so is progress. If one or a few people do not agree, allow a little extra time to resolve the differences. If it still does not resolve, the leader or leaders will need to make a call. It may be appropriate to remind the team that once the options have been aired and discussed, the co-creators have a duty to support judgment calls. In Chapter 2, we discussed how collaboration is not consensus but rather an opportunity to participate fully, think together, and then co-create the future.

Discussing the criteria in detail gives team members an opportunity to clarify what's most important by adding essential details or identifying and removing extraneous elements that might contribute to confusion.

Agreeing on and internalizing the criteria are essential pieces of the overall process. Individual team members will draw on their internalized criteria to inform and guide the selection of the one best strategy from the final strategy options. They'll also use the criteria as a decision-making guide downstream during the execution of the project. Your team's ability to select the right strategy is the logical byproduct of each team member having internalized the indicators or aspects of success. Their shared agreement is also valuable because it encourages individuals to support others through the project.

With this in mind, your mission (should you choose to accept it) is to lead your team through the *thinking* process to develop quality criteria. This involves helping each member of your team reach a unified sense of what is most important and why. Although the debate must result in a set of criteria that you as a leader can live with, it's also important that you give the team permission to add to the conclusions. Try to avoid forcing a preset outcome on them. In other words, avoid any tendencies you have to transform into the Chief of Answers!

Envision Roles and Responsibilities

Table 5-3 lists the main leader responsibilities during this part of the criteria tracking step, as well as the responsibilities of your team.

TABLE 5-3. *Step 2: Criteria tracking roles and responsibilities*

LEADER'S ROLE
• Nominate criteria and invite your team to debate reasons why these criteria would either work or not work.
• Share your personal experience and rationale.
• Remind your team of the larger goal for the project/strategy as needed.

COLLABORATOR'S ROLE
• Think about and surface criteria suggestions.
• Make tacit assumptions explicit.
• Question or challenge any criteria that do not seem legitimate.
• Understand and agree on the final criteria. Ultimately support the selected criteria.

Identifying the criteria openly is also important because it allows people to state what is important to them as a team, as a division, and as an organization, and it helps them internalize why the strategy is important (that is, not just because "Bob said so"). When everyone is able to express their ideas for success, you win in two ways. You gain the advantage of potential upsides: some of the ideas will be very good. And you eliminate some downsides: later on, people won't spend a lot of time fretting over whether their idea might have made things better, because they will know. For additional ideas on how to help teams develop criteria, see the "Tips for Criteria Development" exercises in Appendix A.

Imagining what success looks like can seem strange if you are not accustomed to it. Many organizations use phrases like "getting traction" and "achieving momentum." These sound positive and successful, but they are not specific enough to allow people to steer their activities in alignment with the overarching goal. Instead of "getting traction," we need to talk about how many new customers we are looking for. Instead of "achieving momentum," we should look at specific quarter-over-quarter growth targets. The more specific and quantifiable the various dimensions of this project are in people's hearts and minds, the better they can make decisions that support success.

When you are capturing criteria, the debate is often as valuable as the actual result. The outcome itself may not come as much of a surprise to you, but your team's discussion as you're developing criteria will give each individual on the team time to internalize what is important and why.

What's most important about criteria tracking is that you turn unspoken assumptions into explicit and shared insights.

Managing Temptation:
Claiming to Know What Matters over Trusting the Group to Complete the Decision Collectively

During criteria tracking step, you may think you know what success looks like. So you will be tempted to make your views known and then move directly on to what you might mistakenly believe is the actual work. Don't leave your team out of the criteria tracking process. Even if you're right, when you act like the Chief of Answers, the team will miss an important opportunity to internalize what they need to know. This will compromise their ability to make excellent decisions and trade-offs later on. And, more than likely, you might miss something critical or supply extraneous elements. Most leaders find value in the trust and shared ownership that are developed by letting their team help them vet the list.

The Goal: Achieving Viable Options That People Believe In

During the Envision phase, you'll generate, capture, and articulate a full range of options that create potential strategic solutions. Because of the way people have been asked to participate in creating this option, you'll have some buy-in within the organization. Because you'll have a way of actually picking the one right option for this organization, you don't need to be afraid of having many options.

Once you've successfully guided the team through this phase, you'll have some viable choices for consideration (Figure 5-3).

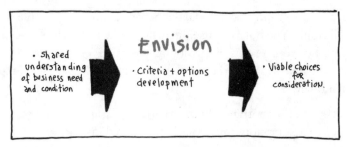

Figure 5-3. Envision creates options and criteria to feed the Select phase

When you have completed the Envision phase, your team will have generated a rich set of possible criteria and many options to explore. At this point, your job is to migrate the team's attention toward the third phase of the QuEST process framework: Select.

CHAPTER 6

Phase III: Select

> *Freedom is not merely the opportunity*
> *to do as one pleases;*
> *neither is it merely the opportunity to choose*
> *between set alternatives.*
> *Freedom is, first of all, the chance to formulate*
> *the available choices, to argue over them—*
> *and then the opportunity to choose.*
>
> —C. Wright Mills

Killing Off Bad Ideas So Good Ideas Can Thrive

At a three-year product strategy meeting at Apple during the early 1990s, the McKinsey hired guns presented something I now refer to as the "99-idea slide" as the final summary of a strategy presentation. It was chock-full of information, presented in a visually compelling way. It showed all the viable product strategies we could pursue. With its combined richness and graphical simplicity, the 99-idea slide wowed all of us.

Shortly after the presentation, the meeting broke up. Apparently, we were "done" with our strategy process, and we had an impressive PowerPoint deck to show for it. I was befuddled. I wondered what I was missing. Maybe other people had a larger view or perspective— some special awareness—that helped everything make sense. It didn't seem like we'd actually made any decisions, but perhaps we had and I had missed it. The 99-idea slide was impressive, but I wasn't sure what it meant for the work I was leading. Was someone going to tell me what the implications were? Or was it assumed that I already knew?

As it turned out, it wasn't just me; we were all unclear. Not one of the participants knew how to put the strategy into practice. So, like many consulting reports before them, the binders moved from the desk to the bookshelf and, finally, out of view. A few years later, Apple lost that particular market to the competition—exactly the outcome we had sought to avoid. It wasn't for lack of trying, or interest, or even willpower.

In this instance, the strategy was considered crucial, so we had taken a very different tack than we had with prior product strategies. In the past, a few execs had gotten together and quickly come up with some options, and the rest of us were told what to do. With help from the consultants, we had done a great job of whiteboarding and research to generate a vetted list of many viable options. These myriad options had opened up a Pandora's box, however. Having such a huge list to choose from was, in some ways, worse than having a shorter, less-considered list of options.[1]

So what was missing from our strategy? Perhaps it is obvious, but it took me some time to figure out that we lacked an underlying process that would have allowed us to winnow the many options down to the right option (Figure 6-1).

Figure 6-1. *The search for strategy*

What was missing was a way to decide which of the available strategic options made the most sense for *us* to do. We had no organized way to select a strategy from the list. And, at least as important, we needed a way to determine which of the available options we should *not* pursue. In other words, we needed a way to kill off options so we could focus on moving forward.

Selecting "The One"

Perhaps you are thinking that any one of the options on the table in a given situation would have been good enough, and in fact that might be true. Sometimes good enough is indeed enough. But more often, choosing the best option matters. In this case, the "best" option is whatever makes the most sense for this organization, at this particular time, given the market conditions, matched to internal capabilities, considering allocated resources, and so on. By selecting the best option, you have a higher likelihood of achieving the vision behind the strategy.

Imagine your goal is to cross a vast expanse of territory to acquire something of value and return safely. The kind of vehicle you select to achieve this goal will depend on what particular territory you're crossing—its topography, climate, and obstacles—as well as the cargo you need to transport, the amount of risk that's acceptable, and the resources you have available.

If you have mountains to traverse, for example, you might choose a helicopter. If you are facing frozen tundra, you might choose a snowmobile. Each vehicle has particular characteristics and strengths that make it the right vehicle for a particular terrain: its rate of speed, its ability to move past obstacles, the number of people it can carry from here to there.

Strategy development works in much the same way. By the time you arrive at the 99-point slide, what you find in front of you is the equivalent to a fine array of nice-looking transportation vehicles that you've worked very hard to assemble. Each of them will appear to get you from here to there. But which do you choose? Helicopter? Biplane? Humvee? Hovercraft? How will you decide? Might you need to involve a person who knows the details about the terrain, the cargo, and your resources? In practical terms, obviously, it's essential to make a decision. It wouldn't work to have half the team prepare the hovercraft and the other half jump in the helicopter. Unintentionally pursuing multiple options in parallel will waste resources and put your best people in competition for no good reason. Failing to choose means failing to achieve the goal.

With respect to strategy selection, deciding on one strategy option will dramatically improve your chances of getting where you want to go.

For any given situation, one option is superior to all others. The question is, which one?

And is there really just one answer? I think there is. But let me be clear that by *one* strategy I mean an inclusive and complete strategy. So "one" is not about a singular idea. One strategy can contain many different ideas, but they must come together in a unified way. At an operating level, this might look like one channel strategy, or one retail strategy, or one enterprise strategy, or a combination of ideas, as long as they work as a unified whole. Using our prior example of transportation vehicles, we would use the word "helicopter" to describe the capabilities and discrete items that come together to form an entire strategy. The word itself is simply a container that combines many things within it. It's the kind of "one" that poet Walt Whitman evokes in "I contain multitudes." And when I use "one," I am using the word as a kind of logical handle that lets us simplify the way we talk about the array of complex options we ultimately need to prioritize.

Most organizations can align with only a certain number of efforts at a time. Thus, figuring out which vehicles—or which strategies or options—*not* to take is also key. When the issue of "what not to do" is left unanswered, strategies get interpreted many different ways and can fail as a result.

Under the time pressure of everyday business and in the absence of a good selection process, teams tend not to build a rich list of options, since doing so often seems to make the decision process harder. That is, organizations and teams that have a selection process actually do a better job of *generating* options to win.

So what you need is a process framework that allows your group to kill off ideas and get to the right strategy for that time and that situation. You need an agreed-upon way to work with the necessary mix of people to align with what's important so you can shorten the list, dig into the details of the remaining options to figure out what's doable, and finally, fix what's not quite right to get to a limited set of truly interesting options. If the limited set has only one option, you're done. Otherwise, you and your team need to weigh the items against each other and *make a decision* so that you have a single agreed-upon strategy. Not only that, but you have to do it fast, or the next time people will revert to the command-and-control option of deciding and telling others.

The framework that can help organizations make complex yet subjective strategic decisions is one I affectionately call Murder-Boarding. You might think it sounds a bit sinister, but successful businesses use this framework strategy for good purposes.

MurderBoarding: What Is It?

MurderBoarding is a kind of counterweight to whiteboarding as a brainstorming tool. Instead of creating an unbounded set of new ideas, its purpose is to enable teams to evaluate many options effectively, yet still converge on the winning choice in a bounded time-frame. It's a framework to help you make the best decisions that affect large groups or social systems, for the good of an organization. It's also a crucial step in the collaborative strategy process, because it allows a decision to be made around *qualitative* messy choices. Thus it overcomes some key obstacles to effective team collaboration, namely the "Kumbaya" consensus orientation that often besets teams.

MurderBoarding highlights the focused, methodical, and premeditated mindset required for killing off even worthy ideas. It's not just the weak ideas that get killed; good options or ideas at the wrong time also need to go. Decent, but not great, ideas put forth by very nice people are also a target. MurderBoarding is not about team spirit in any way. It is about a selection and decision framework that lets you and your organization make tough choices amongst good options.

As a reminder, all of this fits into the QuEST process as the third phase, Select (Figure 6-2).

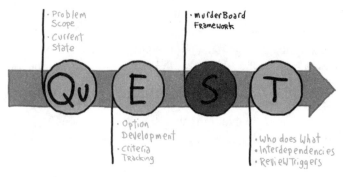

Figure 6-2. *Select (via MurderBoarding) is the third phase of QuEST*

We need a framework to allow organizations to move past the fact gathering and options development steps (embodied by either the 99-point slide or the criteria tracking step of the Envision phase) to achieve convergence. The framework must take into account the many reasons why people have a tough time making choices. We need to work fast, navigate the complexities of an organization, and ideally enable the organization to make interdependent downstream decisions in alignment with the core strategy. The MurderBoarding framework addresses these needs by:

- Doing adequate discovery of what makes sense
- Transforming often-tacit beliefs into explicit decision criteria
- Debating and understanding what matters and why

Sometimes it helps to know how this fits into other management tools. MurderBoarding is not like scenario planning or decision-tree analysis; it's not meticulous quantitative analysis or a predictive modeling tool. Instead, the goal of MurderBoarding is to enable critical conversations between people so that they can explore essential success criteria, evaluate trade-offs, test ideas, understand one another, and work together to pick the best strategy.

MurderBoarding is about optimizing your selection, *not* "maximizing" or "satisficing," which only aims to meet a minimum set of requirements. Using our example of transportation options, satisficing would be the equivalent of choosing the first or easiest option that seemed to work (biplane?), and being done with it. By contrast, with maximizing, a person wants to make the *absolute ideal* decision. Even if they review several choices and find a great option that seems to meet their requirements, they can't make a decision until after they've *fully* examined *every* option. This sometimes means never making a decision, and always means driving the average forward-thinking business executive crazy. *Optimizing* a decision is about making the decision based on a preselected set of criteria (including schedule) that you and your team can debate.

MurderBoarding is important because it ensures that collaboration actually makes sense for strategy creation, in the following ways:

- People can define, debate, agree upon, and ultimately communicate the criteria for success for any given strategy. This lets everyone be thinking partners, rather than having one (executive) group that "thinks" and another (lower-level management) that "does." This, of course, lets organizations close the systemic Air Sandwich mentioned earlier.

- People and teams have confidence that they will be able to move quickly from a rich list of viable options to a single strategy, so they are willing to build this list rather than go on gut instinct.

- Strategies are chosen based on their merits, risks, and feasibility.

- Strategies have more legitimacy because teams can see and understand the robust, transparent process. Substrategies can then be created in support of the core strategy.

- Resources are not squandered, since teams understand the activities they *shouldn't* do.

The last point about resources is worthy of elaboration, especially considering our current economic climate. Many companies have been forced to cut costs, but they have often lacked a way to intelligently discern what should be cut. MurderBoarding provides a way to do resource alignment intelligently rather than randomly.

If you're asking, "Which one makes sense?",
you need MurderBoarding.

Using MurderBoarding

MurderBoarding is a valuable tool when you have one of the following:

- Too many ideas at once. You know you're at this point when you find yourself asking, "Which one makes sense?"

- A situation that has changed in a variety of ways since the last business review.

- The organization seems to have lost its focus.

- A high-stakes opportunity (millions of dollars) that justifies the investment of a thorough review.

- A new vision that requires people to stop doing what they've been doing and shift to something new.

Here are some sample questions that may signal a need for Murder-Boarding. If your division could focus on only one thing in the coming year, what would it be? Should you take your product to another country to further develop and invest in it? Do you want to focus on your existing franchise and expand the customer base to mid-markets? Should you make more product improvements to keep up with the low-end competitors entering the space? Which idea makes sense? Has the organization lost its focus?

MurderBoarding will help you understand how each option serves the larger goals of the organization and decide the course of action that will serve your situation best. Being clear about a course of action means knowing both where you will focus your resources and where you will *not* spend time and energy. When you don't rule anything out, your organization or team won't know where to focus their attention, and can't act in support of the goals of the organization.

People tend to resist change fiercely when they don't see what's in it for them, and MurderBoarding provides a structured way to align people to a new strategy. The sidebar "Turning Around a Big Ship" on page 165 illustrates a situation in which a new leader used a framework to reach a common understanding of what success looks like. This situation had a key element that signaled a need to do MurderBoarding.

When you have too many ideas to act on and you need to focus, MurderBoarding is a razor-sharp tool to help you slice away at fuzzy thinking. When gut feelings no longer provide enough clarity about which direction to take, MurderBoarding helps you make tough choices and can give you the confidence to move forward in a definitive way. When people see things differently and can't agree, Murder-Boarding provides a mental elevator that your team can board together to rise above the individual perspectives, so that everyone can align to a common, higher-order vision of success.

There are many situations where teams should engage in the Murder-Boarding process framework. But some situations do *not* call for MurderBoarding:

- When a straightforward change is being considered that clearly has no cross-functional impact.

- When the criteria for success are known, shared, and have not changed.

- When the stakes are low and consequences are minor.

When the decision makers have the full faith of the team, and alignment issues will clearly not be an issue during execution.

Steps to MurderBoarding

There are four basic steps in the MurderBoarding framework (Figure 6-3):

Decide what matters

> This step is about gaining agreement and making explicit the things that all your stakeholders care about. It is figuring out, as a team, what is important to the business and determining the must-have criteria that should shape the strategy selection decision. Deciding what matters means explicitly setting aside the nice-to-have items. Once an organization is aligned on what it wants to do (or be), it can make the tough choices.

Sort

> This step is about organizing ideas. It involves making a first-pass comparison of options against the criteria of what matters. Sorting helps to triage possible solutions, and to find out whether additional criteria will be needed to further evaluate the options.

Test

This step is about applying strategies hypothetically in context to see what insights develop. It is about going out in the organization to learn more, gather additional facts, and refine criteria further. Within the testing process, you fix, toss, tune, and merge ideas, molding them into fully vetted, executable strategy options.

Choose

The last step is about making the decision—sometimes easy, often messy—together. It is about selecting the most appropriate idea given the situation you face today. Choosing is the last and most vital phase of MurderBoarding because the result defines your strategy. If you don't choose and you don't converge, then you don't have a strategy. And you can't win.

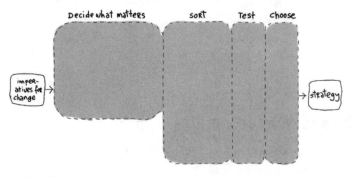

Figure 6-3. *MurderBoarding framework*

If you don't choose, you don't have a strategy;
you just have a set of options.

Step 1: Decide What Matters

When a team can say clearly what matters in the decision, they will be able to see their strategy options with sharper focus and make important distinctions between the options. Deciding what matters is about getting to the heart and soul of an issue, enabling you to see the difference between an adequate strategy idea and an extraordinary one for a specific situation.

Turning Around a Big Ship

Rita was a newly hired VP in a Silicon Valley Fortune 500 enterprise software company. The C-Suite brought her in as a "change agent" to lead an existing 700-person team with a new charter to establish the company's platform in the face of such titans as Adobe, Google, and Microsoft. Her mission was to retake command of a market that the company had actually initiated, but long ago lost.

The good news was that the company's competitors were all building their platforms from scratch, and Rita's company already had a platform in place. The bad news was that the company had a legacy platform, and people would need to change what they were working on. Rita was having a hard time implementing this shift, with her people saying they were too overwhelmed with their current work to even have a meeting to explain all the things that were on their plates. They implied that the organization had a responsibility to hire more people, not just ask them to do more.

Rita took me to breakfast in Sunnyvale, and shared the story with irritation. "How do I get them to stop what they're doing so we can focus on this new mission and become a real player in the marketplace again?" Rita believed her next action was to get the team to stop doing what they were doing.

But the team thought they were doing what mattered. They couldn't imagine stopping "just because." That would mean deciding to do nothing instead of something important. Before she could get the team to make a decision to stop something, she needed to get them to revisit and agree upon what really mattered to them.

I counseled Rita that this was in fact her next move. And she was able to use the MurderBoarding framework to get her team clear on the imperative to change, to agree upon what success actually looked like (beating those titans and reinventing their platform!), and then to choose what they would start and stop doing to refocus. Because the MurderBoarding framework engages the team in identifying what's important, they were able to get aligned without the normal political infighting. Without that alignment around the imperative, they couldn't imagine that there might have been something better to do than what they were already doing.

—continued—

Rita needed to ask questions about the new strategy and what the team felt mattered:

- Why are we doing what we're doing now?
- How is this serving us?
- How well do we understand the new objective?
- Do we agree the new objective is important?
- What is the gap between today and that new direction?
- What would success look like in the new future?
- Why do we want the new outcome?
- And specifically: what do we need to start and stop doing to get there?

Rita felt that if she didn't get traction quickly, the opportunity would be lost. She needed a lightweight framework for gaining alignment in a short timeframe. I showed her why and how to do MurderBoarding, and within five weeks, she was able to reallocate resources aligned against a clear strategy, with great buy-in from her people. It was the MurderBoarding framework that allowed her to make what was clearly a tough set of subjective decisions.

Your own experience may have already taught you that successful strategies are those where the whole organization knows the answers to questions such as: Where do we want to be? How will we know when we're winning? What does success look like? The answers to these questions become a cohesive understanding that drives the team's choices. The previous chapter already covered the need to track what matters in the context of developing strategy ideas, but deciding what matters (and criteria tracking) is actually applied here as part of the MurderBoarding framework (Figure 6-4).

Typically, there are only two or three things that really matter when distinguishing between strategy options. Getting to "what really matters" requires some detective work to determine what is important in your specific circumstance, with your team, and in your market or company at this particular moment.

Before considering the options, start by figuring out what should shape the decision. Ultimately, this increases the relevance of the final idea or choice. These criteria remind you, as the leader, that

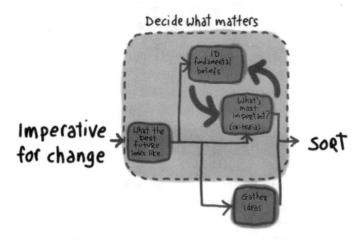

Figure 6-4. *Step 1 of the MurderBoarding framework: Decide what matters*

you're not seeking some theoretical "best strategy," but rather the most appropriate strategy for your specific situation. It isn't about good or bad, right or wrong—it's about which one fits your goals most closely.

Every organization has a number of belief systems that influence which criteria will be chosen. Some beliefs are explicit and therefore largely shared, but many are unspoken (tacit) and are typically held inconsistently throughout the organization. The tacit beliefs usually tie in to people's underlying sense of identity and of what the firm/product/business "is." Tacit beliefs can be problematic when they anchor people—and therefore the organization—to the past, thinking about what they've done or have been rather than what they could do or be. The analogy of an anchor is appropriate because it's the anchor that keeps a ship stuck, unable to maneuver away from an oncoming storm or seek out new harbors. Some organizations are so anchored that new strategies are hard to find.

Beliefs profoundly influence the organization's vision of what success looks like. Whereas explicit beliefs are often fairly consistent across the team, tacit beliefs differ across the organization and can lead to "hidden agendas," which are, effectively, different tacit criteria. You'll often see tacit beliefs in teams that have been siloed and stable for a long time. The team's criteria for success will be driven by belief systems both tacit and explicit. A common agenda is essential to implementing a successful strategy, so it is important to ensure that you surface all the tacit beliefs and the resulting hidden agendas so that the teams can align.

When beliefs are tacit, they can influence a group's unconscious decision process.

Tacit beliefs left unidentified can subtly lead the group to choose a strategy that is aligned with the unspoken beliefs but is less optimal for the situation at hand. It is critical, then, to identify existing beliefs, and to surface tacit beliefs and make them explicit. Surfacing tacit beliefs allows them to be reconsidered, checked to see whether they are commonly shared, and evaluated to determine whether they are still applicable or need to be changed. Writing beliefs down and speaking them out loud allows a group to understand the intent behind historical decisions and to evaluate whether those beliefs still hold true or need to be adapted to move forward. Of course, this requires a discussion to take place with the involved parties. Exploring these beliefs will lead to an understanding of what matters to this organization, and why.

Saying things out loud allows you to bring clarity of thought to what you are saying, and gives others the opportunity to challenge the ideas. This explicit dialogue can prevent a whole team from making decisions based on false assumptions, or coming to the mistaken conclusion that people are aligned in purpose when they are not.

So how can you find those tacit beliefs? What telltale signs give hints about those submerged ideas? And how do you identify the explicit beliefs so that you can make a thorough inventory of them, to help distinguish them from the hidden ones? It turns out that many clues are present in the language people use.

When executives are sharing ideas with the larger organization, they quite often embed their belief systems within their comments. These belief systems are subject to interpretation, and interpretations can vary, leading to misalignment and causing well-intentioned people to execute poorly.

Expressed organizational beliefs typically use the language of needs:

- "The solution needs to be funded by organic growth."
- "The fix needs to fit with our current channel model."
- "We cannot create new product offers until the second year of the existing product line."
- "Product Team A's requirements need to be paramount because they provide the cash to support the other businesses."

Tacit beliefs are typically notions of identity or unwritten rules for how the organization does things:

- "We make products—things you can touch, feel, and see."
- "We compete on price."
- "We must do things through the retail channel."

These expressed organizational beliefs and tacit beliefs can represent criteria. Being alert to the hints in the language that people use is useful to a degree, but it's passive and therefore somewhat limited. You will also want to engage in active digging. Here are some helpful hints for unearthing important beliefs:

- List out beliefs as a group, and then deputize members of your team to search for any additional beliefs held in the wider organization.
- Ask people open-ended questions. For example:
  - What gets rewarded around here? By whom?
  - What is "sacred," "off-limits," or "untouchable"?
  - Similarly, *who* is "sacred," "off-limits," or "untouchable"?
  - What is worth staking your reputation on?
- Ask people to talk about their own experiences. It is also interesting to have people express what they believe others think of their views, whether they are shared views, heretical, etc. Often this can illuminate hidden issues that less introspective people tend to miss.
- Ask questions one on one or in small groups. Find a neutral, private venue where people can feel comfortable talking. Take a shared walk around the block, or grab lunch at a place not-so-close to the office so you won't be constantly checking over your shoulder for colleagues wandering by.

Bringing these criteria to the forefront at the start of the process enables you to fully consider what would be best for the business before the team gets wrapped up in one or two compelling ideas. By contrast, when criteria are *not* made known and explicit early, people tend to invest in ideas first and then let the ideas drive their criteria selection later in the process. ("We must pursue this idea!")

There are two tempting simplifications that commonly arise in dealing with success factors. First, people tend to lump all success factors together and see them as equally important. This is attractive because you don't have to wrestle with ranking the factors. But this approach does not help the selection process, so it's actually a losing model.

The second simplification is establishing a hard-and-fast ranking. For example, suppose revenue is listed above affinity. A simplistic approach would resolve all conflicts between the two in favor of revenue, when in fact there may be cases where revenue is covered and you can afford to address affinity.

When you're done with Step 1 of the MurderBoarding framework, you'll have a clearly identified list of beliefs and criteria. It's often tempting to jump the gun at this point and "make the decision." Don't do it! Making a decision at this stage will usually take you to a second-rate option. Instead, it's important to take a reasonable amount of time to understand and improve your options. Step 2, Sort, is key to understanding.

Step 2: Sort

Step 2 of the MurderBoarding framework pushes teams to use the chosen specific, practical criteria to understand the merits of one idea compared to other ideas. This avoids the problem of "shoot-from-the-hip" final strategy decisions based simply on someone's "gut instinct." Once it's clear what success will look like and the team knows what matters to the final strategy selection, they need to test the options against the criteria, represent the results in a coherent way, and sort the options into buckets ("strong," "possible," "weak") based on how they measure up against each other. In this way, the team can identify which subset of ideas they need to stop pursuing (kill) and which ones they need to explore further (Figure 6-5).

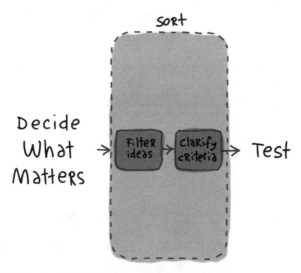

Figure 6-5. Step 2 of the MurderBoarding framework: Sort

Newcomers to the sorting step sometimes have trouble getting a sense of how much is enough and how much is too much. To clarify, a deeper example is worth pursuing here. In this case, a team looking at geographic market expansion came up with criteria for what success would look like when establishing a presence in another country. The team developed this list based on what they knew about their previous successes in other vertical markets. For them, going global meant having:

- Different types of buying options (enterprise licensing, shrink-wrap, etc.)
- The right channel in place
- Dedicated headcount
- Budget requirements that fit within the parameter of revenue/expense ratio
- A product that worked in the local language
- An online store where people from that country could buy the product

In the sorting step, the team needed to test options against the criteria. In our example, the options were the different countries under consideration. The team evaluated each country by the criteria just listed and built a thorough description of the current landscape, shown in Figure 6-6.

Sorting together will result in everyone knowing why one thing is more important than another.

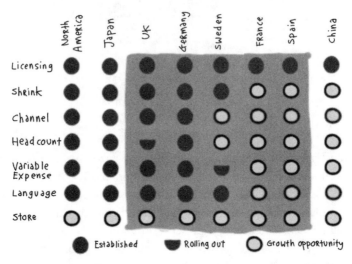

Figure 6-6. *Doing the first sort*

This picture drove the next level of questions and decisions. The team believed that some countries that appeared similar could be distinguished with the addition of one or two well-chosen criteria. After some discussion and data gathering, they added these two criteria:

- Country sales leadership's readiness to commit to increased quota in exchange for investment
- Acceptable expected level of in-country piracy

After the facts were gathered, it was clear which countries would be able to drive growth. Regions such as North America and Japan already had nearly all of the criteria in place. Some countries had little investment in place to support vertical expansion, and conversations with the heads of those regions were marked by enthusiasm and interest. They were willing to commit to growth targets in exchange for incremental dollars. The qualitative discussions with the heads of the regions gave the team a clear understanding of the current state and enabled some early decisions.

Unsurprisingly, surfacing the criteria early in this process helped make sure people were, in fact, making decisions based on identified criteria. The sorting process involved many people bringing different points of view and understanding what mattered to the business. Filtering through these points of view brought up more discussion items, which ultimately led to revisiting and revising the criteria that drove their decision:

- Use the proven model they had already created for North America. Don't customize for each country.

- Drive revenue in relationship to the investment made. Some countries could be more expensive, and there had to be some "fairness" in the way investment dollars were allocated.

- Focus on "easy wins" first so each dollar invested brought maximum gains.

- Go global quickly to prevent competitors from winning chosen verticals first. Speed matters.

The reason you do all this as an open exercise with the team is for *shared understanding.* By explicitly naming criteria, then sorting, then identifying the reasoning, everyone involved knows *why* something is considered important. This is crucial in building an organization of co-thinkers and collaborators.

Sorting often drives more fact gathering, such as identifying which teams wouldn't sign up to a bigger quota in exchange for additional resources. When different options impact different parts of the organization differently, the sorting process can spark trade-offs and bartering. Basically, this amounts to negotiating within the organization for additional criteria and rethinking "facts," such as how much additional investment is appropriate. In our example, the team then summarized the results of the sorting step into a table that reflected their next level of alignment (see Table 6-1).

TABLE 6-1. *Strategy rationales for country prioritization*

STRATEGY	MARKET AREA	PROPOSED ACTION
Profit	North America, Japan	Keep investment as-is.
Invest for revenue growth	France, Germany, Spain, UK, Sweden	Create a quota relationship between dollars invested and expected quota assignment so growth is assigned with investment commitments.
Market development	China	Early conversations suggest that launching programs in China will take too much investment to enable a fast return. Recommend reviewing decision in 1 year when piracy rates will drop and market maturity will rise.

The sorting step gives you a set of options clearly ranked in terms of your criteria. As the situation changes or new information comes to light, you know what options to favor. For example, if the company was interested in profit first, then they would know which countries to focus on. If they had additional resources, they could invest for future revenue growth. And if they had even more dollars, they could do market development. Options were both ranked (top to bottom) and named with an action so the business leaders could see the available choices.

Take a moment to consider that the sorting step does not merely produce a document. It has a profound impact on the team in the form of a deep and shared understanding of what is at stake. The next step, Test, will involve discussions by many team members throughout the larger organization. If a dry document of sorted options had somehow been lobbed in by "experts," how prepared would the team members be to fully vet the feasibility of various options? Make no mistake: the document is important. But an aligned team is equally important, particularly as you move forward to engage others in your organization.

Step 3: Test

Step 3, Test, is about maturing the ideas that were ranked in Step 2 (Sort), based on the criteria developed in Step 1 (Decide what matters). In Step 3, you will explore how those ideas can be implemented within your particular organization. You do this by floating the ideas by people who can lend perspective on how they will or won't work. Organizational testing is the specific set of activities that explore what conditions exist *in your company* to make one course of action better than another. This step may require you to consider different options for addressing the reality of what exists in your organization. The question for Step 3 is: how do you avoid getting completely bogged down by the challenges you uncover? You may unearth the unexpected, which is why many organizations hesitate to "test" before pulling the trigger. Luckily, we take that obstacle into account in this step of the MurderBoarding framework (Figure 6-7).

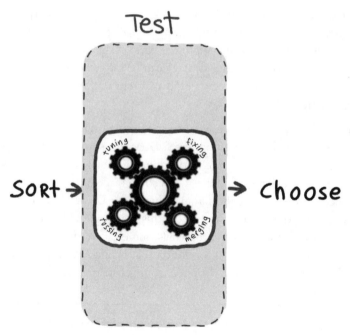

Figure 6-7. Step 3 of the MurderBoarding framework: Test

Organizational testing is a process of preselling ideas to test their ability to work. During organizational testing, you'll uncover operational points of view that didn't arise during the generation of ideas, but will be vitally important for the final step of the four-part Select phase, Choose.

The key benefit to organizational testing is that it forces you to think cross-functionally. It helps you avoid the kinds of problems that occur when any business unit or functional area optimizes for their own needs. We've all seen business problems where marketing creates demand at such a high volume that operations can't deliver, and then the company's brand is negatively affected by this poor customer experience. This comes out of siloed behavior, though it doesn't mean that all silos are bad. Silos can be efficient when situations are stable, and everyone can focus on their task without being distracted by activities elsewhere. But when it's time for change, silos are one reason why organizations can make poor strategy choices.

Strategy fails when the keys to making a strategy operational cross-functionally are not uncovered soon enough. So by doing organizational testing, you are surveying other parts of the business that could be affected, to see whether a strategy can be implemented or to better understand how the strategy would play out and affect those other business areas.

The kinds of questions you want to ask during organizational testing are typically at the operational level. Does our supply chain support this? Did we think about the implications to our IT team? How will we merge our existing pipeline? Does some piece of this new strategy conflict with existing contractual obligations? Do we have what we need to provide product support in this new region? Each conversation uncovers more data: more details, more criteria for success, and more obstacles. This new information that is uncovered will result in options being improved or dropped from consideration.

Organizational testing cuts across silos to see what the company can do when working effectively as a whole.

Imagine, for example, that a team decides that the right thing to do to enable their next level of growth is to expand into Asia. Before presenting the decision to the senior executives, the operational leader will do an organizational test and bring the idea to the finance leader. The dialogue might look something like the following:

Operational leader	We're thinking about going to Asia. We've narrowed it down to Japan or China, but we still need to know more to choose.	*Nice and open-ended. This is where discovery happens.*
Finance leader	Have you thought about currency?	*Bingo!*
	Because we don't actually know how to support a different currency. We don't do that right now.	
Operational leader	Tell me more about what's involved with a new currency.	*More open questions.*
Finance leader	Well, I expect we'd have to set up a subsidiary to accept local currency; we don't have one yet in China. And how will you take orders? Direct or online?	*Turns out the finance leader has done some thinking already, too.*
Operational leader	Both are interesting....	*Short answers, keep them talking!*
Finance leader	Will inventory levels require us to set up an exchange rate hedge?	*Another discovery!*

Organizational testing is essentially intelligence gathering to collect a set of frank, detailed comments—positive and negative—from the organization. As any tactical commander worth their salt knows, you have to do your recon before heading onto the battlefield. An organizational test generates a new list of requirements that the team must manage in order to:

- Modify ideas
- Kill them outright
- Come up with new ideas

This is typically the messiest step of the MurderBoarding framework, and it can be frustrating to reach the middle of the process and realize that you need to adjust your criteria *yet again* (Figure 6-8). Try not to get discouraged! Strategy creation is inherently a messy process. It's supposed to be; you're inventing the future of the company. This is exactly the time when you need to trust MurderBoarding. Have faith that this iterative process of tuning ideas and criteria drives convergence and makes the difference between fair strategy decisions and great ones. Having this step be time-bound (say, for one week) is useful because it helps everyone stay engaged.

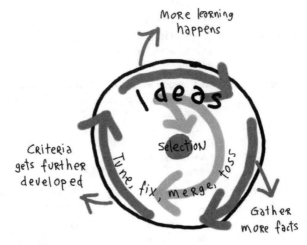

Figure 6-8. Organizational testing can be highly iterative and messy

Step 3a: Reshape ideas

A successful organizational test typically prompts some additional evaluation of your ideas. Based on what you learn, you may need to reshape an idea and then drill down again to confirm its viability, which in turn may uncover more details, which then may require additional configurations.

Reshaping an idea is essentially a process of:

- Pulling components apart
- Understanding what parts are distinct
- Segmenting out things that no longer matter
- Getting rid of redundant options
- Restating the idea as something that more closely fits what you need

Figure 6-9 illustrates several ways that ideas can be shaped, including splitting a single idea into multiple ideas, adding distinctiveness, segmenting, culling variants, and restating. These help people to develop a shared, clear understanding, which will be incredibly important when they are doing the tasks.

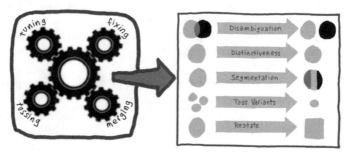

Figure 6-9. *Details of reshaping ideas*

Being able to reshape ideas is critical to selecting your preferred strategy. In fact, reshaping good ideas based on new information is so vital that Google, a company known for allowing many to innovate, includes it as one of 18 principles baked into the company model.

Jonathan Rosenberg, Google's SVP of Product Management and Marketing, recently spoke to his alma mater, Claremont McKenna College (CMC), and had this to say about reshaping ideas:

> The next big idea is to morph ideas.... I've talked about how different inventions come on, and we don't foresee their real economic impact for some time: the transistor; the laser; the VCR. I also talked about the steam engine, which was originally developed for pumping water out of flooding mines, and once you connected it to the railroads, basically you tamed the west. There are all of these technologies that are proposed as point solutions to very narrow problems.

What we have today is fast change with the underlying technology: the CPU power, the storage requirements. You're constantly revisiting ideas that didn't work before and reapplying them. Blogs were originally about publishing information so that people could reach niche communities. But the whole blog systems that we developed are now the engines behind publishing information in Google docs and spreadsheets, which is the next evolution for those of you who are using Gmail.[2]

Decoding

You need to decode what people mean and understand the nuances of options so you can tune, fix, toss, or merge them. There are five common elements of decoding:

- *Disambiguation.* Often a term may mean different things to different groups. Localization means one thing to Software Development and another to Fulfillment. Disambiguation means eliminating fuzziness in speaking or writing so that everyone will understand it in the same way.

- *Distinctiveness.* Shave the fluff off an idea so that its unique, particular information is distinctly called out.

- *Segmentation.* Often ideas are nested within a larger item, but to fully understand the flavors of any idea, it needs to be broken into different parts.

- *Tossing variants.* Narrow what you are talking about to the discrete item that matters. Customization is a big term, and customizing a website is different from customizing a physical package. If you care about only one of these, be sure to exclude what you don't mean.

- *Restatement.* As a conversational tool for testing, restatement can help make sure the situation is well defined. Have you ever had a conversation with someone where you thought you both were talking about the same thing, only to later realize you each meant something entirely different? Restating an idea is a way to uncover these potential misunderstandings before they cause problems.

The philosophy and approach that Jonathan describes for product reinvention is exactly what happens during Step 3 of MurderBoarding. As you learn more, you go back to original ideas to morph them. You blend many ideas together, or you take one part of one idea and merge it with another. The final picture may not look like any one element that entered the process, but that's perfectly all right.

It should be noted that as you refine ideas, you can decide to fix part of an idea or not. By making these refine/fix decisions as a team, you will not only make more informed decisions, but you will also eliminate doubt for many people within the organization when they later make interdependent decisions. For example, a team expanding from consumer software to enterprise selling may uncover that their ordering systems are not set up to handle enterprise-wide order processing. Instead of killing the idea, they may simply decide not to fix this problem. They may decide that instead of investing in a $50M IT system, they will outsource the order processing for enterprise deals.

By contrast, a team wanting to do business globally may discover through its finance department that they are legally required to set up a separate entity to process local currency. The team may decide to invest in this separate entity because *not* doing it is a deal-breaker for the idea, and the idea is compelling enough to justify the investment. The point here is that trade-offs are an essential part of this tuning, fixing, tossing, and merging process.

Eliminating doubt allows for the freedom and speed to move forward rapidly.

The beauty of this process of tuning, fixing, tossing, and merging is that once an idea is ready for selection, your whole team will know, *beyond the shadow of a doubt*, that this idea has been made the best it can be with respect to your organization and your circumstances. Your team will have engaged in the rigorous debate of ideas, tearing them apart and reassembling them in new configurations, and discussing what works and what doesn't. They will have asked all the critical questions, so that when you do select one final strategy in Step 4, everyone is clear on the reasoning without a shred of doubt.

Because MurderBoarding requires a team to test and refine ideas carefully, a particular idea can become so lightweight that it no longer retains its power. Be sure to ask yourself: Is this idea elegant and powerful in its simplicity? Or is it simply hollow and empty of value? If it feels lightweight, it might have gotten that way because people discarded its challenging aspects in order to avoid debating its complexity.

Remember that it takes strength to be open to new ideas. It takes courage to rethink ideas that you may have already invested in, or to sign on to a truly powerful new idea. Be sure to stay patient as you test ideas in the organization, and try to stay open to altering ideas as you learn more. Also keep in mind that there may never be enough data. Strategic decisions involve incomplete or changing information, so learn to make a choice given what you know, and identify triggers so that you can reevaluate if you learn more down the road. Stay as flexible as you can, and be ready to trim away things that might be good but not great.

The output of the organizational testing step is a set of reshaped strategic options with a reasoned understanding of what it will take to deploy each option (resources, people, costs, time, etc.). In addition, Step 3 has the curious extra benefit of creating even more permission for people to highlight or appropriately fix any problems when they come up later. MurderBoarding empowers people to be more responsive and avoid the dysfunctional, passive, "it's not my job" bystander behavior.

Step 4: Choose

Step 4, Choose, is the last and most crucial step of the Murder-Boarding framework and is how you complete the Select phase of the QuEST process. If you have performed MurderBoarding correctly, the right strategy for your situation will be clear to you and your team by the time you reach this step. You will know that you have a strategy that meets your explicit goals, and you will have thoroughly explored the implications of this strategy throughout your organization. Everyone will know the reasoning behind why this strategy was selected over the others and what makes this strategy best. Choosing is a remarkably straightforward step in the MurderBoarding process because of the work done in the preceding steps. In organizations that lack the MurderBoarding process, choosing is much more painful and tricky.

It is human nature not to want to end something that looks viable or already has momentum. But choosing is about the survival of the fittest, and *only* the absolute fittest. Remember, by choosing what to do, you are also choosing what *not* to do, allowing the winning options to thrive. Many people wonder what to do with the options that did not get selected. I've found that if you refer to "killing" them, it can sometimes cause some backlash. So, don't kill them. Simply set them aside, for potential future use. Just as it is hard to prune a rose bush when there are flowers blooming, it is hard to make these decisions. This is because the act of cutting can appear to be destructive rather than constructive. But the difference between one strategy option and many options is the difference between winning and simply being in the game. Reframe MurderBoarding as a constructive process, and be willing to convince reluctant people.

Let's look at the MurderBoarding framework as a complete picture (Figure 6-10).

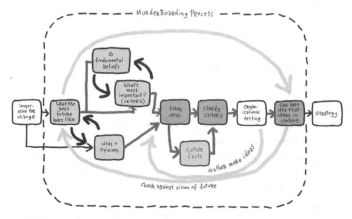

Figure 6-10. MurderBoarding overview

After performing the multiple steps of MurderBoarding, you'll have both organizational alignment and organizational commitment. Everybody on the team will be able and willing to state what the strategy is and how the key criteria explain why that strategy was chosen. That's incredibly powerful, and it also requires that our responsibilities be clear.

Select Roles and Responsibilities

It's important that everybody knows the key parts of their roles. Table 6-2 illustrates your main responsibilities in the Select phase, as well as those of your team.

TABLE 6-2. *The Select phase roles and responsibilities*

LEADER'S ROLE

- Be the facilitator of the whole process. Manage the framework process for others.
- At first, your job is to get clarity, not agreement. So ask, "What else?" What else would we need to resource here? How do you understand that to work? What else do we need to change in the company to support this idea? What additional conversations do we need to have to be sure this idea will work?
- Make sure necessary debates take place. Take the contra-position on an idea everyone supports. For example, "We all love this particular idea, and we're already looking at ways it can work. If we were to kill this idea, what would it mean?" Or, "We're all in love with this notion, but before we marry this idea, let's spend time figuring out where it would fail."
- Be attentive. Stay present and listen when someone has to let go of an idea he has built, lobbied for, or worked hard to ideate. Often people will hold on to their "baby" until they believe that you hear them and understand them. Pay attention to people's emotional needs around their ideas and offer your compassion, so that they can feel heard and find a way out of their own gridlock.
- Identify what is out, being parked, or being killed. Name it so people can internalize the decision.

COLLABORATOR'S ROLE

- You are a co-thinker, not a champion of one idea or one function.
- Discern what can be added/shaped/eliminated.
- Be willing to let go of your favorite ideas. It might be "your baby," but it's not an actual baby!
- Be a collaborator in building up the best idea (for the organization as a whole) together.
- Ask a ton of questions so people's *shared* understanding grows.

To be sure, during the process of developing a new strategy, you will see many possible options for addressing your problem. However, choosing the right strategy means selecting one that embodies a single, unified, coherent set of choices.

Part of your responsibility is to make sure that everybody is crystal-clear about the reasons the final strategy choice is the right one. It will be far easier to get everybody in the organization to commit themselves to actions that align with the strategy when they understand it and feel like they've been part of the process. As we've covered in different parts of the QuEST process, openly documenting key decisions is crucial. Publishing key decisions reinforces the choices made by everyone who was directly involved in the process, and it significantly improves the communication with others who were not actively included.

The leader's final role is to "make the call" when needed. If and when your team finds itself at an impasse as to which strategy to select, it will be your responsibility to make the final decision. Sometimes this means that you need to paint a compelling vision for the team, and sometimes it means that you have to "burn the boat." Burning the boat means being willing to destroy the precious vehicle that kept you safe as you crossed uncharted waters. It's about creating a reason to do something dramatically different. It works because it helps motivate people to move from the current, comfortable state to more unknown, unchartered areas. (See "Burning the Boat" on page 247 in Appendix A.)

Most of the time, after traveling through the collaborative strategy process together, you and your team will end up agreeing about which strategy is best. However, sometimes this is not the case. Either way, the decision about which strategy to pursue is ultimately yours to make. Take special care to do this in such a way that everybody on the team understands why the decision is being made.

Sequences of Select

The newcomer to MurderBoarding may believe that signing on to this framework will mean endless meetings and "design by committee." So it might help to know there are also times for one-on-one meetings and for group deliberations, and certainly a cadence of meetings that works to set the pace.

The MurderBoarding framework can be applied to many different types of strategies—business, channel, product, market, pricing, etc.—but to describe the flow of forums, let's walk through an example using the product strategy type.

In Step 1, Decide what matters, the product manager sets up some one-on-one meetings with key experts in the business and influential people who have insight into what should shape the strategy criteria. Though these are one-on-one meetings, this stage can happen quickly if planned well. The idea is to have private conversations to gather information, anonymize contributors so the issues can be discussed openly (if needed), and then share a document of key findings, either as an email or an official report.

In Step 2, Sort, the product manager then brings together the involved parties to sort options against criteria and filter them into buckets. This becomes a way of learning which trajectories could be followed. This step typically consists of two meetings, and produces a work document that can be reviewed with the business unit head or general manager as appropriate.

In Step 3, Test, the product manager or her operational leader pulls together the cross-silo review to do more discovery and shape options. Often this can be done by having the cross-silo staff work 1:1, to understand what can be done and what is needed. Then, they report on those findings to the decision makers, who shape the strategic options based on what the organization is willing or unwilling to do.

In Step 4, Choose, the operational leader brings together the necessary functional heads, typically in an already established forum, such as a quarterly business review or an exec team staff meeting, to review strategy recommendations.

The most important part of sequencing is to make sure each person who participated in the earlier steps is updated on what took place. This maintains alignment from concept through decision.

Table 6-3 captures these steps and some key forums, and summarizes the outputs.

TABLE 6-3. *Sequencing Select steps with roles, forums, and output*

STEP 1: DECIDE WHAT MATTERS

Who			Forum	Output
Initiates	Consults	Decides		
Product manager	Experts; multilevel influencers	BU head/GM	One-on-one meetings	Discovery document shared broadly

STEP 2: SORT

Who			Forum	Output
Initiates	Consults	Decides		
Product manager	Sales VPs, director of engineering, director of marketing, managers	BU head/GM	1–3 group meetings	Filtered ideas sorted into buckets

STEP 3: TEST

Who			Forum	Output
Initiates	Consults	Decides		
Product manager or operational leader	Cross-silo senior staff	Cross-silo VPs/GM	One-on-one plus 2–3 group meetings	Identified organizational interdependencies and reshaped strategy options

STEP 4: CHOOSE

Who			Forum	Output
Initiates	Consults	Decides		
Operational leader or GM	Functional heads (CTO, CMO, VP of engineering, senior staff)	CEO/Board	Larger operations meeting for transparency; participants witness how decision gets made	Strategy with transparency on why "best" options

The entire sequence of MurderBoarding can take as little as 2–3 weeks or as long as 1–2 months, depending on the complexities of how many people are involved and the impact of the decision. But, unlike what we sometimes fear, it won't take forever.

The Goal: Selecting a Winning Strategy

MurderBoarding is about making the best decision as an organization, for the good of the organization. To manage the inevitable messiness, here are some guidelines that can help make the whole process proceed more smoothly and effectively:

- Keep the end in mind. The goal is to select the one powerful, inclusive, and complete strategy and kill off the others, so that the one gets the attention it needs to thrive. Remind people of this end goal as often as you need to.

- Be time-conscious. Allow reasonable time for people to come up with ideas and criteria, but be quick to cut off discussions that rehash closed topics. Discourage deep investigations into issues that won't matter much either way. Notice when the new ideas have slowed or stopped entering the conversation, like when the popcorn is done popping. Maintain the message: we need to do the full process. And remember that you need to do it quickly, or people get into the mindset that collaboration really isn't worth the time investment.

- Set the ground rules. Since this process is about the best idea winning, ask people to agree to let go of personal ownership of ideas, political games, or wishing-it-were-true. Ask them to enter the exercise with an honest intellect and clear vision. Encourage them to ask tough, realistic questions.

- Use anonymous judging when needed. Especially when probing the depths of team beliefs, feel free to let people contribute or vote anonymously if you believe it will help the team be more candid.

- Move the nonviable (recently killed) ideas to a physical list, wiki, or other container (away from the main list) that you can come back to later. Since certain people may be attached to ideas that they worked hard to propose, putting these ideas in a "place" reassures them that their ideas are being shelved for now instead of being left for dead. This often allows people to move on to the next task at hand. This list is also useful to have as a reference, because occasionally you will find that a rejected idea resurfaces as a winner after it is revisited and refined, or when the business environment changes over time.

- Merge/build new ideas. Use the talent of your group to tune your ideas to your specific situation or come up with new variations (optimized to your outcomes). The idea isn't to kill one another's ideas, but rather to build on one another's ideas.

- Turn over lots of rocks. Test your ideas with other people. To offset your closeness to your own situation, request that outside colleagues be your audience as you frame the options. Ask them to roleplay people in your eventual key audience and invite them to test your thinking. Encourage them to ask you "zinger" questions. This is an opportunity to test your thinking once again.

- Make the call. Choose the best alternative and say it out loud. Build your muscle for saying "this matters more than that."

- We'll talk about how to handle conflict in these discussions in Appendix A. It's very important to know how to make use of and manage tension in these discussions.

The beauty of the MurderBoarding process is that once you select a best idea and implement it, you will be able to reach new goals. Over time, selecting and developing new ideas will allow your organization to coalesce around a business focus as strategies cluster and gain momentum (Figure 6-11). Of course, the business will constantly flex, and strategies will need to be updated as the organization responds to market opportunities. You will be able to create the capacity within your organization to reinvent itself collaboratively from the inside out.

- Above all, remember that a strategy is not a strategy until you've chosen something. You must choose what to do and what not to do, and you must make your decision knowing that your organization can realistically implement it. A strategy that you can't act on is just a massive anchor holding back your organization's progress.

Figure 6-11. *When we choose to kill options, we can keep the best ones*

Moving On

Let's put to rest the notion that the goal of strategy creation is to get one big win. The ultimate goal is not to win once, but rather to build both the capability and capacity that power our organizations to win *repeatedly*. In other words, getting strategy right depends on creating the conditions that let us outshine our competitors, and to outshine them on many levels—to out-think them, out-create them, and out-innovate the other players in the market. MurderBoarding plays into that specifically because it allows you to collaborate organizationally, pick from a relevant set of ideas, and then quickly and efficiently make decisions in the open. The framework of MurderBoarding allows a whole organization to *think* and to make tough qualitative decisions, which is the key to winning strategies.

The MurderBoarding framework can be challenging, because it is our human nature to resist squashing something that looks viable or is already in progress. Killing an idea or program with momentum can also be very difficult to explain and justify. And although many leaders take the "let's cut equally" approach in order to share the pain, let's remember that even though it might be easier to spread the pruning cuts uniformly across the tree, the result would devastate the tree's ability to bear fruit. It's the same with business. It's hard to do selection because it forces clarity, and you will need to make difficult trade-offs. However, it's better to do that early, with focused effort, so that downstream results are aligned. Otherwise, your strategy is based on the hope that decisions made later by others will get you where you need to be.

You haven't reached the finish line yet, but you've made a lot of progress. Once you've done the hard work of the Select phase of the collaborative strategy QuEST process, there is still one more phase before execution. The Take phase is about ownership and responsibility.

CHAPTER 7

Phase IV: Take

Some favorite expressions of small children:

"It's not my fault... They made me do it... I forgot."

Some favorite expressions of adults:

*"It's not my job... No one told me...
It couldn't be helped."*

*True freedom begins and ends with
personal accountability.*

—Dan Zadra

Eliminate Gaps by Owning Outcome

Remember in the introduction, when I told the story of my part in a huge strategy debacle? The CEO's new vision had given us the direction to move from a single-product to a multi-product company. It was a big change. Strike that: it was a *huge* change.

I had questions about how the different organizations and teams would line up to ultimately deliver, but I kept quiet. I thought then that "someone else" had it under control, and I wasn't the only one who had questions. But everyone charged forward without knowing who owned what, or which interdependent parts had to be strongly connected. Each of us, and the leadership involved, delivered on the parts we *individually* owned. We did what was on paper as our job description or area of responsibility. The executive team had done what it needed to do at the top of the Air Sandwich, and the doers at the bottom kept on doing. The sandwich was becoming super-sized!

The problem was, we lacked the responsibility for determining how to achieve success *across* the organization rather than only for our individual components. In effect, we were looking at the middle of that Air Sandwich, and each of us was thinking, "This is not the part that matters to *me* because *I* don't own it" (Figure 7-1). In effect, the middle of the Air Sandwich is the part that no one owns. If no one owns it, each party is saying that it must be irrelevant, rather than what we actually know by now: that it is absolutely essential.

Figure 7-1. *The middle of the Air Sandwich looks irrelevant at first*

Of course, we know better *now*. And, oh, the heartache it could have saved if I had known it then.

The key issue, of course, is that there was a gap in the way the strategy was formed, which ultimately resulted in strategic company failure. Representing a lack of thinking, debate, and understanding, the gap *also* results in a lack of shared responsibility. And as long as the gap exists, alignment of downstream activities won't take place, no matter how good the people.

In Part I of this book, we spent time defining how each of us owns responsibility for participation and engagement. In Part II, we've talked about how the QuEST framework enables responsibility and accountability in each preceding phase.

- In Phase I, Question, we got responsibility by having everyone participate in defining the problem and jointly knowing what needs to get solved.

- In Phase II, Envision, we enabled everyone to provide options and envision solutions so that they shared responsibility in coming up with the fix.

- In Phase III, Select, we made sure everyone had responsibility for debating the best option for the company at this time, in this context, for this situation, and for making sure the "why" was something they could get behind.

So at this point, we want to complete the flow of accountability by focusing on the final phase, where we take ownership of the success of the overall strategy—not just our individual parts. In this phase, we take responsibility for who needs to do what, and identify the interdependent linkages across silos, people, functions, and so on.

The Goal: Taking Ownership

The last part of the collaborative strategy process is the Take phase. This is where you translate "The One" strategy idea into action and come to agreement about who should own what, in clear and measurable terms, so that the parties involved know what to do next and can stay in alignment with each other (Figure 7-2).

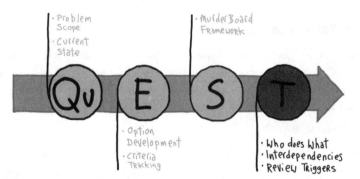

Figure 7-2. Take is the fourth and final phase of QuEST

By the time you've arrived at the Take phase, you will already know the "real" problem that needs solving, have solid, viable options created by people within the organization, and have made the tough choices based on shared criteria of what success looks like.

Implied in all that work is that, by the very way the strategy has been created, the people involved believe in the strategy. People will not only understand its rationale, they will have internalized the rationale so that they can make important decisions in the field that support the new change. That's important to call out as a prerequisite to the Take phase. The Take phase builds on the collaboration throughout the QuEST process to identify any needed commitments.

Take is about people signing up willingly for what they need to do. Avoid the "no one told me, I didn't agree" excuse.

One thing that Take is not is assigning or telling others what they need to do. This can be a subtle distinction, but it's important that people sign up willingly and are not coerced. This avoids the "no one told me, I didn't come to that meeting, I didn't agree" thing that can happen. The Take phase is all about personal responsibility, so we need to insist on it to get it.

Why Take Is Important

The primary goal of this phase is to specify, with as much fidelity as possible, the accountability and responsibilities of people. It also involves identifying the interdependencies between players so that handoffs go smoothly in real time. This includes finding the answers to these questions:

- Who has responsibility for what?
- What big bucket actions will be required to manifest the strategy?
- What are the interdependent tasks/responsibilities/actions?

- What organizational changes, if any, are needed and where in the organization are they necessary to enable the strategy?

- What are the triggers that would alert us if/when a reassessment is needed, should the strategy not hit the intended target?

How to Do It

Although the Take phase is not complicated, it does require some crisp operational work. Imagine, for example, that your team has decided to launch a mobile product as a market expansion play. You and your strategy team have diligently gathered facts, developed solid criteria, creatively generated ideas, and rigorously selected one idea as your strategy. If you did the process right, you have likely created the best strategy given your capabilities. You have arrived at the strategy that best fits your goals *and* your specific capabilities as a company. You also know the criteria by which you'll achieve victory.

Identify who/what/interdependencies

Now it's time to sit down with every part of the implementation team (sales, marketing, engineering, customer service, finance, legal) where there are interdependencies, to determine who needs to do what to make this strategy a reality. You can do this in small groups or all at once.

Each function or division should address these questions:

- What key things do you need to do to make this a reality? List up to five.

- Do you need to *change* anything organizationally to make this happen?

- What specific dependencies do you have on deliverables from other groups?

- What specifically do you need to do?

- What risks do you need to account for?

Next, each group should use a responsibility grid. A sample of a partially filled-out grid is shown in Table 7-1. For this example, Sales has committed to four action steps in support of a new mobile product.

TABLE 7-1. *Responsibilities (with preliminary mock data)*

SALES			
Takes	*Interdependencies*	*Deliverables*	*Dates*
1. Identify the partner candidates for this new business.		Partner candidates identified and profiled by Sales.	4/10
2. Figure out what the core value proposition will be and test in focus groups.	Budget TBD for research.		6/10
3. Create momentum of revenue for FY10.		Define a plan within 30 days. Get approval. Execute within 60 days.	ASAP
4. Address marketing needs of these new ISP accounts.	Sales and Marketing co-own this action.		

Using a grid is an easy way to name the key next steps by group and then compare these next steps between groups where any interdependencies lie. Without such a process, some tacit expectations for what others need to do gets lost in translation, and thus a gap is created. We limit these grids to five responsibilities because that's about as many as any group can realistically track. If the rest of the process has gone well, the Take phase goes really quickly because everyone is already thinking about what they need to do to make the larger strategy a success, and they likely started to identify interdependencies during the Select phase.

The Take phase grid can be filled out in a face-to-face working session, or completed independently by each functional group. Now, you might be wondering why we are asking you to do a template model when earlier we trashed templates. The key here is that you're not being asked to fill in the blanks. You are being asked to discuss (and then document) key things for each group. There is value in asking each group questions such as, "Do you need anything from engineering?" If the answer is no, then you can confirm, "So you have no dependencies on engineering?" The point is that you want to ultimately meet and talk about the action steps, because this discussion irons out the interdependencies between the various functional units and makes all parties aware of any changes that need to happen in the organization.

> The key is not to fill out templates, but to ask questions and discuss key issues that iron out interdependencies.

This is also the place for critical negotiations about trade-offs, resource allocation, and agreements that need to be made before you focus on action (not three months later when the problems start happening). This discussion is essential for the strategy to function properly, and its importance cannot be overemphasized. Completing the interdependencies, deliverables, and targets sections of the grid lets you clearly and specifically articulate expected commitments (Table 7-2). Details and dates are vital here, because the specific commitments become the way to measure progress once the strategy has been launched. For example, "first week of March" is much better than "Q1" if other people are expected to act on that deliverable.

TABLE 7-2. Completed responsibilities grid (again, mock data)

SALES			
Takes	**Interdependencies**	**Deliverables**	**Dates**
1. Identify the partner candidates for this new business.	None.	Vetted list	Present to Tiger Team at the first week of Q1. Approval second week of Q2.
2. Figure out the core value proposition and test in focus groups.	Budget to be allocated within 15 days of agreement.	Tested value prop	Deploy Pilot by Q2. Debrief lessons learned at E-team meeting end of Q2.
3. Create momentum of revenue for FY10.	Legal resource allocation.	Contract	Contract signed by both sides by first week of Q2.
4. Address marketing needs of these new ISP accounts.	Marketing and Sales co-own this deliverable.	Requirements document	Defined and iterated within Tiger Team. Owned by Director of Marcom.

Sometimes strategies affect many parts of an organization. This take-ownership system can work in a cascading fashion, so you can fill out the grid at the VP level, then again at the director level, then at the team level, and even at the individual level as necessary. There are various ways to do this. You can do it interdepartmentally at a low operational level and then bubble up, or it can be top-down. But be sure no member of the team is saying to themselves, "There's no way this is going to happen," without raising the issue. That is, be sure not to stay locked into VP commits, because if you do, you could be right back in the "6x product expansion in 18 months" situation. When Take is done, the defined actions create a "nesting" effect, which aligns everyone in the organization along the same goals. It provides a way to check whether the individual actions (at any level) add up to the expected outcome.

Specifics are important because once this list of actions has been agreed to, everyone can get to work. Everyone knows what needs to happen when, and the focus can now be on execution. In terms of progress and status, the roles are clear, the goals have been specified, and at any point in time, anyone can assess how well the strategy is being executed. You can keep the strategy alive by using these Take documents to review where you are, whether anything in the market has changed that warrants a review or change, and then tune your commitments as needed.

While the Take phase is critical in supporting a successful implementation, some teams may complain, "Why do we have to write this all down?" The real objective of this process is to catalyze the right kinds of conversations *ahead of time*, and create a visible action system that can be made visible within the company. You may find that some people need coaching to see the benefits of this system, why it is important to be extra-specific when making commitments, and why this process is important.

Explicit and visible commitments drive
accountability in the Take phase.

One thing that I've seen teams do is name a "take" item for beliefs/ activities that have to be given up. I've seen it work or not work, depending on the culture. For example, if a company is shifting from a mostly services company to a product company, there is a big change in how they think about customer requests. In a service company, you say yes to just about anything as long as it's profitable. In a product company, you often want to standardize feature sets, and that forces a different discipline. In this example, the "what has to be given up" is custom orders/product customization. I recommend you have discussions during the Select phase about what you will stop doing, but if you fear something won't stick inside the organization as a key "stop," you can name and capture that "stop action" here as a major take.

At the conclusion of this final phase, you will fully understand:

- The actions required to execute the strategy, and who specifically owns them
- The interdependent parts of all the moving components
- Any beloved beliefs and activities that have to be given up
- Budget or resource implications
- How the organization will know when it has hit the intended target

Take roles and responsibilities

To reiterate, the goal of the Take phase is for everyone involved in the collaborative strategy creation and execution be able to state what the strategy is and what critical actions they will need to complete to make the strategy a successful reality. By doing this well, we are fixing the "5% know the strategy" issue for your organization.

> *Watch out for the total picture and not just "your part," because your part is the total picture.*

The leader's role is to keep facilitating what at times becomes tedious attention to detail. This doesn't mean that the leader does or does not have to focus on the details. Either approach can work. But the leader must confirm that the right people are focusing on the details.

That may mean that the leader openly probes into the details of one or two issues, which signals their importance, and then asks generally about whether other issues have been covered at this level of detail. As the effort moves from collaborative strategy creation to collaborative strategy execution, the leader's job is to champion the work of the team, making sure that everyone involved understands the direction the strategy sets forth and its purpose. Remember, if you skip a crucial conversation here, you pay for it later with many more. Take the time and have the right conversations; this creates alignment and shared responsibilities.

For each of us collaborators, this is the time we get to show up to make sure we co-own the success. The Take phase is where the rubber meets the road, and every person—from executives to individual contributors—makes sure things tie together, and then commits openly to his or her actions.

Table 7-3 lists the leader's main responsibilities in the Take phase, as well as those of the team.

TABLE 7-3. *The Take phase roles and responsibilities*

LEADER'S ROLE

- Be sure to involve everyone who is important for making the strategy real. Some of this will take place before the Take phase, but if there are other people who are even minimally impacted, they need to be brought into the final fold.
- Include everyone at this phase; this is not the time for leaving people out of the process. If anything, be an over-communicator.
- Ask people to discuss key interdependencies and then fill out the responsibility grid. (Again, this is not the same as filling in a template.)
- Ask people to commit openly to these deliverables, milestones, and targets.

COLLABORATOR'S ROLE

- Sign up to the things you need to own.
- Make sure you identify interdependencies early and often. Watch out for the total picture, not just "yours," because yours *is* the total picture.
- Know the signals or early signs that can let anyone in the team or business know if you're "off track."
- Openly communicate your and others' commitments. Over-communicate to make sure there is real understanding.

Managing Temptation:
Choosing Your Individual Status over Team Results

After having labored so hard during the Select phase, there is a natural tendency to want some personal credit. Some leaders find it hard not to want to pass out cigars and receive personal congratulations. Leaders, you'll want to resist this temptation because, once again, the organization and the people involved need to own the strategy and continue feeling responsible for every aspect of it. If you fall prey to grandstanding "your achievements" over the team's contribution, your team will feel betrayed, devalued, and unmotivated at the crucial moment when they need to begin the heavy lifting of implementation. There's a balance to be struck between getting acknowledgment for your leadership and stealing the show.

As the leader, you will want to champion the efforts of the team, and then drive accountability. Having people commit to what they will do gives individuals a chance to show up.

If you can find a way to add transparency and make commitments visible so anyone can see who is responsible for what, it will help ensure accountability throughout the organization. This might involve publishing agendas or notes, reiterating commitments at key meetings, or creating some kind of business review (some companies use a quarterly business review) where key decisions and next steps are communicated.

Make key decisions and next steps specific enough to show who is responsible for fulfilling each commitment. This helps make people accountable to their peers (and perhaps to their bosses), and it enables effective progress tracking later without to the appearance of micromanaging the effort. Good progress tracking is key to surfacing issues during implementation so that those issues get the attention they need. By increasing the transparency of the collaborative strategy as it unfolds, each person is now in the driver's seat of changing how work gets done at your company. And because of the way you are doing these discussions, you are driving a cultural shift in your organization toward shared ownership of success.

The Artifacts of the Take Phase

The work of this phase makes resource commitments open and clear, so that any resource issues can be resolved before the plan is in place.

Specifically, the Take phase is important because the artifacts:

- Create a common vocabulary around what needs to happen and who is doing what
- Prompt teams to understand and negotiate the interdependencies across divisions or departments
- Allow dialogue on how to deliver (instead of why we can't) by raising obstacles and issues early
- Give everyone a process tool to assess whether the strategy is on track
- Help people be objectively clear on achievement against goals

There are two key points to remember about the Take phase (see Figure 7-3). First, the Take phase is about being explicit and open with commitments. Explicit and open commitments are important because people tend to do those things that they have to report on to others.

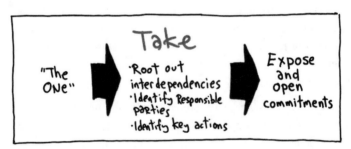

Figure 7-3. The Take artifacts

Second, this phase is about specifics. Before everyone forgets what was decided, what needs to be managed, and the reasons for key decisions, you need to *write it down*. Be specific about what your milestones are. For example, a statement such as, "When this strategy is successful, we will be playing nice with the product people," is not specific. (Which product people? Are there 6 people or 600?

What does "playing nice" mean?) Specifics are always who, what, when, where, and why, so that everyone understands the milestones in the same exact way. When you know the specifics, you also know when you need to reevaluate the strategy.

Managing Temptations Overall

In Chapters 4 through 7, I've highlighted the common temptations you will find along the way. These temptations are real, and unless you are from the planet Krypton and have escaped all human foibles, you will face them. There is no guarantee about whether it'll all work out, but these tools and process frameworks will certainly help you do strategy better than you would have in the Air Sandwich days.

As we lead this process, we aim for the organization to think strategically. This is a different way of being, and because it involves people, it has its own challenges. We've named the issues that will often arise, and I want you to remember that these temptations are very easy to fall into. Keep in mind that you want to avoid them; it might help to have your colleagues join you and point out that they are happening in case you get tempted.

Both clients and colleagues have used this process to defend themselves against these alluring temptations so that they can shift toward better outcomes. The QuEST process acts like a defense shield in this way (Figure 7-4).

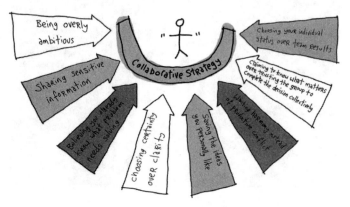

Figure 7-4. Defense shield against common temptations

Wrapping Up

Developing a New How of doing strategy creation in which people can come together to create the ideas that will drive the company to win is one of those "simple, but not easy" things. The four phases we've just covered give the practical tips and approaches that will let you do this well. However, any process framework is only as good as what you put into it, so of course the talent of your team and the organization will make a difference in how well your strategy turns out. But the New How is the new black. How good you get at it is up to you.

Sure, this kind of strategy creation better aligns your team. Equally important, it enhances the effectiveness of the entire organization. Slowly, each person becomes empowered (Figure 7-5) to make decisions more independently—decisions that align with larger company efforts. With their newly expanded perspective, each person becomes capable of making more informed trade-offs and adjustments on the fly as challenges pop up during the execution of collaborative strategy because they "get it." They see the big picture and they know what matters and why. As a result, the entire organization can respond quicker, invent faster, and win.

Figure 7-5. QuEST is empowering

What has permeated all of this work is the notion of co-creation of solutions, and ultimately the co-ownership of winning within your organization. With a full complement of engaged contributors, you'll be in a far stronger position to build winning solutions. And as a byproduct, you are building a team that is fluid, responsive, and working within a creative organization that knows how to win again and again.

As we exit the process framework section, we proceed to the final section of the book, which is focused on the company-wide rules of engagement that enable winning at the highest levels. You will definitely arrive in Rome.

PART III

Foundations to Successful Collaborative Organizations

We're getting close to the finish line.

In Chapter 1, we made the point that most organizations are using outdated systems that derail effective strategy creation. We looked at the pieces of organizational systems and identified three chunks. The first belongs to the individuals in the organization, which we covered in Part I. The second chunk, process methodology, is shared by the individual and the organization, and we covered that in Part II. It's time to look at the third chunk of system elements, which belongs more to the organization than it does to the individuals.

If we take a metaphorical perspective, we can view the process creation system as a cathedral. The individuals represent the bricks, and the process phases are cross-timbers. To build a robust edifice, we obviously need quality bricks and excellent timbers. But we need more. Something must fill in the cracks between those structural elements and hold them together; we need bolts and mortar. Similarly, the third chunk of our system ties all the other pieces together. Also, it's best to figure out the other parts of the structure before we try to figure out how we're going to glue them together. The mortar fills in the gaps and the bolts link where we need linking. We've done the big pieces of structure for six chapters, and now we're down to the last few crucial parts.

Enough said. We won't hold you up any longer. Let's move on to how organizations enable collaborative strategy to create winning solutions.

CHAPTER 8

Collaborating to Win

Hell, there are no rules here,
we are trying to accomplish something.
—Thomas Edison

What Makes It Work Inside the Corporation Context

Every one of us who has spent time in the workforce has participated in co-creating how business works today. Some of our contributions have been positive, and others have been negative. Sound harsh? Perhaps. But I'm not trying to pick on anyone. (Think back on the stories from my own experience, and you can understand how that is true for me.) The point is not to judge, but to illustrate a point.

Every time an executive asked for participation ("Any questions?") and we stared at a crack in the ceiling rather than taking on some issue that we were conscious of, we let the culture of poor strategy creation continue. Every time we cut out relevant raw data or sugar-coated the "issues slide" as we passed content to our manager, director, VP, or GM, we let it happen. Whenever we allotted a key issue insufficient time on a meeting agenda, we let it happen.

Our legacy of hierarchical structures and decision making has out-lasted its value, and in doing so has encouraged a culture of failed strategies. For us to change, we need to change the rules. Part I of this book described how we can promote an inclusive culture of participation in which each of us steps up and the leaders move from being Chiefs of Answers to being cultivators of involvement. We also talked about the need to challenge, debate, and create new options that represent a far better range of solutions than would be created by a few folks in an ivory tower. Part I was about ways of *being*, and how behaviors and attitudes support collaboration.

Of course what we do also matters, and so Part II described a rich process framework, QuEST, that enables effective, open collaboration. QuEST is flexible and dynamic, and allows you to go fast by going slow, balancing the need for action with the need to be thoughtful in your decision making. By providing a way to make the tough, messy choices together, the framework aligns everyone in your organization on the "why," so that they in turn can line up substrategies accordingly. So Part II was about the *doing*—the New How.

But we're not 100% there yet. In order to fully enable a New How, we need a few more "contextual elements" broadly embedded in the organization to glue it together. I call them *organizational principles*.

First Principles of the New How

Teams that are consistently successful have a shared set of norms—a unified sense of purpose and a common vision for what they need to do. Through their common rules of working together, they form a "community of purpose," not just a random clump of people under the same roof. The community is a unique entity with shared beliefs: a shared purpose, shared values, and a shared approach to winning. The more aligned the community is, the more smoothly they collaborate. This is the "forming, storming, norming, performing" sequence that Bruce Tuckman first established.[1]

Where does a team get its shared beliefs? For "organically grown" teams, they may develop out of some jumble of the stronger personalities of the team's founding members. Or they may be explicitly "synthesized" as part of a scripted team-building exercise. Either way, shared core beliefs help to build trust and allow a team to take risks with each other and create together. The shared beliefs help to provide a sense of identity while encouraging shared ownership of the work product. Any core set of beliefs is useful to some degree, but high-performing teams have core beliefs that align with their responsibilities (see Figure 8-1). Through my experience, I have found several key principles that help collaborative strategy teams become high-performing teams.

Figure 8-1. *We believe*

Although I am introducing these principles near the end of the book, in my mind they are the very foundation of the New How. If you took the actions discussed in Parts I and II of this book, without also applying these basic principles, you likely wouldn't be embodying collaborative strategy. That is, they are central to how people create and carry out strategy. These principles form the common thread that weaves together the way people work, through codes of conduct. The principles of collaborative strategy involve five aspects of a shared worldview that everyone adopts if they aim to be part of a high-performing collaborative strategy team:

Distribute decision making

> As much as possible, organizations that want to move fast must support decision making closest to the related part of the organization. Both the number of individual decisions and the bias of shared decisions should spread throughout the organization. This means that less focus is put on title and level than on the area of focus to drive new growth.

Demand good followership

When a decision is made, everyone aligns behind it because they had their voice in shaping it. Even those who disagree know how to do good followership. We reward and support a culture where differences are raised up front.

Reward co-ownership

Everyone owns the outcome of a strategy or business success. The notion of "I did my part; I should get rewarded" won't hold water. Rewards and compensation are predominantly based on the collective business performance.

Set clear goals and then improvise

For people to collaborate in creation, they need to have a clear destination to aim for, and the freedom to create. The leader (CEO/GM) needs to define the destination well enough for others to aim for it, even when they don't check in for weeks at a time.

Be students of the game

We know that teams and people will make mistakes and that things change fast in the marketplace. This is reality. We also know that *learning* organizations get better over time at innovation, disruptive change management, and operational excellence. We say "whoops,"[2] learn from the error, realign to our compass, fix our approach, and keep going because we have work to do. We don't insist on definite answers; we welcome questions. We enjoy exploring ideas and weighing the merits of multiple options. We like turning over rocks and exploring new frontiers. We embrace being "students of the game."

These first principles are organizational norms that lead to winning results. You'd be hard pressed to find a winning company that doesn't embody most, if not all, of these principles in some form, even if they have not explicitly adopted collaborative strategy.

All of this is in support of a larger intention, of course. The New How is based on the premise that strategy is not "Strategy" until it has become real. We believe that a strategy becomes reality when people create and support it so that it achieves the intended outcomes.

We understand there is no such thing as creating a strategy and "throwing it over the wall," or thinking about strategy as a collection of ideas, or a set of PowerPoint slides, or a turn-the-crank meeting where templates get filled out. A strategy is legitimate only when it is ready to generate results.

Let's dig into all these first principles in more detail.

Distribute decision making

The first principle is that people are expected to work together so effectively that they can make decisions closer to the source of the relevant action. We don't make fewer decisions (we might make more), but we make them where they need to be made. This means that we move the locus of control. We don't approach the world with the notion of "that's above (or below) my pay grade." Similarly, we as execs must not dismiss an activity as beneath us if it is important to the business, because that models the wrong behavior. Instead, roll up your sleeves and set an example.

Strategy creation can happen anywhere in the organization where the talents, information, and wisdom exist to address a particular need. Whenever a decision is needed, the issue is not immediately escalated to the top. Instead, the team reaches out locally until it finds what it needs to make that decision.

Ellen's story (scrubbed of identifying information) in the sidebar "Hey, Wait...Do We Do That?" on page 216 shows how having a process for shaping strategies on the fly makes a company more responsive to the marketplace. The events in that story took place in 2008, and represented a shift in approach for a company aiming to win new markets.

If Ellen's company had adhered to a traditional strategy creation model, Ellen's pursuit of a new market might have taken six months to a year or longer. Her time, and that of her colleagues, would have been spent trying to build consensus and getting approvals rather than inventing on the fly. She would have had to wait for the planning cycle, create a business plan, and get high-level sign-off before taking any definitive action. Some execs might challenge assumptions or data, and others might cleverly take the credit.

Hey, Wait...Do We Do That?

Ellen's company delivered PC support services. On a recent review of customer calls, Ellen noticed that customers were consistently having issues with creating and managing networks in their homes. They were repeatedly asking for help in troubleshooting these problems. Although Ellen's company didn't "do" network management, Ellen knew that the higher-level strategic goal of her division was to grow the nascent services business.

Ellen assembled a small group of colleagues and direct reports, and then stepped through a logical process framework to explore the potential opportunity. They evaluated the facts and weighed the options of launching a network management services offering. In concert with her team, Ellen decided that adding these services to the company's menu was a good idea. She corralled internal experts, put together an operations plan, trained a group of customer service representatives, and quietly piloted the offering so that when customers requested support, the company could present this new offering as appropriate.

Ellen's boss, the VP of Global Services, discovered this was happening only when a customer commented that he had tried the company's new network service and liked it. The VP was a little hesitant to reply, thinking to himself, "Do we *have* a network service offering?" But the customer enthusiastically showed him the support link on the company website.

Perhaps Ellen could have communicated earlier or more effectively with her boss, but the point here is that Ellen and her team's initiative to develop a new opportunity expanded the market they were serving in alignment with the higher-level strategic goal. Soon, the services business expanded to become PC *and* network services. The new offering was profitable almost immediately and helped differentiate the company from its competitors.

This story is a classic example of effective collaborative strategy. Ellen was empowered to respond to what customers were telling her, and she was empowered to find and engage with the right people to experiment and try new ideas. Ellen didn't need to prove that a network services market existed or check in with many layers of executives to see what she was allowed to do. How much time would have been wasted if she had taken that approach? Instead, she simply saw what looked like an opportunity, understood that it was aligned with the larger strategic goal, vetted the idea with people close to the action, and then took the initiative to test it—ultimately shaping the future of the company.

Instead, Ellen used her domain knowledge to create a strategy that fit with the clear mission of the business. She had the roadmap on how to think about the situation. This allowed her to test an idea quickly and prove its worth in the marketplace (which is more compelling than survey results or dubious analyst forecasts), making the company more responsive to its customers and therefore more ready to win.

Ellen used a process that allowed her to invent on the fly. She and her team had a set of shared core beliefs—beliefs about her role, what her organization would allow, and what ultimately mattered to her company. These beliefs enabled her to focus on value creation first and approval second. These first principles were the driving force behind her ability to invent. Knowing that her principles were shared with the larger team, Ellen had the permission she needed to innovate, without even asking. It was in the culture.

Permission to innovate without asking happens when the strategy is co-owned.

Stepping back from Ellen's story, it's important to note that each company will have their own mix ratio. One firm might have 90% of the decisions approved by the C-Suite, but could be better served by a number like 70%. Another might be at 70% today and benefit by moving to 50%. You and your organization must look at the kinds of decisions you face and consider where they need to be made.

Demand good followership

Strategy conversations are creative discussions. We contribute to this creative process by bringing our experience and wisdom, our *point of view*, to the table. Our point of view is based on our experiences and observations; it may be a keen awareness of something the rest of the group is not thinking about yet. And our strongest points of view are usually the mostly deeply held. That's all well and good until our strongly held opinion turns out to be in conflict with someone else's. This tension can pose quite a challenge, but when handled well, it can be very productive.

For effective collaborative strategy, we must embrace tension, engage questions, serve as thinking partners, and abide by the result. In short, we must engage in good followership, and we must insist on it from our teams. Let's make sure we cover each of the elements.

EMBRACE TENSION. We recognize that we will never have unlimited resources to do all the things we want. We see limited resources as creative constraints[3] that spark conversations and new ideas; the constraints form the box we need to think outside of. Our naturally differing points of view will ignite creativity, innovation, and problem solving. We get that the kinds of complex business problems we face today are inherently about tensions, and we welcome them as the fuel to create new solutions. To move from theory to plan and from plan to reality, we must appropriately challenge ideas that sound wrong or that clash with what we believe to be true.

Constraints form the box we need to think outside of.

We understand that it's OK to disagree, and that how we offer up disagreement matters. We never blame, accuse, yell, or humiliate. Instead, we respect one another's personal dignity and identify specifically where our disagreements are—between our facts, opinions, feelings, or needs. When we fight fair and deal with tension above board, we enable good followership later. We can challenge ideas respectfully without making the challenges personal, and we look for the constructive ideas when others challenge our ideas. Raising concerns with an idea doesn't have to mean confrontation. Table 8-1 shows some ways to make room for feedback on ideas.

TABLE 8-1. *Questions to help "call it out"*

Care for a bit of free advice? (It's worth what you pay for it!)
There seems to be an assumption here. Can we dig into that for a minute?
This reminds me of an experience I had that might be relevant. Can I share it?
Would you like to know my point of view?
You know, something about this is rubbing me the wrong way. It could be my bias, but I think it's better to get it out in the open. Is now a good time to do that?

Notice that each question asks permission to test receptiveness to the feedback. This shares power with others and allows them to choose. Asking permission also signals that we care what others think and don't necessarily regard our own ideas as inherently superior. In addition, it provides a kind of peaceful early warning that a challenge is likely to occur.

Occasionally, a team member will solicit input and then proceed to shoot it down. When this happens, call it out. Sample phrases include, "It seems like the time for new ideas is over. Is that the case?" or "Would you like some more input?" In creating strategy together, we understand it is our duty to engage fully in the discussions. We honor the distinction between shooting down and challenging.

VALUE QUESTIONS. We ask many questions and are comfortable answering many questions. We don't use questions to attack each other, but to examine ideas carefully and understand their merits and pitfalls.

BE THINKING PARTNERS. We are co-creators. We recognize that challenging one another's assertions, conclusions, and data in good faith is actually our duty. We welcome diversity of opinion as the source of more fully formed ideas. We want to know more so that we can create more as a team—more solutions, ideas, and alternatives. We are all responsible for applying what we know, what we believe, and even what we suspect to the discussions at hand so that new ideas align to the reality of the company. We know that if we do not "call it as we see it," the game itself doesn't work. We show up to the strategy conversation ready to contribute at the highest performance level possible.

ABIDE BY THE RESULT. When we sign up for collaborative strategy, part of the price of admission is to support the judgment calls of those who carry that responsibility. Because in the end, there will still be judgment calls. Is there a 10% chance or a 40% chance that the product team will miss the date for the key deliverable? What are the odds our competitors will announce a product in this space in the next 12 months? How quickly will buyers switch to/from our product if X?

Sometimes the judgment comes down to: we can do X or we can do Y, but we don't have the resources to do both. Ideally, there is a clear consensus decision, but sometimes not. As a part of Murder-Boarding, our pet project may get shelved or tossed. This isn't fun, but it *is* necessary.

On any messy decision, it will not be clear what is "right" or "wrong" (that's what makes it messy), and the person leading will need to make the call. Some days, that could be you; other days, it's someone else. If you have done the process right and heard everyone out and vetted the ideas, then you need to buy in on the decision. The key to collaborative strategy working is that you decide to have the fair debate and let your voice be heard to shape the outcomes, but when it comes time to make the call, you align behind the leader.

That's good followership. And just like we need to have good leaders, we need to cultivate great followers.

Reward co-ownership

Companies often set themselves up for failure by saying they want people to co-own success, but then routinely rewarding individual efforts through both recognition and economic payoffs. To get co-ownership, we've gotta incentivize co-ownership. Say the company has 15 objectives. Pay 100% at 15, 50% at 12, and 20% at 10. Everyone will support all 15 objectives, not just the one they own more directly.

And it is not OK to have people do their part right without co-owning the success of the company's end goal. We've covered this kind of accountability and personal responsibility in Parts I and II, but it is worth saying again: people participate based on their ability to help build the future together.

Rather than naming an employee of the year, choose a department of the year or initiative of the year. Or make 50% of any person's success tied to the company's success. Make sure groups don't sandbag by recognizing in advance those groups that are taking on aggressive goals.

In short, make sure that incentives line up with what your company values in a collaborative set of goals.

Set clear goals and then improvise

Ever been to a symphony? How about an improv session at a comedy club? The difference between traditional strategy and collaborative strategy is like the difference between these two performances.

At the symphony, the more exactly a performance matches the director's vision, the more perfect it is. Flawless execution occurs when each talented performer performs precisely as practiced under the meticulous attention of the maestro. Rehearsal is essential and virtuoso skill with the instrument is valued, but deliberate deviation from the score is taboo.

In stark contrast, improv has a very different performance process. The group's players improvise and play off each other to create the piece, building on what others have created with a "yes, and..." style. The performance is less scripted, and the process of creation is fluid. In improvisational art, collaboration is unique, built on high engagement, and allows individuals to contribute something to the larger whole. Each performance has common themes, but is unique to the situation at hand. In both types of performance art, the players bring their unique talents, but they use different methods to "create" the performance.

Improv relies on a method that requires less formal planning and prep time. It goes faster from concept to execution. But it does require a clear objective or structure so the players can act and respond interestingly. Improv, therefore, is akin to collaborative strategy because it is constantly creative and depends on the process of aiming and adjusting (Figure 8-2). Collaborative strategy lets you aim toward a business outcome and then move forward without having to step out of the scene to check in with others for specific direction.

Figure 8-2. *The relationship between strategy and improv*

Consider for a moment what might happen to these two performances if something were to go wrong—someone falls down, for example. How would each performance be affected by something it didn't anticipate? The orchestra would struggle to gloss over it, fumbling and straining as best they could, looking for direction from the maestro. The improv players, on the other hand, would roll with it, incorporating it into the story to add new layers to their performance.

Like improv, every strategy creation effort is brand new. We can't rehearse it. Effective strategy creation must be adjusted in real time to the events in our world. Aiming and adjusting requires being watchful of the situation, and revisiting ideas, assumptions, and plans in an ongoing fashion as a matter of practice. Of course, it's not pure improv. The destination is a guideline in improv, but an essential shared target in strategy creation. Without that clear latitude/longitude direction, what follows is chaos.

Be students of the game

Making learning a core competency can be a strategic advantage. As the Rumi poem aptly states, "It's in the rub that the stone gets polished." We need to spend more time polishing our stones—interacting with one another as we solve problems. Many corporate cultures seem to value "getting along." I believe that worldview comes at a high price. I believe that it's when we address our disagreements that we find the insight we need. It rests on certain philosophical assumptions, best practices, roles and responsibilities, and methods for getting stuff done and making things happen. Let's explore them.

> *Our purpose in meetings isn't talking; it is learning.*

DON'T DWELL ON THE PAST. Examine your experiences, find the lessons, and learn from them. Then move on and focus on what is actually happening in the organization today. Take your cues from what is going on around you, and play off events in the moment. Don't say, "This doesn't include"; say, "It needs to include." Go forward in problem solving, not backward in nit-picking mistakes. Constantly ask, "Who are we now?" and "What do we want to create now?" Use the past to help you create the future by what you do now, in the present.

CREATE EXPERIMENTS. Embrace the notion that it's not possible to get it right the first time every time.[4] This is especially true with new approaches that no one has thought of or tried before. Your goal in these cases is not so much "get it right" but "get the ball further down the field" and learn in the process. As such, you invite each other to play with ideas and try different things as part of the creative process.

Experimentation searches for useful ideas that can be built upon and incrementally improved. A question like, "What about that idea could work?" is inviting and provocative. Taking this approach prompts others to share their ideas, insights, or points of view so that they can be blended into a larger understanding of what everyone knows.

Inquisition favors the status quo by searching for flaws and putting the burden of proof on new ideas. Questions like, "Why do you think that will work?" are intimidating, and no answer seems adequate. It's hard to know even where to begin! Table 8-2 is a summary of the distinctions between experimenting and running an inquisition.

TABLE 8-2. *Experimentation versus inquisition*

EXPERIMENTATION/INNOVATION SOUNDS LIKE	INQUISITION SOUNDS LIKE
What would make that work?	Why will that work?
What if it were to look like this?	This is missing X, Y, and Z. Why?
Can we show an example of it working? Can we do a pilot and let it run for a quarter and see how it goes?	Can you prove it can be done? If we can't prove it can be done, let's not do it.
Could we consider...?	This is wrong.
Let's change Paragraph B so it ties to our larger goal...in this way....	Paragraph B kills this thing for me. Period. End of discussion.

We've all seen people "do inquiry" with an inquisition approach. It can show brilliance but not wisdom. Let's use experimentation and innovation language instead. It helps bring out our unique points of view. One is open and creates new options, whereas the other shows off what one knows but not what one can create.

Collaborative strategy is a creative act that depends on the ideas of many people throughout the organization. Because collaborative strategy places significant value on what might be possible versus what is certainly true, the nature of the conversations around ideas and feasibility matter deeply. Codes of conduct support us to offer up insights, remote associations, and clever concepts so we can co-create with many different people, regardless of status and titles.

INVOLVE OTHERS. In discovering what is possible, who does the talking and who does the listening are just as important as the conversations that take place. Involving others means having fewer conversations with people who share similar points of view or areas of expertise, and actively initiating conversations with people in different functions and levels within the organization to explore possibilities.

Involving divergent points of view quickly exposes biases and assumptions, and provides a counterweight to the human tendency to fall in love with one's own ideas. You want to expand the facts, needs, and issues that are considered, and this expanded view contains the key insights that often make or break a strategy. Involving others also sets the stage for collaboration by bringing people together to engage and explore. The following are five questions you can use to encourage involving the right people:

- Which stakeholders or business units might have an opinion here?
- Which stakeholders or business units are we assuming will not be affected? How can we check this?
- Who have we left out of the discussion?
- Whose combined insights might be valuable?
- Where do we anticipate the most conflict?

To see an example of how unexpressed needs bubble up in strategy conversations, let's look at Sabrina's story in the sidebar "I Want Something" on page 226.

The Payoff

Suppose you decided to live by the New How methodology and approach that you've just learned. Wouldn't it change how you work? Suppose you could collaborate to set direction. Wouldn't it improve your chances of achieving success? When collaborative strategy takes place within a firm, I've seen the pace of action go up, even while team members are more thoughtful about their work. A motivated and aligned powerhouse of people is formed. Table 8-3 shows us more benefits that come when an organization drives collaborative strategy.

I Want Something

Sabrina was a member of a $2B company that recently gave her the go-ahead to create a brand-new derivative business. The only stipulation was that she had to use the company's existing sales and marketing organizations so that the resources could be leveraged to help her, and also so the derivative business could help the company. No problem, right? Wrong.

First, the marketing team wanted a planning document that would be stable for 6 to 12 months so that they could cascade it through their big organization to coordinate messaging, box designs, and retail displays. But Sabrina's new business was changing so quickly, she couldn't tell them what the next 12 months would look like. She needed to do a pilot first, see what happened, and then tune the approach. The conversations with marketing went round and round. She felt the traditional business was being old school. They felt she was being demanding and flaky. Both parties seemed to want to work with each other, but the relationships were getting strained.

The conversation became heated around an end-cap retail display stand. Sabrina saw one in the lobby of the company, and wanted to see if that might work for her product, so she sent one of her people to find out if the vendor could do a prototype. This kicked off a whole series of meetings around the requirements, whether it would go nationwide or international, which languages were needed so that legal could weigh in, and more. Sabrina's quick experiment turned into a missile program. She was ready to bypass the company altogether and have her 17-year-old son whip up a prototype in their garage over the weekend.

Sabrina thought her problem was the end-cap stand. It wasn't. Sabrina's problem was that she and the people she was working with wanted incompatible things. The existing company players wanted to follow proper procedures so that the product could scale and to avoid surprises. They wanted to minimize risk. But for Sabrina, risk wasn't even part of the picture. She simply wanted to play with ideas, because she couldn't know what she wanted until she saw what worked. Sabrina needed to experiment, but she was trapped in a process-oriented culture that had no way to deal with experimentation.

Both parties were so enmeshed in their points of view that they never realized they had skipped a crucial conversation about what each side needed. Consequently, they had not identified the core issue, and that left them wrestling with the details instead of proposing ways to balance their fundamental differences.

TABLE 8-3. *Results of the New How*

ORGANIZATIONAL CAPABILITY	BENEFIT	WHAT IT LOOKS LIKE
Invent on the fly	The organization as a whole reacts quickly to competitive actions and other changes in the market.	The organization is in a perpetual state of renewal and reinvention. The executive team defines a strategic direction and then communicates it to the organization. The larger strategizing team constantly gets new information, adjusts course, incorporates feedback, and readjusts.
Act in real time	Everyone tracks the current strategy, enabling the organization to respond faster and more precisely and reducing the need to constantly "take it to the top."	Decision making happens close to the action. People from the middle of the organization are empowered to identify opportunities and make decisions so that the organization can respond to what is happening in the marketplace.
Develop radar	Constant intelligence gathering enables the organization to identify new opportunities as they are developing.	Every member of the organization acts as a "node" in the system to gather information about evolving threats—landscape, trends, issues, and consumer behaviors. Members constantly sift the information to uncover nuggets of insight and opportunity.
Harness the power of the modern workforce	People learn, grow, and contribute at the highest levels they can.	People have the charter, the power, and the permission to use their talents to make the decisions that drive strategy as it is forming. They create the future while staying aligned with the larger whole.

TABLE 8-3. *Results of the New How (continued)*

ORGANIZATIONAL CAPABILITY	BENEFIT	WHAT IT LOOKS LIKE
Marketplace-winning focus	The focus of winning is in the marketplace and on the competition. Everyone owns this goal.	People leave behind the infighting and CYA activity. The CEO and other leaders spend less time managing and more time leading, freeing up cycles for innovation and inventing the future.

Underlying the benefits described in this table is this: collaborative organizations focus less on politics and more on substance (Figure 8-3). We focus less on why things don't work and more on what will make it work, and we come together as people who have a shared mission. It's a healthy organization that brings out the best in people. Each of us has experienced times when collaboration worked, and times when it hasn't worked. It may seem like there is some secret sauce involved, but we all know it's not magic. Or, more accurately, the secret sauce is a critical mass of people committed to the right principles.

Figure 8-3. *We focus on substance*

We can see the behaviors, processes, and organizational principles that enable collaboration. When we see this full collection, we have the opportunity to put them all in place so that we can experience the benefits of collaboration most of the time.

Organizations That Win Form Winning Cultures

Collaborative strategy relies on a defined set of principles that enable the team members to engage in strategy creation together. If you have ever sat down to play a favorite card game with someone new and gotten frustrated when you realized the two of you played by different rules, you know that these principles matter. It feels like the other guy is cheating! Who wants to play in that kind of game? But when you and your colleagues are aligned on the rules, it's fun and exciting, regardless of the outcome.

Agreeing on the rules of the game is essential because the process of creating strategy does not come with a standard board we can look at and easily wrap our brains around. While strategy creation requires all the smarts—from data, insights, and models—to achieve results, it must also involve working intimately with human beings and their ideas. To get their insight and creativity and enthusiastic contributions, we need them to enjoy being in the game.

We covered five first principles earlier in this chapter. They span a range of how culture gets shaped within an organization via power, people, change, decision making, process, and idea generation. Each of these areas comes into play during collaborative strategy creation, and we need shared understanding of the code of conduct to simply manage them. Otherwise, we get unnecessary conflict, confusion, and the erosion of a shared sense of purpose. So take those principles and make them your own, and embed them in your organizations. Because when companies have good, shared bedrock principles, they establish the foundation for a culture that fosters and reinforces winning.

You might recall from Chapter 1 that strategies fail for many reasons that have to do with how people relate to one another, respond to change, make decisions, and generate and share new ideas. We can change our systems to fix those things, and we've now covered all three parts of that change: how people act and behave, how people do the work of strategy creation, and the first principles that organizations need to share.

Imagine what can happen if you and your colleagues work in this collaborative environment. For most of you, strategy creation and strategy execution would look very different. People with positional power would no longer drive the company in arbitrary directions, ignorant of what really works. Leaders in high places would no longer make ill-advised unilateral decisions on how to deal with significant challenges facing the organization, and then drop the new direction like a bomb on the company at large. There would be no silent majority aware of a different "truth," knowing the new plan won't work and quietly making side bets on when the trainwreck will occur. People wouldn't have to sit and wait for umpteen levels of management approval to pursue a new idea, watching as competitors steal the match.

Instead, we can move to a place where ideas, debate, engagement, and tension are valued as contributing to a better outcome. With shared rules of engagement permeating the organization, each of us can develop ideas and react to changing conditions with confidence and experimentation.

So will you join me at the party to celebrate the death of traditional strategy creation? You bring the philosophy of collaborating to win; I'll bring the hors d'oeuvres. (I heard there'll be a great group doing improv!)

Let's party on.

Epilogue:
It's What We Make of It

Throughout this book, I've shared the ways business can improve, how we reinvent work together, and how collaboration in the form of co-creating business solutions can fundamentally improve outcomes. Let me share with you now the backstory of why I believe what I believe.

I was in my final quarter of graduate school, feeling ready to be done with the tightrope act between working and studies, when I got the assignment that transformed my perspective of how business works.

Standing regally at the podium, my white-haired professor, Andre Delbecq, dean of management studies, gave us our last assignment: study a tree, reflect on how this tree relates to business and leadership, and then write an essay about it. And, no, it wasn't a joke. "Easy A, here I come!" I thought, already picturing how this cake-walk assignment would free up the necessary time to focus on my more important paper, an HBR case study about how company strengths are manifested in business outcomes.

Though I considered the tree assignment a waste of time, I went through the motions, diligently studying a large oak tree near my home. I'd been staring at that tree for some minutes when I suddenly realized: the tree essay and my case study work represented the *same darn thing*. (Wouldn't ya know it, I learned something after all?)

What (I asked myself) is the basis of a tree? The roots and the trunk. Sure, the leaves and the fruit are the eye-catching bits that come to mind when we think of a tree. They are what my six-year-old son will sketch if you ask him to draw you a tree. Yet the enduring elements that survive the storms and winter frost are the unsung roots and trunk, which produce and nourish the leaves and the fruit.

The parallel in business became clear to me: companies often focus their attention on the eye-catching business results of profits and stock price (the leaves and the fruit), rather than the organizational systems and processes (the roots and the trunk) that generate those results. In both cases, it's the unseen and unsung parts that drive the fundamental health, growth, and results of the system. Just as roots derive nutrients from the soil, so businesses draw upon ideas to feed growth; as the trunk supports and defines the tree shape, so people innovate and set direction for the company. When you prune the branches judiciously, making tough decisions to make room for future growth, the trunk will support the branches that bear fruit, and nutrients will go to all the right places.

As I studied that tree, I realized how simple it was.

All the complicated and sophisticated models I'd been learning in business school and applying inside notable companies were, by themselves, not enough to create success. The models and analysis missed the very basics of what created strong business outcomes. The roots of the tree represent the individual team members in business. To harness the power of ideas, you need people to capture them, debate them, and shape them into the substance of competitive advantages. People are the roots that enable organizations to thrive.

Just as a single root can feed a tree, any one person can prompt a business to reinvent. Change begins with the actions and attitudes of people like you—driven people, looking to tackle challenges—who choose to work in a new way, creating a New How. We feed and water the tree, or in this case, our organizations. We make the choices to pursue results that support the health of our companies.

The idea that any or each of us can reinvent business to work better is both daunting and inspiring. But anyone who has picked up this book and studied its contents this far is plainly interested in driving change and adopting new approaches that create more winning outcomes.

There is much to do; where do we begin? Well, we begin as we already have, by understanding what is possible. What comes next depends on you and your situation. But it is about taking action (Figure E-1), as cultures and companies change when any one shift happens.

Figure E-1. *Culture change begins with one person*

Most of my career has been about problem solving and creating winning strategies. I also have a growing passion for understanding what can enable the people in organizations—people like you and me—to improve how business works. That passion has driven me to develop the tools and practices that fill this book. So, this book is not just about making your business more successful; it is also a manifesto.

I've shared this approach with you not merely so we can achieve better business results, but because it can create better work environments where people can rise above and thrive. I want everyone to step up their game, bring their full abilities to work, and stop abdicating responsibility to "the other guy." I want companies to thrive because they are able to come up with great new directions and make them real in the marketplace. Those successes will, in turn, challenge each of us to be more active, creative, and engaged members of our business world. The more we bring our unique creativity, personal ownership, shared purpose, and collaborative spirit to our work, the more the institutions we work within will embody those characteristics.

Our organizations will grow nobler in their methods and outcomes. I hope you will join me in this quest.

There are no signs that our world is going to move slower, or become simpler or less competitive. On the contrary, the problems ahead will likely be intensely challenging. As we in business choose flatter, more collaborative models in our organizations, we are designing the future. We can take Gandhi's advice and remember, "The future depends on what we do in the present." We can create better and faster organizations. You are not merely allowed to participate; you are called to participate in creating a New How for your business.

Thank you for reading this book. But please don't stop here. Go make a difference in the world.

Acknowledgments

The New How is not a memoir. Still, many of the ideas in this book developed gradually in my mind over the last 20 years, so writing it has been a clarifying view of what makes me believe these ways work.

This book emerged from a conversation with Harry Max in early November 2007. Having recently joined my Rubicon team, Harry and I were talking about my approach to strategy development, which I see as a deeply creative act—one that not only focuses on business concepts, frameworks, and ideas, but also the process through which strategies are formed, shaped, chosen, and made real by people.

Harry had recently written "the book" on how DreamWorks Animation collaborates internally in creating films. He raised this question: did successful business strategy really involve the same kind of creative acts as film development? And was the creative process itself crucial to successful outcomes? Of course, the answers were yes and yes.

Building successful strategies is deeply creative, and it's when we blend the what *with* the how *and* the who that success is more likely to manifest. But this idea had a genesis long before my high-tech career. These beliefs were ingrained in me early. In 1987, as a community college student trustee, I was unexpectedly selected by my chancellor, Tom Fryer, to be given a seat at the table hashing out the future of the California community college system for a piece of reform legislation called AB 1725.

Tom was a notable national leader in shared governance, so everyone in the room—the governor, legislators, faculty leaders, and me—participated as equals. It was a completely collaborative effort. Each time we had a policy decision to make, Tom would put together a three-inch-thick binder of notes, articles, and opinions we needed to read the week before the meeting, then follow up with a phone call. He wanted to know my opinions, along with everyone else's. He wanted to know my thoughts and the ideas his materials had sparked. I was 30 years younger than Tom, but he spoke to me as an equal, and I worked hard to have an opinion worthy of his attention. We each had responsibilities. We were deeply accountable for having and holding opinions and of course for achieving results. Because it was something we were jointly creating, none of us would have "credit," but we would all end up having great pride in the work we did.

Tom once explained his methods at a meeting, and I was lucky enough to find the file that held those notes:

> When we, as the administration, don't talk to faculty and students as equal members, they see themselves as passive participants and victims of the decisions of the administration. As a result, they don't understand the decisions, or feel like the decisions are theirs, and they won't contribute themselves to the effort. Our community doesn't exist until everybody creates something together.

Looking back on that experience, I can see the thread of my own story, and why I believe that collaboration and shared governance can create that elusive "buy-in" that every organization seeks as it innovates and sets direction. It's when we co-own the outcome of success together that we co-create that future of success.

In my 20 years since those community college days, I've participated with nonprofits, educational institutions, and, of course, business. And one thing stands out across all those leaders and people involved: most of us believe in the idea of collaboration as a way to get better results. Yet most of us don't take a collaborative approach. From that, I draw the conclusion that we don't work collaboratively because we don't know how. It's not a lack of will, but a lack of way.

Finding that way has been a learned thing. Not surprisingly, it's been a process of both successes and failures that have led to the clarity I have today. And so I'll only refer to the companies rather than the individuals that have helped make this book possible. To my clients and colleagues at Adobe, Apple, Autodesk, Openwave, Symantec, Logitech, HP and others: thank you for being co-conspirators in creating these ideas. You have given me the opportunity to learn with you, through both failures and successes, what will work for others.

Thank you to the O'Reilly team for believing in this idea. From the original email exchange with Tim O'Reilly to meeting his capable and seriously kick-ass COO, Laura Baldwin, this company has helped to make this work a product worth sharing. Mike Hendrickson has become more than an editor to me, and without his insightful and clever guidance, I don't think this book would ever have been completed.

I am grateful to everyone at Rubicon; no one could ask for a better ensemble of people to work with. As you already know, your ideas have shaped mine, and although my name is on the book, your ideas and values are embedded within these pages. Working together to solve the tough(est) problems in high-tech companies is incredibly fun and joy-filled, and I am grateful to do it. I don't have anything more to ask for.

Notably among that team is Harry Max, who started this whole endeavor, as I've already said, and encouraged this work. And his perpetual deception—"It'll get easier soon"—was probably needed to get me to finish.

To Hugh MacLeod, artist extraordinaire: your love for your craft shines through here.

No leader succeeds without a supportive team in his or her personal life. And I am no exception. My husband, Curt Beckmann, and I are lucky to have met in grad school. He was the first to sign me up to do this work, the first to listen to my cranky complaining that I really didn't want a second job while I was CEO of a company, and the one to keep nudging me on. Along with him, my son, Andrew, provided unwavering support and personal sacrifice during too many nights and weekends so I could try to do this creative effort.

Special thanks go to friends, family, church community, the Vistage #34 CEO group, clients, and countless associates who endured the "book excuse" for a million misdeeds, large and small—from pushing off key meetings to forgetting the sweet potato pie at Thanksgiving. (Sorry, Jennifer Stern!)

And, finally, thanks to my many reviewers and advisors who helped me take something inherently "in my bones" and get it into the world: Gloria Chen of Adobe, William Irvine, Peter Ebert of SAP, Tammi Madsen from Santa Clara University, Kathy Chill of Citrix, Robin Beers of Wells Fargo, John Hagedorn, Eric Zarakov of Tessera, Taylor Ray, David Chun of Equilar, Brian Fitzgerald, Mary Walker, Mark Interrante of Yahoo!, Jeffrey Pugh of Sun, Sonnie Sussillo, Bill Oyler, Susan and Mark of StartWorks, Nehal Gajjar, Tony Nemelka, Genevieve Haldeman of Symantec, and Padmasree Warrior of Cisco. And, to my friend and stepdaughter, Julie Beckmann, your selfless support of this book was an incredible gift. If this work is useful to others, it is thanks to all of you, because you helped me to make what I know clear and cogent.

To the degree we're always learning, I'm sure that what I've written today will seem hopelessly limited by some future understanding. Please forgive me for all the limitations held within it, and Twitter me ideas to make it better. You can find me *@nilofer*.

Tools

This appendix covers the following list of tools:

- Tips for interviewing
- Building a findings framework
- Speaking truth with clarity and power
- Tips for criteria development
- Generating options
- Burning the boat

Tips for Interviewing

Interviewing is often like an archeological dig: all of the pieces may be there, but they are scattered across the landscape. Because interviewing involves people, the approach you use to conduct interviews affects the quality of the information you gather (and your ability to create a well-formed strategy).

Intention

The purpose of interviewing is to get a current picture of what needs to be addressed, and to assess the emotional readiness for change in your organization.

Approach

1. Have a sponsor set up the meeting. Sponsor introductions can go a long way in emphasizing the importance of the interview and acknowledging the value that people have to add.

2. Prepare an interview guide (not a script) beforehand. Usually you should share it with the interviewees ahead of time so that they have time to think. But don't share this guide if you think it will tempt people to give "prepared" answers, or consult others for the "right" answers.

3. Doing interviews with two interviewers (i.e., two-on-one) allows one person to focus on listening and note-taking. If you use this approach, the note-taker/listener should keep a relatively low profile to encourage the interviewee to speak freely. Interviewing alone is better if you expect delicate or risky topics to come up. If, in a two-on-one interview, you get the sense that the interviewee is holding back, consider rescheduling a one-on-one interview.

4. Spend a moment at the beginning of the interview to let people know that their information is valuable, and it will not be used to get anyone in "hot water."

5. Start with a warm-up question that is open-ended and allows people to state their point of view. Typically, people need 5–10 minutes to get their brains engaged on the topic at hand.

6. Start the interview with the easier topics first. Leave more sensitive issues for later.

7. Don't ask too much. Ask one question at a time. Go slowly. The speed at which you ask questions can signal to the interviewee whether you are more concerned about your own agenda or more interested in his point of view.

8. Simplify questions to keep learning and discovery focused on small pieces of the problem. Exploring smaller pieces allows you to see the nuances of the problem.

9. Briefly paraphrase what you've heard from your interviewee to affirm your understanding and so they can correct you in the moment.

10. When interviewing, be sure to listen, not lead. Focus on learning, not demonstrating your intelligence.

11. Use an indirect approach. Ask "What bothers you most?" (instead of "When do you hate your job?").

12. Use a "Colombo" tactic: act dumb but keep probing.

13. Show respect for what people can contribute. People at all levels have something to contribute.

14. Always send thank-you notes. You may find that you need the help of your interviewees later, and courtesies such as thank-you notes go a long way toward making people feel acknowledged and appreciated.

Building a Findings Framework

Building a findings framework gives you a way to create a snapshot view of the current situation, so people can begin to understand the issues.

Intention

The purpose of a finding framework is to help you organize what you've learned and synthesize it, so you can report it back to your organization. It also gives you a framework to test your own logic and understand the proof points of what you've just learned.

Approach

1. Organize all your findings.

2. Take a day and reread everything. Invest the time.

3. Then, using an outline format, ask yourself:

   A. What did I learn?

   B. What do I believe to be true or not?

   C. What are the implications?

4. Make a list of the key points of your findings.

5. Seek at least three supporting references or data points for each key point. Make sure they are distinct, and yet capture the comprehensive situation.

6. Review your sources. Check to be sure they are solid and that you have documented them (subject to confidentiality). Identify the gaps and where you need additional info.

7. Talk with additional people if you need to fill in the gaps.

Speaking Truth with Clarity and Power

Conversations about "the state of the state" should not be focused on pushing information at people; they are about getting people to recognize what is happening in the current situation. Your goal in these conversations is to inform people about what you see, why you see it that way, how you feel, what you believe to be true, and what you believe is important for them to understand. The following tips help you speak about the truth clearly and powerfully.

Intention

When speaking truth, it is very important to leave room for people to think their own thoughts and have their own understandings. Words like "respect" and "dignity" are useful in this context to remind people that honoring differences and perspectives is necessary for driving change. The words you use, the tone you use, and the context you set will all make a difference in how others respond.

Approach

1. Start with what matters most, and set the context for what you want. This can sound like: "For me, what I most want to do is to create a shared understanding...." Sharing what is important to you may seem like common sense, but without it, people do not know your intention. It is not enough to know your intention; you must communicate it to the group.

2. Say exactly and specifically what you want people to understand. Use as many distinctions as needed. It is not enough to describe something as "blue" if what you really mean is "turquoise." Don't rely on subtext. Don't expect them to "figure it out." You are responsible for calling a spade a spade. Use proof points when you can. For example, "I believe the issue is turquoise because of these three points of fact...."

3. Present everything as "early findings," not truth. The word "truth" has a charge to it. The phrase "early findings" suggests you are doing good discovery and your observations are for the team to understand together.

4. Avoid easing in. The work of Chris Argyris has introduced this concept of "easing in," which is where you try and soften a message by delivering it indirectly through hints and leading questions. Easing in conveys that you have a point of view you are unwilling to share directly, which suggests that the issue is embarrassing or shameful. A better approach is to make the subject clear and discussable by stating your thoughts straight out and indicating that you are interested in working on solving the situation.

5. Avoid using the word "you" when you are about to critique something. Rather than saying, "Your ideas are unclear," you can say, "I need more clarity on those ideas." You can state your perceptions, feelings, and assumptions, but you should not state other people's assumptions and feelings.

6. Remember that people will take in different pieces of information at different speeds and in different ways. You want to think about presenting findings at a summary level and at a specific level, with both qualitative and quantitative facts. Look for ways to paint a picture or use an analogy.

7. Ask people to comment on what they see differently and why. Remember the goal is a shared understanding. You want to make sure everyone sees things fully and expansively (versus agreeing). Clarity and understanding is what you seek.

Tips for Criteria Development

When a team has a "feeling" for what they want, but cannot express this feeling clearly in words, these exercises can be helpful. They reveal tacit beliefs and perceptions, and elicit criteria that will ultimately help the team select a winning strategy.

Intention

The purpose of criteria development is to surface tacit assumptions about what matters, so the organization can know why one thing is more important than something else. Being explicit about assumptions allows you to test them and challenge them as a group.

Approach

Exercise #1: Imagining the future

This exercise allows a team to dream, but without having to "own" the wording or the grandness.

- Have each person write ideas on Post-its and submit them into a pile.
- One idea per Post-it. The Post-its must all be the same color.
- Guiding questions:
    - What would you do if you had a magic wand and could solve anything for our customers, the whole industry, or one product line?
    - If you were king of the universe, what new thing would you want first?
    - If you were king of the universe, what would you not want touched?

Exercise #2: Developing competencies

This exercise looks at competitors for ideas about where a team can excel.

- Have each person write ideas on Post-its and submit them into a pile.
- One idea per Post-it. The Post-its must all be the same color.
- Guiding questions (preface each with "Compared to our competitors..."):
    - What do we do well?
    - What don't we do so well?

- What could we do differently (e.g., technologies, culture, partnerships)?

- What do we have that we never want to let go of?

- What do we love about what we have (e.g., ease of use, fraud management, underdog status, brand power)?

Exercise #3: Exploring new models

This exercise[1] looks at parallel industries to brainstorm ideas about what could be emulated. For example, do we want to deliver like FedEx? Design like BMW?

- Have each person write ideas on Post-its and submit them into a pile.

- One idea per Post-it. The Post-its must all be the same color.

- Guiding questions:

  - What are 10 companies you admire?

  - Why do you admire them?

  - What things would you like to see our company do as well as another company?

Generating Options

Brainstorming is a great way to generate options and ideas. During the brainstorming process, you need to give free rein to people's creativity and avoid criticism. Criticism can hamper creativity.

Intention

The purpose of generating options is to make sure you have fresh alternatives to today's problems and that you are pulling these options from an expansive pool of ideas.

Approach

1. Clearly define the problem to be solved, as explicitly, concretely, and politically incorrectly as you can. Lay out the criteria to be met. The best problem statements focus outward on a specific customer need or market-facing goal, rather than inward on

some organizational view. For example, "We want to serve our mid-market customers with a new online service" is better than, "Our division has to grow by 20%." Keep the session focused on the problem you want to solve.

2. Have ground rules. Just like a great game, you need to know how to play. Some sample ground rules are:

   — Defer your judgment.

   — Turn off all electronic distractions (phones and computers).

   — Don't use "but..." to destroy an idea.

   — Use "and..." to build on ideas.

   — No criticism.

3. Pace it out. The best facilitators nurture the conversation in its early stages so that the session allows people to start generating ideas and helps people find their groove. Make sure that no train of thought is followed for too long, because people start to check out. You want to manage the flow but not over-engineer it. Change the pace if you want to change the outcomes. If people are stuck, have them do something different: get them to work together or apart, outside or inside, at the whiteboard or at their desks.

4. Introduce inspiration. No team can come up with stuff out of the blue, so a good way of spurring really great and inspiring ideas is to introduce a new element. A book, a speaker, or some "homework" to get fresh points of view are all useful. As the leader, you influence the team's ideas by what you put in front of them. Speakers can be someone within the company or out; books can be on point or far afield (hint: children's books can spur great ideas).

5. Make a record. People can be very fearful of losing an idea if it is not in writing. Knowing that it's being captured frees people up to focus on idea generation. Appoint one person to note down ideas that come out of the session. Avoid the temptation to evaluate the ideas during the session, and remind people the session is for creating, not critiquing.

Burning the Boat

Burning the boat is about creating a compelling reason for people to move on and incentives for them to adopt a new direction. The term itself comes from Thucydides, in his *History of the Peloponnesian War – Book III*,[2] written about the solution one general came up with in ancient Greece: "...burning their boats so as to have no hope except in becoming masters of the country." This legendary military decision eliminated all possibility of retreat. The troops knew there was no way out but through, and they performed because the situation left no alternative.

Intention

Burning the boat is about setting a new direction and rewarding all actions that support that new direction. It is an all-or-nothing approach that must be chosen with care.

Approach

Specify the destination
> The team needs to know what the new destination is and how to get there. How you communicate the new direction will matter significantly in whether you get there. Why that particular direction? Why is it important? Announce the new move and make sure there is a specific launch date or even an event that will cause the team to remember that a large change has occurred.

Make the move necessary
> There must be a penalty for clinging to the old. For example, the point of demarcation between the old and the new might be a change in procedure, such as people will not be able to get into the building without the new identification badges. The change should be marked by tangible and intangible elements so that there is reinforcement of the change.

Create a crisis

I recently had an executive bring in a high-priced consultant to tell her board why the current business was limiting growth. The executive needed a third party to carry the message and signal loudly that the old business didn't support the future direction of the company. Employees understood the seriousness of the change because they saw "the suits" walking around holding meetings.

Talk about the new

With every meeting, there should be a conversation that acknowledges and brings the new direction into focus. You have to reiterate how important the new direction is to bringing in revenue and to the future of the company. Relate the new direction to current operations. Spend time talking about the new. As a leader, you will signal to your team what's important to you (consciously or unconsciously) by how much time you spend on the new direction. Tune in and talk about it, and your team will, too.

Only hire in the new focus

Look for people that match the new direction. Make sure that each new hire extends your reach into the new space by providing knowledge and capabilities that will help you get where you're going.

Reward people based on the new focus

Compensation can sharpen performance. Salespeople in particular have an amazing ability to focus on their compensation plan. Use the plan to guide behavior so that your company reaps the rewards and gets the kinds of results you wanted when you first determined what the new direction would be.

Dismantle the old infrastructure

Don't continue to support the old business. If you've decided to let go of a product line, consider selling it, renaming it, or otherwise getting the point across that things have changed in a fundamental way. Don't feed the old systems by providing them a large slice of the budget, mentioning them in company-wide meetings, or including them in the sales offsite.

Minimize maintenance of the old

In the midst of a large change, it's easy to spend too much time and money on something you're trying to put on life support. Determine the appropriate level of maintenance so that customers are taken care of, and then don't spend a dollar more. Refer customers to new models and new services so that they migrate to what your organization is fully involved with.

Put a process behind it

A process concentrates thinking and is a subliminal message to the team: "This is not a passing fad. It is valuable and it's here to stay." Make sure the team knows you think the new direction offering is important by using a process for reinforcement.

Resources

In this appendix, I share with you some favorite resources for your library. These were chosen because they have shaped my thinking and perspectives and benefited my clients greatly. I've categorized them as follows:

- Strategy
- Collaboration trends and tools
- Leadership
- Tough conversations
- Creativity
- Facilitation
- Decision making
- Change management
- Listening

Strategy

Chan, Kim and Renée Mauborgne. *Blue Ocean Strategy: How to Create Uncontested Market Space and Make Competition Irrelevant.* Harvard Business School Press, 2005. [Good for identifying new market opportunities.]

Christensen, Clayton. *The Innovator's Dilemma: The Revolutionary Book that Will Change the Way You Do Business*. Collins Business Essentials, 2003. [Good for Global Giants to understand how markets often move out from under them.]

Collis, David J. and Michael G. Rukstad. *Can You Say What Your Strategy Is*. Harvard Business Review, April 2008.

Matteson, David and Jim Mattheson. *The Smart Organization: Creating Value through Strategic R&D*. Harvard Business School Press, 1998. [Excellent way of knowing how to build wisdom and intelligence through systems.]

Mintzberg, Henry, Bruce Ahlstrand, and Joseph Lampel. *Strategy Safari: A Guided Tour through the Wilds of Strategic Management*. Free Press, 1998. [One of the best books with a comprehensive view of strategic frameworks.]

Various authors. *Harvard Business Review on Corporate Strategy*. Harvard Business School Press, 1999. [Landmark reading across a 20-year horizon.]

Collaboration Trends and Tools

If you want to know how collaboration, community, and our digital world will change how business is done, some good resources are:

Locke, Christopher, Rick Levine, Doc Searls, and David Weinberger. *The Cluetrain Manifesto*. Basic Books, 2001.

Surowiecki, James. *The Wisdom of Crowds*. Anchor, 2005.

Tapscott, Don. *Growing Up Digital: The Rise of the Net Generation*. McGraw-Hill, 1999.

Tapscott, Don. *Wikinomics: How Mass Collaboration Changes Everything*. Portfolio Hardcover, 2008.

Weinberger, David. *Everything Is Miscellaneous: The Power of the New Digital Disorder*. Times Books, 2007.

"Best Online Collaboration Tools 2009 – Robin Good's Collaborative Map," *http://ow.ly/gAbk*.

Leadership

Choosing definitive leadership books to share is akin to answering the question, "Which is your favorite child?" That said, I recommend anything from Barry Posner, dean of the Santa Clara University Business School, and a few others that decode why "how we lead" matters.

Frisch, Bob. "*When Teams Can't Decide*." Harvard Business Review, November 2008.

Kouzes, James M. and Barry Z. Posner. *Encouraging the Heart: A Leader's Guide to Encouraging and Rewarding Others*. Jossey-Bass, 2003.

Kouzes, James M. and Barry Z. Posner. *The Leadership Challenge*. Jossey-Bass, 2008.

Kouzes, James M. and Barry Z. Posner. *Credibility: How Leaders Gain and Lose It, Why People Demand It*. Jossey-Bass, 2003.

Lencioni, Patrick M. *The Five Dysfunctions of a Team: A Leadership Fable*. Jossey-Bass, 2002.

Pruzan, Peter and Kirsten Pruzan Mikkelsen. *Leading with Wisdom*. Greenleaf Publishing, 2007.

Seidman, Dov. *How: Why How We Do Anything Means Everything...in Business (and in Life)*. Wiley, 2007.

Streatfield, Phi. *The Paradox of Control in Organizations (Complexity and Emergence in Organizations)*. Routledge, 2001.

Tough Conversations

In business, people often avoid tough discussions, but as the poet Rumi would say, "Without the rub, you cannot get to a polished stone." These books might give you some tools and things to consider in defining your own approach.

Blanton, Brad. *Radical Honesty: How to Transform Your Life By Telling the Truth*. SparrowHawk Publications, 1996.

Haugk, Kenneth C. and Ruth Koch. *Speaking Truth in Love*. Stephen Ministries, 1992.

Matthies, Dennis. Precision Questioning Workshop. Vervago, Inc. http://www.vervago.com.

Noonan, William R. *Discussing the Undiscussable: A Guide to Overcoming Defensive Routines in the Workplace.* Jossey-Bass, 2007.

Patterson, Kerry, Joseph Grenny, Ron McMillan, and Al Switzler. *Crucial Conversations: Tools for Talking When Stakes Are High.* McGraw-Hill, 2002.

Stone, Douglas, Bruce Patton, and Sheila Heen. *Difficult Conversations: How to Discuss What Matters Most.* Penguin Books, 1999.

The Hoffman Institute Foundation. In the Hoffman Process, scientifically proven benefits applied on the professional level result in increased self-confidence, greater ease in times of ambiguity, and the ability to stay centered under stress. In short, The Hoffman Process provides a practical way to apply self-awareness in a performance environment. *The Hoffman Quadrinity Process.* http://www.hoffmaninstitute.org.

Creativity

Three outstanding books on how your stance and approach can infuse creativity into your work:

Deep, Sam and Lyle Sussman. *Power Tools.* Addison-Wesley, 1998.

de Bono, Edward. *Six Thinking Hats.* Back Bay Books, 1999.

Kelly, Tom and Jonathan Littman. *The Ten Faces of Innovation: IDEO's Strategies for Defeating the Devil's Advocate and Driving Creativity Throughout Your Organization.* Doubleday Business, 2003.

Facilitation

People often think of facilitation as a "soft people" thing because HR people do it, but the skill of facilitation is akin to learning how to lead an improv performance.

Interaction Associates. *Facilitative Leadership®: Tapping the Power of Participation course.*

Neuhauser, Peg C. *Tribal Warfare in Organizations: Turning Tribal Conflict into Negotiated Peace.* Harper Business, 1988.

Decision Making

Biz culture frankly sucks at making tough choices and getting people to step outside their own learned "best" approaches. Sometimes it seems like they'd rather peanut-butter-spread resources and fail slowly. We collectively must change that; these books are an amazing set of tools to do it:

Ariely, Dan. *Predictably Irrational: The Hidden Forces that Shape Our Decisions.* HarperCollins, 2008.

Howard, Ronald A. and Clinton D. Korver. *Ethics in the Real World: Creating a Personal Code to Guide Decisions in Work and Life.* Harvard Business School Press, 2008.

Schwartz, Barry. *The Paradox of Choice: Why More Is Less.* Harper Perennial, 2005.

Change Management

Business cannot achieve new growth without change. After all, we have to stop doing some things to do things anew. And while we all "hate to change," it can be done well or not so well. These compelling authors have given some great tools for leading a change effort:

Collins, Jim. *Good to Great: Why Some Companies Make the Leap... and Others Don't.* Collins Business, 2001.

Gardner, Howard. *Changing Minds: The Art and Science of Changing Our Own and Other People's Minds (Leadership for the Common Good).* Harvard Business School Press, 2006.

Moore, Thomas. *Care of the Soul: A Guide for Cultivating Depth and Sacredness in Everyday Life.* Harper, 1994.

Senge, M., Art Kleiner, Charlotte Roberts, Rick Ross, and Bryan Smith. *The Fifth Discipline Fieldbook.* Doubleday Business, 1994.

Listening

Quite often, what stops people from being on the same side of the table is the listening skill set. We ought to add it to the education curriculum in every country. By listening well, people can move from the us-versus-them understanding to an us-versus-problem perspective. These have been instrumental in shaping my worldview:

Goleman, Daniel. *Emotional Intelligence.* Bantam, 1995.

Hart, Thomas N. *The Art of Christian Listening.* Paulist Press, 1980.

Notes

Introduction

1. *http://discussionleader.hbsp.com/hbreditors/2008/10/cisco_ceo_john_chambers_on_tea.html*

Chapter 1

1. Dan Ariely's book *Predictably Irrational* (HarperCollins) says we spend too much time and energy keeping our options open. We'd be better off narrowing sooner.

2. As mentioned in the introduction; see *http://discussionleader.hbsp.com/hbreditors/2008/10/cisco_ceo_john_chambers_on_tea.html*.

Chapter 2

1. Tim O'Reilly (who founded O'Reilly Media, coined the term *Web 2.0*, and is the publisher of this book) has great wisdom on this: create more value than you capture. I agree that's a great principle, because it creates personal satisfaction, and I believe the money follows passion.

2. Stimson, William R. "How to Move a Tree," *Ode*, April 2008.

Chapter 3

1. Kaplan, Robert S. and David P. Norton. The Strategy-Focused Organization. Cambridge, MA: Harvard Business School Press (2000).

2. TED (Technology, Entertainment, and Design) is a thought-leadership conference with a focus on ideas that will change the world. The talks are posted on *http://www.ted.com/* so ideas worth spreading can be seen by everyone.

3. See *http://www.lifeplays.com/aboutus.html* and *http://www.onetaste.us/ ?page=CIA*.

4. Schwartz, Barry. "The Tyranny of Choice." *Scientific American Mind* (December 2004).

Chapter 5

1. If you would like more information on brainstorming or creative idea generation, check Appendix A for some resources.

2. For specific information about brainstorming creative options in inclusive and complete ways, see the exercise called "Generating Options" in Appendix A.

3. Edward de Bono has some good approaches on how to do this, so check Appendix B for more information.

Chapter 6

1. According to a McKinsey Global Survey (*McKinsey Quarterly*, April 2008), most companies assess three or fewer options and look forward no more than two years when responding to a competitor's move. A significant number rely on intuition, and the most frequent response is the choice that is most obvious at the moment the decision is made, for example, answering a price cut with a price cut. Perhaps most alarming, if faced with the same situation again, 60% of executives would respond with the same or even less analysis.

2. Source: Video of Jonathan Rosenberg at Claremont McKenna College on March 19, 2008.

Chapter 8

1. See *http://en.wikipedia.org/wiki/Forming-storming-norming-performing*.

2. Or perhaps "#%!&@!!", depending on the price of the mistake!

3. See *http://www.wired.com/culture/design/magazine/17-03/dp_intro*.

4. If you're getting everything right the first time, chances are, you're being very conservative and missing upside opportunities.

Appendix A

1. FedEx came from a version of Exercise #3. Fred Smith applied the hub-and-spoke idea from the telecommunications and banking industries to his logistics and transportation business.

2. For more background, see *http://www.greektexts.com/library/Thucydides/ History_of_The_Peloponnesian_War_-_Book_III/eng/61.html*.

Index

C

cadence, managing, 82–84
calling out practice, 51–54, 219
case studies
  "Hey, Wait...Do we Do
    That?", 216
  "I Want Something", 226
  "Profile of a Collaborative
    Leader", 87
    (see also Grande, Hans)
  "What They Mean to Say", 58
cathedral metaphor, for process
    creation system, 209
Chambers, John (CEO of Cisco
    Systems), regarding
    business climate
    changes, 18
change
  behaviors needed for (see
    behaviors conducive to
    collaboration)
  in business climate, examples
    of, 18, 165
  incentives for, 247–249
  managing, books about, 255
  quote by Margaret Mead
    regarding, 60
  resistance to, MurderBoarding
    helping with, 162
  in strategy creation, reasons
    for, 25
Chief of Answers role, 73–77
choices of individual
  impact of, 50–51
  practices for, 51–66
  quote by C. Wright Mills
    regarding, 155
  (see also behaviors conducive to
    collaboration)
Cisco Systems CEO, regarding
    business climate
    changes, 18
co-creator role, 46–50, 219
collaboration
  for assigning
    responsibilities, 202
  behaviors for (see behaviors
    conducive to collaboration)
  books about, 252

for fact gathering, 129
importance of, 23
leaders' difficulty with, 71–74
for option development, 147
for problem scope
    identification, 115
in QuEST framework, 104
for selecting options, 184
(see also participation and
    ownership; process for
    collaborative strategy)
communication
  decoding, 180
  in difficult situations, books
    about, 64, 253
  frequency and duration of, 82
  listening, books about, 256
  truth of situation, informing
    people of, 242
completion, determining, 90–91
conflicts
  communication in difficult
    situations, books
    about, 64, 253
  contradiction, embracing, 63–66
  engaging, 91–96
  identifying and resolving, 36
  tension, handling, 218
  (see also blaming others)
connections, developing, 89–90
contradictory data, sharing, 60
contributing (see participation and
    ownership)
co-ownership, rewarding, 214, 220
creativity and improvisation
  books about, 254
  freedom to use, 214, 221–222
  leaders creating environment
    for, 80, 85
  results driven by, 47
  strategy creation using, 109, 218,
    224
  translating problems into
    opportunity for, 35, 65,
    218
  (see also Envision phase, QuEST
    framework)
criteria for success of potential
    options, 147–153, 243–245

About the Author

Nilofer Merchant is the founder and CEO of Rubicon Consulting and a noted strategist, global high-tech industry thought leader, and trusted advisor to an elite set of entrepreneurs, officers, and CEOs. The New How process was built as she worked with or for companies such as Apple, Adobe, Logitech, Symantec, HP, Nokia, and others.

Colophon

The cover, heading, and table font is Franklin Gothic; the text font is Birka.

Get even more for your money.

Join the O'Reilly Community, and register the O'Reilly books you own. It's free, and you'll get:

- 40% upgrade offer on O'Reilly books
- Membership discounts on books and events
- Free lifetime updates to electronic formats of books
- Multiple ebook formats, DRM FREE
- Participation in the O'Reilly community
- Newsletters
- Account management
- 100% Satisfaction Guarantee

Registering your books is easy:

1. Go to: oreilly.com/go/register
2. Create an O'Reilly login.
3. Provide your address.
4. Register your books.

Note: English-language books only

To order books online:
oreilly.com/order_new

For questions about products or an order:
orders@oreilly.com

To sign up to get topic-specific email announcements and/or news about upcoming books, conferences, special offers, and new technologies:
elists@oreilly.com

For technical questions about book content:
booktech@oreilly.com

To submit new book proposals to our editors:
proposals@oreilly.com

Many O'Reilly books are available in PDF and several ebook formats. For more information:
oreilly.com/ebooks

O'REILLY®

Buy this book and get access to the online edition for 45 days—for free!

The New How

By Nilofer Merchant
December 2009, $24.99
ISBN 9780596156251

With Safari Books Online, you can:

Access the contents of thousands of technology and business books

- Quickly search over 7000 books and certification guides
- Download whole books or chapters in PDF format, at no extra cost, to print or read on the go
- Copy and paste code
- Save up to 35% on O'Reilly print books
- **New!** Access mobile-friendly books directly from cell phones and mobile devices

Stay up-to-date on emerging topics before the books are published

- Get on-demand access to evolving manuscripts.
- Interact directly with authors of upcoming books

Explore thousands of hours of video on technology and design topics

- Learn from expert video tutorials
- Watch and replay recorded conference sessions

O'REILLY®

Spreading the knowledge of innovators   oreilly.com

©2009 O'Reilly Media, Inc. O'Reilly logo is a registered trademark of O'Reilly Media, Inc.